Virtues and Economics

Volume 4

The series is dedicated to virtue ethics and economics. Its purpose is to relocate economic theory to a domain where the connection between the virtues and economic decisions, as that connection is actually experienced in everyday life, is an organic component of theory rather than some sort of an optionally added ingredient. The goal is to help develop a virtue-based economic theory which connects virtues with the contents of economic activities of individuals, unincorporated and incorporated economic agents. The primary context is Catholic Social Teaching but other faith traditions (especially Judaism, Islam, Hinduism, Buddhism, and Confucianism) will also be explored for their construction of virtues in economic action. Special attention will be made to regulatory and policy issues in promoting economic justice.

The series connects virtue ethics with the core of economic theory and practice. It examines the basic and irreducible intentionality of human activities concerned with the production, distribution and consumption of goods and services. It considers the incommensurability of values as the central problem of economic decision making and examines whether that problem can be overcome by any means other than practical reason.

This series will cover high quality edited volumes and monographs.

More information about this series at http://www.springer.com/series/15627

Luigino Bruni

The Economy of Salvation

Ethical and Anthropological Foundations of Market Relations in the First Two Books of the Bible

Springer

Luigino Bruni
GEPLI Department – Economics
Libera Università Maria SS. Assunta
Roma, RM, Italy

ISSN 2520-1794 ISSN 2520-1808 (electronic)
Virtues and Economics
ISBN 978-3-030-04081-9 ISBN 978-3-030-04082-6 (eBook)
https://doi.org/10.1007/978-3-030-04082-6

Library of Congress Control Number: 2018964120

This Springer imprint is published by the registered company Springer Nature Switzerland AG.
The registered company address is: Gewerbestrasse 11, 6330 Cham, Switzerland

Acknowledgments

I thank Marco Tarquinio, the Director of the Italian newspaper Avvenire where most of the chapters of this book have been firstly published. Thanks also to Alessandra Smerilli, Antonella Ferrucci, Anouk Grevin, Iolanda Martins Tovar, Luca Crivelli, Muriel Fleury, Rosanna Virgili, Sergio Premoli, and Tommaso Reggiani. I especially thank Peter Róna, who has believed in this project and has helped me a lot both for the content of the book and for the English language.

The book has been translated from the Italian by Eszter Katò.

Introduction: A Journey to the End of the Night

> Have you not heard of that madman who lit a lantern in the bright morning hours, ran to the market-place, and cried incessantly: "I am looking for God! I am looking for God!" As many of those who did not believe in God were standing together there, he excited considerable laughter. (F. Nietzsche, Thus Spoke Zarathustra).

Abstract Why then the Bible and Economics? To say Europe and the West is to say Judeo-Christian humanism in its various forms, contaminations, cross-fertilizations, diseases, and reactions but especially in its copious and extraordinary fruits of civilization. This humanism has its own articulate foundational codes. One of these, the deepest and most fruitful one, is the Bible, from Genesis to Revelation, which provides us with the words with which to speak of politics and love, death and economics, and hope and doom for millennia. In an era in which our "words are tired" and do not speak anymore because they are "worn out" and reduced to a "breath of wind," it is necessary to start the search of words bigger than our age. The words of the Bible have nurtured and inspired our civilization. They were revived and reinterpreted by many generations, they have filled up our most beautiful works of art and the dreams of children and adults, and they made us hope during the many painful times of exile and slavery that we have gone through and are going through still.

There are historical passages in which people realize that old things have passed away, the previous world is about to end, and there is a yearning desire for something new. Our time is one of these times (that the old Greek would have called *kairoi*). An essential resource in these ages of cultural crisis is the "narrative patrimony," a necessary asset needed for imagining and then writing the requisite new stories. Human beings like many things, but overall we like the amazing stories, to tell and to listen to. Without amazing stories the economy and business also suffer, because entrepreneurship and consumption are essentially storytelling, narratives about firms, markets, and commodities. "I had something to tell, but I was not good at writing, so I made a company," said to me an entrepreneur friend. This book is written in the belief that the Bible can offer some of the new generative words for imagining, telling, writing, and incarnating new economic life and new collective social and political actions and narratives.

In the last two decades, thanks mainly to the work of the philosopher Giorgio Agamben (1998, 2005, 2011), there is a new interest in the theological roots of modern economics.[1] *Economic theology* is today something similar to Carl Schmitt's *Political Theology* (1922/2005), i.e., the attempt to find and show the theological origin of some of the fundamental concepts of Economics, i.e., spontaneous order, debt, and the original meaning of the Greek word for economy (*oikonomia*). This book goes in the same direction, by searching in the Bible the roots of other key-words related to the Economy and Economics, such as market, salary, contract, pact, reciprocity, gratuitousness, and meritocracy. It is an essay of *archeology* of Economics and, more generally, social sciences, in the sense specified by Agamben, namely, the search for the *archè* (principle) of our categories. Agamben and the other scholars of the Economic Theology research project find the economic *arché* in the theology of the so-called fathers of the church (Tertullian, Cyrillus of Alessandria, Origen, Irenaeus of Lyon, etc.), those who made the first theological-philosophical mediation of the event of Christ. My goal is less ambitious, surely different, since these roots of economic concepts are searched directly in the Bible, neither in the Hebrew nor in the Christian theology. The book is an exercise of *narrative* Biblical Economics, where the arguments are not justified nor proved on the basis of academic footnotes and references. I have tried to keep the text plain and easy, although in the bibliography the reader can find the books and papers for further reading. I followed what the economist Alfred Marshall suggested to his fellow economists in relation to mathematics, a suggestion that I have applied to biblical studies: use the mathematics (i.e., Biblical studies) for the scientific rigor of the reasoning, but don't put them in the text, in order to make possible the reading even for the "laypeople" (not familiar with mathematics, theology, or Biblical studies).

Why then the Bible and Economics? To say Europe and the West is to say Judeo-Christian humanism in its various forms, contaminations, cross-fertilizations, diseases, and reactions but especially in its copious and extraordinary fruits of civilization. This humanism has its own articulate foundational codes. One of these, the deepest and most fruitful one, is the Bible, from Genesis to Revelation, which provides us with the words with which to speak of politics and love, death and economics, and hope and doom for millennia. In an era in which our "words are tired" (Ecclesiastes) and do not speak anymore because they are "worn out" and reduced to a "breath of wind" (Ecclesiastes), it is necessary to start the search of words bigger than our age. The words of the Bible have nurtured and inspired our civilization. They were revived and reinterpreted by many generations, they have filled up our most beautiful works of art and the dreams of children and adults, and they made us hope during the many painful times of exile and slavery that we have gone through

[1] See also Foucault (1999), Leshem (2013, 2014, 2015), Nelson (2004, 2017), Dean (2012), Toscano (2014), Bruni (2008, 2012a, b), Bruni et al. (2014), Bruni and Porta (2015), Bruni and Smerilli (2015), Bruni and Zamagni (2007, 2014, 2016), Bruni and Milbank (2018), Bruni et al. (2016).

and are going through still. There are no stories of liberation that could be greater than those of the Exodus, no wounds more fertile than those of Jacob, no blessing more desperate than that of Isaac, no laugh more serious than that of Sarah, no contract more unjust than that of Esau, no obedience more blessed than that of Noah, no sin more cowardly than that of David against Uriah the Hittite, no misfortune more radical than that of Job, no crying more fraternal than that of Joseph, no paradox larger than that of Abraham on Mount Moriah, no cry more piercing than that of the cross, and no disobedience fonder of life than that of the midwives of Egypt. There are many reasons that make these narratives "greater." One is their radical ambivalence, which, if accepted and understood, makes it possible to avoid the dichotomies that are often the first root of every ideology. These stories tell us, for example, that fraternity/sorority always borders on fratricide and that these are the two paths that form a fork in the many crossroads of the stories of individuals and peoples. All the great stories are above all a gift of words that without them, we do not have words donated to us to think, feel, speak, pray, and love. When these great stories and words are missing, we tend to borrow the words from gossip and TV fiction, and with these bricks we can only build a small house.

The Bible has always inspired a lot of literature, a great deal of art, and sometimes law, sociology, or politics, too. Modern economics, however, has never let itself be inspired by the Book of Books. One reason for this absence is the choice Economics made at the end of the nineteenth century to abandon words for numbers. A science with no room left for words cannot understand and dialogue with the Bible that is all about Word.

Along the history of both economics and its practitioners, there have been very few attempts of dialogue with the Bible, and in general with religion. One of the few, Henry Wicksteed (1910), a leading neoclassical English economists, tried to combine the Biblical tradition with economic tradition.

Later, the American Jacob Viner wrote *The Role of Providence in the Social Order* (1970), and in many other economists we find references to Adam and Eve in the Garden of Eden, to the good Samaritan (Buchanan, Sen), to Abraham's sacrifice, to the book of Job, and to the many parables and episodes of the gospel. Most recently, books such as *Biblical Games* (Brams 2003) or *The Economy of Good and Evil* (Sedlacek 2011) have tried to deal directly with the Bible, and not just with religion or theology. However, there is still a huge continent of possibilities to explore.

The Italian economist, Emanuele Sella, wrote a book in the 1930s trying to build a "Trinitarian economics" (*La dottrina dei tre principii*). He wrote something that is still valid, for both theology and biblical studies: "Economics, as a possible Trinitarian system, is not there (neither among catholic economists!), because the theological culture of economists is nothing, and the economic culture of theologians is poor" (1930, p. 113).

The Economy and Economics had been "under the guidance" of the sacred texts (i.e., on credit, interest money) for many centuries, but as soon as the discipline reached adulthood in the Modern Age, it sought and wanted its freedom. Today, a few centuries later, it is possible, and I believe necessary, to start a new lay dialogue.

The idea inspiring this book is that the Bible has many words to offer to our economic life and ideas. It can tell us things it has not said yet, because for too long no one has asked it to speak to us. But if it is true that reading the Bible can enrich the economy, it is equally true that new "economic" questions can make those texts say things that they have not yet said.

Finally, human history has always been a dialogue composed of new questions and new answers; and if on the one hand the Word has pushed forward humanity, on the other hand, and on a different level, the history of mankind has also allowed us to understand ever-new meanings of the scriptures (this is where the enormous dignity of history lies). If the Bible starts to speak again in the streets, in business, and in the markets, all these human-inhabited places will have great benefit from it; but the biblical text will also be enriched, and it will offer new answers that it has not yet given because the questions have not been asked. Without the nourishing environment of the squares and markets, without the *humus* of everyday life and the fatigue of work, the Bible does not become the tree of life. The St. Matthew Passion has become more splendid after Bach, Jacob is better after Rembrandt, and Joseph is more beautiful after Thomas Mann. If it were not so, history would be an unnecessary background of a theater piece, of a script that is already completely written, and those early Biblical books would no longer be alive.

With this background and perspective, this book contains my reflections on the first two books of the Bible. The Part I of the book is the systematic comment (chapter by chapter) of the book of the Genesis, and Part II is the comment of the Book of Exodus. The *Genesis* is the "first" book of the Bible, for many reasons. It is the *foundation* of the entire Bible, because it contains the great narratives of creation, Cain and Abel, Noah, and later Abraham and the Covenant, and the sagas of patriarchs of Israel, up to the marvelous cycle of Joseph in Egypt.

The book of *Exodus* is about empires and liberation. The Exodus starts in Egypt, where the Genesis ends, and it can also be seen as a sort of continuation of that story, around the fundamental figure of Moses and his journey toward the Promised Land. There have always been empires, and they still exist. But today we are getting used to them – which makes it increasingly difficult to recognize them. And since we do not recognize them, we do not call them by that name either, we do not feel oppressed by them, and we do not start any process of liberation. There remains only the "sovereignty" of consumers, who in turn are more and more unhappy and lonely sitting on their couches. The reading of the Book of Exodus is a great spiritual and ethical exercise, perhaps the greatest of all, for those who want to become aware of the "pharaohs" that oppress us, to feel the desire for freedom inside themselves again, to hear the cry of the oppressed poor, and to try to liberate at least some of them.

I will try to make these old and still fertile Biblical narratives say some contemporary economic and civil words by asking questions to them; but the most interesting questions will be those that these texts will pose to us. The greater part of the challenge will be not to try to update those ancient pages but to make ourselves their contemporaries. And we will read them along with thousands of years of history, in the company of many, believers and non-believers, who have entered into dialogue with the Bible and, by enriching it, have enriched the world.

A final note.

In the following pages, there are some recurring keywords that have been introduced, discussed, and developed in those years of my personal and collective research on *Civil Economy*. The main frequent and relevant ones are *reciprocity* (Bruni 2008; Bruni and Tufano 2017; Bruni and Zamagni 2007, 2016), *gratuitousness* (Bruni and Smerilli 2015), *pacts* (vs. contracts: Bruni 2012a, b), and *awards* (vs. incentives: Bruni et al. 2018). As discussed in the last 15 years of research, the way I use these words is in general different from their commonsense meaning. Reciprocity requires a certain degree of gratuitousness and is not fully instrumental and extrinsic; gratuitousness is not the gratis (for free) but has to do with intrinsic motivation; the presence of gratuitousness makes pacts (or covenants) different from contracts; awards are the acknowledgment of intrinsic motivated actions, whereas incentives are contracts. To keep light and enjoyable the reading, these keywords will not be analytically discussed in this book, where instead these words are taken as primitive; at the same time, at the end of the reading, the different bits will converge toward a puzzle, where it would be possible to see a first grammar of a biblical economy.

References

Agamben, G. 1998. *Homo Sacer: Sovereign power and bare life*. Stanford: Stanford University Press.

———. 2005. *State of exception*. Chicago: University of Chicago Press.

———. 2011. *The kingdom and the glory: For a theological genealogy of economy and government (Homo Sacer II, 2)*. Stanford: Stanford University Press.

Brams, S.J. 2003. *Biblical games: Game theory and the Hebrew bible*. Cambridge, MA: MIT Press.

Bruni, L. 2008. Reciprocity altruism and civil society. In *Praise of heterogeneity*. London: Routledge.

———. 2012a. *The genesis and ethos of the market*. London: Palgrave Macmillan.

———. 2012b. *The wound and the blessing*. New York: Newcity.

Bruni, L., and J. Milbank, eds. 2018. Martin Luther's heritage in modern economic and social sciences. Special issue of the *International Review of Economics* (forthcoming).

Bruni, L., and P.L. Porta, eds. 2015. Introduction: From happiness to trust and gratuitousness in economics. Special issue: Trust and gratuitousness in economics. *International Journal of Happiness and Development* 2/3: 193–203.

Bruni, L., and A. Smerilli. 2015. *The economics of value bases organizations. An introduction*. London: Routledge.

Bruni, L., and F. Tufano. 2017. The value of vulnerability: The transformative capacity of risky trust. *Judgment and Decision making* 12 (4): 408–414.

Bruni, L., and S. Zamagni. 2007. *Civil Economy*. Oxford: Peter Lang.

———. 2014. Economic and theology in Italy since the eighteenth century. In *The Oxford handbook of Christianity and economics*, ed. Paul Oslington, 57–72. New York: Oxford University Press.

———. 2016. *A civil economy. Another idea of market*. London: AgendaPro.

Bruni, L., Oslington, P., and S. Zamagni. 2016. Economics and theology special issue: Introduction. *International Review of Economics* 63: 1–5.

Bruni, L., V. Pelligra, T. Reggiani, and M. Rizzolli. 2018. The pied piper. *Journal of Business Ethics* (Forthcoming).
Dean, M. 2012. Governmentality meets theology: 'The king reigns, but he does not govern'. *Theory, Culture & Society* 29 (3): 145–158.
Foucault, M. 1999. Pastoral power and political reason. In *Religion and culture*, ed. J.R. Carrette. New York: Routledge.
Leshem, D. 2013. Oikonomia redefined. *Journal of the History of Economic Thought* 35 (1): 43–61.
———. 2014. The ancient art of economics. *European Journal of the History of Economic Thought* 21 (1): 201–229.
———. 2015. Embedding Agamben's critique of Foucault: The theological and pastoral origins of governmentality. *Theory Culture and Society* 32 (3): 93–113.
Nelson, Robert H. 2004. What is economic theology? *Princeton Seminary Bulletin (New Series)* 25 (1): 58–79.
———. 2017. *Lutheranism and the Nordic Spirit of social democracy: A different Protestant ethic*. Aarhus: Aarhus University Press.
Schmitt, C. 2005. *Political theology: Four chapters on the concept of sovereignty*. Trans. G. Schwab, foreword by T.B. Strong. Chicago: University of Chicago Press.
Sedlacek, T. 2011. *Economics of good and evil: The quest for economic meaning from Gilgamesh to wall street*. New York: Oxford University Press.
Sella, E. 1930. *La dottrina dei tre principii*. Padova: Cedam.
Toscano, A. 2011. Divine management: Critical remarks on Giorgio Agamben's the kingdom and the glory. *Angelaki* 16 (3): 127–129.
Viner, J. 1977. *The role of providence in the social order an essay in intellectual history*. Princeton: Princeton University Press.
Wicksteed, P.H. 1910. *The commonsense of political economy*. London: Macmillan.

Contents

Part I
Genesis

Chapter 1
Saving Glances in Times of Exile

I took its ancient words and my old questions and compared them with the vicissitudes of history, culture and customs. In short, I used my Judeo-Christian faith as a key, and I was confirmed in the belief that in our days it is the only possible key to use.

(Sergio Quinzio, *A comment to the Bible*).

Abstract In the beginning, there is no Cain. There's something 'good and beautiful' instead, that, on the sixth day, with Adam became 'very good and beautiful'. It is the blessing that hovers over the created world. The beginning of the earth, the living beings and humans is goodness and beauty, which tells us what is the deepest and truest vocation of the earth, the living. It also tells us that the earth is alive because it is located within a relationship of love and mutuality. For the mountains, rocks and rivers are also living things, otherwise those other beings we call the living would be surrounded by death, and the little life that would be left would be just too sad. The first chapter of Genesis is a sublime hymn to life and creation, with Adam, the human being as its climax. And all these creatures are good, very good, beautiful and blessed because they were called to life by an overflow of love.

In the beginning, there is no Cain. There's something '*good and beautiful*' instead, that, on the sixth day, with Adam became '*very good and beautiful*' (cf.: Genesis 1:31). It is the blessing that hovers over the created world. The *bereshit*, the beginning of the earth, the living beings and humans is goodness and beauty, which tells us what is the deepest and truest vocation of the earth, the *living*.

It also tells us that the earth is alive because it is located within a relationship of love and mutuality. For the mountains, rocks and rivers are also living things, otherwise those other beings we call the living would be surrounded by death, and the little life that would be left would be just too sad (as it probably appears to the one who does not know how to see this life). The first chapter of Genesis is a sublime

L. Bruni, *The Economy of Salvation*, Virtues and Economics 4,
https://doi.org/10.1007/978-3-030-04082-6_1

hymn to life and creation, with Adam, the human being as its climax. And all these creatures are good, very good, beautiful and blessed because they were called to life by an overflow of love.

Yet, human history of that time (Fourth–fifth century BC), and of our own, was and is still the scene of fights, murders and death. The first aspect of greatness in this text that I find amazing is its ability not to dedicate the first words to the everyday human relations that the authors of sacred texts saw happening before their own eyes. Instead they had the strength and inspiration to dedicate the first words to harmony, goodness and beauty, to the blessings of the creatures and to the most beautiful and best of all creatures: Adam. We do not find this anthropological (and ontological) positivism in the creation stories from the Near East or India that are contemporaries or more ancient than Genesis. In these, in fact, the world is born out of violence, from war between the gods, by decadence and degeneration. However, the first word on man in biblical humanism is goodness- and-beauty (*tov*). Evil can be tremendous and crazy, but the good is deeper and stronger than any large and devastating evil.

Many of these early passages of Genesis were written during the Babylonian exile, or when its memory was still very much alive and painful. Exiles do not end unless there is faith and hope that the good is greater and deeper than the ills of the present.

In that good and beautiful setting Cain and Lamech, Joseph's brothers who sold him, Sodoma's inhabitants, the golden calf and the Benjamites of Gibea were all already there. But we were there, too, with the concentration camps, the foibe killings, the gulag and the massacres of innocent people, merchants of the poor and gambling, wars of religion, 9/11 and the young people killed in Kiev, and all the evils and mass killings we are committing now, and, in all likelihood, will commit tomorrow, too. But first there was this very beautiful and very good thing, made "*a little lower than the angels*" (Psalm 8): there was a blessing that was given for all times and that cannot be cancelled by all our sins. This very beautiful and very good thing may get ill and it may degenerate, but no illness of soul and body is strong enough to wipe out this beauty and cancel this primordial goodness. It takes a lot of pain and a lot of agape to continue to believe in this *bereshit*, but this tenacious and stubborn faith is the only way to save us from those diseases and from succumbing to cynicism and nihilism that are always lurking in our civilization, especially in times of crisis and exile.

Life does not die, we cannot be put out inside until – despite having to watch the story from the perspective of Cain and his sons – we do not forget that *before* Cain there is Adam. And if he is there first, he may the last man as well, because the darkness of the *eighth day* fails to dim the auroral light of the sixth – this is the main message and the greatest act of love that comes from Genesis and the Alliance. The hope that is not in vain lies in never letting the first chapter of Genesis be just a self-consolatory myth, a paradise lost forever, theological smoke in the eyes of the people, a bed-time story for children or the first fiction.

To believe in this first word about the world and man, however, means not to believe the legions of cynics, the many friends of Job who want to convince us that the first and last word about humans is that of Cain. It is on this radical anthropological pessimism that we have built social contracts and Leviathans, criminal law and the courts, tax designs and tax collection, the banks, the investment fund and euthanasia for children.

However, an economy that proceeded on the primacy of Adam over Cain and Lamech would take the ethics of virtues as its foundation, one that has its real roots in the supremacy of good over evil, and that would not let itself be colonized by the subspecies of utilitarianism that are commanding it right now. And then it would see workers like people capable of good and beautiful things first, and it would design organizations where gifts and beauty could grow and not just cynicism and opportunism produced by visions and theories that do nothing but multiply the children of Cain. Then we would use more awards (the motivational tools of Adam) and less incentives (born from the Cain-like anthropology). The real man is a mix between Cain and Adam, but the Bible's humanism tells us that Adam is the first. If the first and last word about us was that of Cain, no forgiveness and no restart would be real.

Those who take that first word on the human seriously, or receive it as a gift will have their soul's eyes changed. They will be able to see that the world is full of beautiful and good things. They can marvel at sunsets, stars and snow-capped mountains but they also see very good and very beautiful things when they look at their colleagues, neighbours, old people dying, the terminally ill, the many people warped by poverty or by too much wealth, the grandmother who has returned to be a little girl playing with dolls again, John who is drunk and smelly in the metro, Lucia who has not woken up from a coma, Cain who continues to shock us. No Amazon rainforest, no Alpine mountain peak can ever reach the beauty and goodness of Mary, the homeless woman at Termini Station in Rome. Just a few of these 'glances' may be enough for us make us rise every morning, to lift us from every crisis. We are still alive because these glances have been and continue to be taken. They were taken by eyes that may have looked at us unnoticed, starting with the first glimpse of the woman who greeted us when we came to this world. The charismas are above all the gift of these different glances at the world, that by looking at us and saying our name turn us into what we already are. By being there they saved Adam from the murderous hand of Cain.

These Maieutic looks have been and are still there in firms and markets. I have come across them many times: in a contractor who placed his confidence again in a worker after a serious betrayal, in a worker who forgave a colleague after a deception, or in a hug between partners after years of deep and reciprocal hurt. And they are there even in times of exile and crisis when these acts of imprudence cost much. Glances that are agapically imprudent, never naive, always true and saving, capable of miracles when crossing other glances of the same type of eyes. "*And he saw that it was very good and very beautiful*".

Chapter 2
Counterparts – From the Very Beginning

Death will come and will have your eyes.

(Cesare Pavese).

Abstract From the very beginning, Adam is placed in the garden of Eden, he takes care of it and cultivates it. He works. Two of the trees have a name: the tree of life' and 'the tree of the knowledge of good and evil. Adam is allowed to eat the fruits of the tree of life and the other trees but not those of the second tree. And at this point Elohim says: It is not good for Adam to be alone. And Elohim made for Adam his counterpart. For the first time, in a creation that is still all good and beautiful, we find that there is something that is "not good", namely, loneliness, a relational shortcoming. This is where one of the most striking and richest passages of Genesis starts. There is an assembly of animals and birds of the sky in front of Adam. Adam gives them their name, that is, he enters into a relationship with them, gets to know them and discovers their nature and mystery; but at the end of this procession of the non-human creation Adam is not satisfied because he has not yet found any creature that could stand by his side as his counterpart.

"*It is not good for Adam to be alone.*" The creation is completed when that 'something very beautiful and very good' – Adam – is revealed as a plural reality, and becomes a person. The rhythm of the second chapter of Genesis is fascinating and amazingly rich as it leads from Adam (the human being) to man and woman.

From the very beginning, Adam is placed in the garden of Eden, he takes care of it and cultivates it: that is, he works. Two of the trees have a name: '*the tree of life*' and '*the tree of the knowledge of good and evil*'.

Adam is allowed to eat the fruits of the tree of life and the other trees but not those of the second tree. And at this point *Elohim* says: "*It is not good for Adam to be alone.*" And so: "I will make for him a helper as his counterpart." (2:18). For the first time, in a creation that is still all good and beautiful, we find that there is something that is "*not good*", namely, loneliness, a relational shortcoming. This is where

L. Bruni, *The Economy of Salvation*, Virtues and Economics 4,
https://doi.org/10.1007/978-3-030-04082-6_2

one of the most striking and richest passages of Genesis starts. There is an assembly of animals and birds of the sky in front of Adam. Adam gives them their name, that is, he enters into a relationship with them, gets to know them and discovers their nature and mystery; but at the end of this procession of the non-human creation Adam is not satisfied because he has not yet found any creature that could stand by his side as his 'counterpart'.

There is a turning point here in the narrative that pushes the reader to position themselves on another level, to enter into a new dimension of humanity. The *ezer kenegdo* enters the scene, a Hebrew expression that refers to taking a glance of something and the eyes themselves. We could translate it as 'someone with whom you can exchange glances as equals'; someone who stands opposite you at the same level, 'eye to eye'. It is the first human encounter. The first eyes that saw other eyes that are completely the same and completely different: "*Now this is it, at last!*" (Cf.: 2:23) It is also the debut of man (male) and woman: before this first meeting there is only Adam, the earthling (*adamah* means earth).

History does not begin with sin, but with the exchange of looks by counterparts. The *ezer kenegdo* is the woman, the *ishàh* standing face to face with the *ish* (man), just as *ish* is facing *ishàh*: "*man [ish] has a yod more than woman [ishàh], while woman has a he more than man. If we combine these two letters that distinguish the two names we get* יה *i.e. Yah, which is the short form of the sacred tetragrammaton for the name of God*" (Franco Galeone). True human nature is relational, the full image of God in the humans is in their relationship, contained and explained in the male-female alliance (1.27), which is the one founding and generating all other relationships and human alliances.[1]

For Adam's happiness Eden with its trees and its fruits is not enough. Animals are not enough either, because they are not his 'counterparts' and they do not fill the gap of human loneliness (even if there is a certain culture today, with an impressive business, presenting them as perfect substitutes for the eyes of the other). They can only accompany man, providing a company that is sometimes valuable and helps us to live, and is all for the better if embedded within human relationships. For pleasure only, Adam may be enough, for happiness, however, both *ish/ishàh* are needed, just as those special eyes that welcome us when we are born, and are the last ones we'll see on this earth, those that in the end will close ours, and those we would like to see again first upon 'reopening them'. But we must practice it all this life so that the eyes that we seek are those of the other person, not our own reflection in their eyes; and only when we meet and truly recognize each other in our true diversity

[1]The structure of the 1,27 of Genesis contains in itself a clue about the relational nature of the image of God in human beings. It is the semitic rule of *parallelism:* in the first two lines the text puts in parallel 'image of God' and the 'Adam', and in the third final line the place of 'Image of God' is taken by 'Man and Woman": '(1) So God created mankind in his own image, (2) In the image of God he created them; (3) male and female he created them' (Gen 1,27). – A redactional technique utilized to suggest that in this relation male-female is the full image of God. The Biblical anthropology is radically relational or personalist – the person, i.e. the individual in relation, founds also the spiritual value of the individual. I thank Cardinal Gianfranco Ravasi for this suggestion.

will their gaze return to us what is the best part in us. The lack of someone watching us so, someone to recognize us and reveal us to ourselves is among the most severe forms of poverty and deprivation of the person, which is very frequent where there are great richness and great power – and where you are rarely looked at and loved as an equal.

It is striking how even this description of man-and-woman flies higher than its own time. The sacred author could only see a reality of submission and inferiority of women around and behind him, but he was inspired to write a song about reciprocity between men and women. A song of love but also a critical judgment on the world of yesterday and today, as the result of a disorder, a deviation, a downfall. But in the beginning, there was the *ezer kenegdo*. Human history out of Eden was not only the denial of Adam with Cain, it was also the betrayal of the primordial reciprocity of *ezer kenegdo* in the many 'Adams' who desecrated the moral equality, equal respect, freedom and dignity of women.

Men and women have nevertheless cooperated. The woman has always been the first helper of man, and vice versa. In the streets and in our homes our eyes did see counterparts in each other. The differences were too great in work, educational, civic and institutional opportunities and a still remain in too many places. Although, we must not forget, even in the most sexist societies of the past and the present there have always been times and places where a man and a woman could exchange glances at par. Many daughters were saved because sometimes they have could see that original look of Eden through the eyes of their parents. And they still see it, look for it, fight for it to become politics, fully human rights.

The question about the *ish-ishàh* relation is at the core of every civilization, even our own. Some good answers are beginning to arrive, but many forms of deception are still remain just like those that are common in large companies where you think you have reached equal dignity, 'conceding' the (few) women to take leadership roles in organizations where the culture, language, admission tests, incentives and the rules of the game have been entirely written by '*ish*' without '*ishàh*'. When we have to revise not only the language, but the criminal justice systems, schools, politics, finance and tax collection with the *ish-ishàh* reciprocity in mind, the work awaiting us will be huge, but exciting and decisive. When we lack this fundamental reciprocity, women suffer a lot, but men also suffer because the happiness of all is inside this reciprocity between equals. When we lose the gaze of the other who is our counterpart, we lose the sense of the limit, we get lost, we become masters or subjects, we no longer understand who we are and generate a thousand moral and spiritual disorders.

There are a great many of challenges and questions that the humanism of the *ezer kenegdo* poses to our economy and society. Just think of work. Adam took care of the garden and cultivated it even in times of loneliness. You can work on your own, too. But work is a fully human experience and the venue for ethical excellence when we are not alone, and when we, men and women, can work together as equals. If the fruits of labour, even if salaries are measured in millions, are not shared at home in an '*eye to eye*' way, they do not become full happiness – at the most they can get us some comfort and pleasure. The eyes of those we love multiply our salaries, they can make the yoke of unemployment bearable, and when they are missing even the best pay slips become signs of poverty.

'*It is not good for Adam to be alone*' is then also a word addressed to our work. We have worked and are working in the factories, in the fields, in the mines and remained human because we did it together, side by side, because we have crossed gazes at par, even when our eyes were filled with tears or anger. Work culture and its new forms of organization in our days are likely to bring us back to the phase of the lonely Adam. Not only because of the development of new technologies (often without eyes to look and bodies to touch), but even more so for an anthropological vision that proposes to increase the well-being and reduce injuries by simply deleting (or 'procedurising' and sterilizing) the human encounters. And so, we end up recreating artificial Edens around the individual-worker, populated only by trees and snakes, but without the joy of living.

Every time that we do not want or are not able to look each other in the eyes as equals, we end up contenting ourselves with ever lower looks, we ask too little of ourselves and others, and the fruits of the Tree of Life remain unripe. The sad *Ish* is back in Eden without human gazes, and hears it again, echoed in the garden: "*It is not good for Adam to be alone.*"

Chapter 3
The Way Home: Inhabiting the Realm of the Human

The jasmine bush of the house has been completely worn by rain and storms in recent days, its white flowers are floating here and there on the dark and muddy puddles and on the low roof of the garage. However, inside of me somewhere, it continues to flourish undisturbed, exuberant and tender as ever.

(Etty Hillesum, *Diary*).

Abstract The symphony of life, centred on the human being and the relationships of reciprocity, breaks off abruptly with the arrival of pain and then death. This is what happens in the third chapter of Genesis. The first turn of events on the scene is the arrival of the snake that speaks to the woman. The words of the serpent speak of the fruits of the Tree of the Knowledge of Good and Evil, those that Elohim had proscribed for Adam: "You must not eat from the tree of the knowledge of good and evil, for when you eat from it you will certainly die". In reality what we are facing is not so much a ban but a warning, a promise: no human can eat those fruits because eating them would cause him die. The snake is introduced as the "most cunning" of all animals created. The serpent was also part of that creation which was beautiful and good, and the possessor of an intelligence that Adam knew because he had given a name to it. Intelligence is not always used for the benefit of life and the good.

The symphony of life, centred on the human being and the relationships of reciprocity, breaks off abruptly with the arrival of pain and then death. This is what happens in the third chapter of Genesis and in the chapters of our lives.

The symbolic codes of the narrative are already abundant, but here they become rich and powerful, some of them borrowed and intertwined with the even more ancient myths of the Middle East. We have lost many symbolic meanings forever because they were too "*far away*", and we have added others over the centuries, often blotting out the clear features and colours of the original fresco with ideological

L. Bruni, *The Economy of Salvation*, Virtues and Economics 4,
https://doi.org/10.1007/978-3-030-04082-6_3

'stuccos'. These great texts still speak to us "*in the cool of the day*" if, like their protagonists, we get '*naked*' in front of their essentiality and let ourselves be asked the question: "*Adam, where are you?*"

The first turn of events on the scene is the arrival of the snake that speaks to the woman. The words of the serpent speak of the fruits of the "*Tree of the Knowledge of Good and Evil*", those that Elohim had proscribed for Adam: "*You must not eat from the tree of the knowledge of good and evil, for when you eat from it you will certainly die*" (2:17). In reality what we are facing is not so much a ban but a warning, a promise: no human can eat those fruits because eating them would cause him die. The snake refutes that first promise, and reformulates it into something very different: "*You will not surely die.*" *On the contrary!* "*…God knows that when you eat from it your eyes will be opened, and you will be like God, knowing good and evil*" (3:4–5). The snake ends his speech here. But his words had an effect: the woman trusts the promise of the serpent, and regards the tree as something different. Its fruit starts to look good, beautiful and desirable to her, and so she eats of them and offers it to the man. The two do not die, but their eyes open and they start seeing things differently, feeling ashamed of their nakedness. The first outcome in the text seems to contradict the promise of God ("*you will die*"), and confirm that of the serpent ("*your eyes will be opened*").

The snake is introduced as the "*most cunning*" of all animals created (3,1). The serpent was also part of that creation which was beautiful and good, and the possessor of an intelligence that Adam knew because he had given a name to it. Intelligence is not always used for the benefit of life and the good. We are surrounded by people who use the abundant gifts of intelligence to destroy, to evade taxes, to seduce and exploit the weak, to cheat, to refine slot machines and to improve the efficiency of anti-personnel mines. The earth is full of this wrong type of intelligence. There exists the good type of intelligence, the one of and for life, but next to it there is also the intelligence of the snake. This different type of intelligence is manifested as a discourse, a *logos*. The serpent seduces and convinces by way of talking, using the word that created the world, the man, the woman and the snake in a different way. This is also the power of the word, which can create but also knows how to destroy even though the Word that creates is stronger and deeper than the word that destroys.

The story is full of words that create, but also with words that through their naked force have destroyed lives, reputations, businesses, weddings and induced suicides. Being able to distinguish the types of intelligence that belong to the serpent from the good types that belong to life is a fundamental and difficult art of living, but the tree of our life will only flourish if we are in the social, ethical and spiritual conditions of learning and perfecting this art. The history of the people and institutions is marked by decisive encounters with these different types of intelligence. We have all known "*very good and very nice people*" who lost the golden thread of life, just because they did not (or could not) recognize the intelligence of the snake. I have seen entrepreneurs getting lost not due to the lack of orders or profits, but because they trusted a logic that was different from that of life, because they had not discovered the snake behind the promises of big earnings and easy loans, or because they followed the logic and suggestions that ended up destroying the good faith they had reposed in their businesses and their lives.

From the *day* of the encounter with the snake, the good type of intelligence of life and that of the serpent have been coexisting, they are intertwined with each other in the heart of every person, even the best ones. One can learn the craft of living by learning to recognize the presence of this other intelligence primarily in our reasoning, and only later in those of others. And then one must be very careful not to make the common mistake of community or business leaders of considering some employees as permanent holders of the intelligence of the snake (and, therefore, not to be listened to and to be excluded) and others as permanent carriers of the good and wise type of intelligence. Instead, the intertwining of the two types of intelligence is always present in everyone and everything, but – let us never forget – the intelligence of life is stronger, more real and tougher, and in the end, it is the winner.

But there is a further turn of events that could even give reason to some words of the serpent: "*Behold, the man has now become like one of us, knowing good and evil.*" (3:22). The man and woman lost the innocence of Eden and the magic of the first creation forever; but the text suggests that, paradoxically, they also gained something important, because they entered the age of ethics (the knowledge of good and evil) and responsibility: they must now begin to account for their choices ("*Adam, where are you?*", 3,9).

But then it is also possible to deduce something important, perhaps even surprising, from this story of Genesis. Once out of Eden, we can find the wholeness, harmony, unity of paradise lost, by inhabiting the fundamental places of the human realm with love-and-pain: "*the pain in childbearing*", "*your desire will be for your husband, and he will rule over you*" (3:16), "*by the sweat of your brow you will eat your food until you return to the ground, since from it you were taken*" (3:17–19). From the first Eden we are "out" forever, but Adam is not dead; Elohim gave him a second chance: history. And so, the vocation of humanity can no longer consist of a return to that first Eden that no longer exists, by perhaps seeking some sort of purity and innocence while fleeing from the places of human suffering – the begetting of children, relations between equals, work and death. We can try and find again the harmonies of the first garden by loving, and with the good types of intelligence of life, we may find gorgeous and painful locations and the ones belonging to the realm of the human. If it weren't so, history would be but a deception and the world would be but a condemnation. But history is the way home, where everyone brings along their *dowry*: the heritage of all the pain-and-love built up along the way. This is the first great dignity of human love, family, work, and even of the return of Adam to *adamah*. It follows from this that it is a moral duty of every person – and humanity as a whole – to try to reduce the pain in the world.

We can save ourselves by begetting children (and making them grow into great people), by falling in love, by respecting each other reciprocally, by working and by relearning to die in every generation. We have saved ourselves every day with the struggle-and-love of many labours: those of having children, that of work, and the last great labour. These are the ways that we have at our disposal to be able to glimpse a new earth-garden: new Eves and new Adams, in the cool of every single day.

Chapter 4
We Are All Abel's Heirs

You are still the one with the stone and the sling,
Man of my time. You were in the cockpit,
With the malevolent wings, the meridians of death,
-I have seen you – in the chariot of fire, at the gallows,
At the wheels of torture. I have seen you: it was you,
With your exact science set on extermination,
Without love, without Christ. You have killed again,
As always, as your fathers killed,
as the animals killed that saw you for the first time.
And this blood smells as on the day
When one brother told the other brother:
"Let us go into the fields."

(Salvatore Quasimodo, ***Uomo del mio tempo***).

Abstract If the first murder in human history was a fratricide, then *every* murder is a fratricide. Elohim does not abandon Adam, but dresses him with skins. The human being does not depart in solitude: it is a family leaving Eden. The first human journey in the pains of history is not a solitary journey but a journey made together. In addition to the skins donated, there is the great gift of each other's company for the journey to face the night time and the times of night. Even when you cross the hour of misfortune or error, the fact of being able to cross it with someone, 'eye to eye', is the piece of bread and sip of water that won't let you die in the desert – even in the deserts of the crisis of work, of the company, and therefore of life. The blessing on the creation and on Adam does not get removed by disobedience. And a son, Cain, is donated to the human couple. Cain is a gift, even a future murderer will always remain a son. The second born is Abel. Abel is the same word that we find in the book of Qohelet: habel, vanitas, nothingness. Both become working men: Abel is a shepherd, Cain a farmer, and perhaps the narrative itself, too, contains an echo of the conflict among the last nomads and the first farmers, a conflict that was eventually won by the resident ones. Both make offerings to God, but, for reasons that remain mysterious, God did not like the gifts offered by Cain.

L. Bruni, *The Economy of Salvation*, Virtues and Economics 4,
https://doi.org/10.1007/978-3-030-04082-6_4

If the first murder in human history was a fratricide, then *every* murder is a fratricide. Elohim does not abandon Adam, but dresses him with skins (3:21). The human being does not depart in solitude: it is a family leaving Eden. The first human journey in the pains of history is not a solitary journey but a journey made together.

In addition to the skins donated, there is the great gift of each other's company for the journey to face the night time and the times of night. Even when you cross the hour of misfortune or error, the fact of being able to cross it with someone, 'eye to eye', is the piece of bread and sip of water that won't let you die in the desert – even in the deserts of the crisis of work, of the company, and therefore of life.

The blessing on the creation and on Adam does not get removed by disobedience. And a son, Cain, is donated to the human couple. Cain is a gift, even a future murderer will always remain a son. The second born is Abel. Abel is the same word that we find in the book of Qohelet: habel, vanitas, nothingness. Both become working men: Abel is a shepherd, Cain a farmer, and perhaps the narrative itself, too, contains an echo of the conflict among the last nomads and the first farmers, a conflict that was eventually won by the resident ones. Both make offerings to God, but, for reasons that remain (at least partly) mysterious, God did not like the gifts offered by Cain. Cain suffers from this lack of recognition ("*his face was downcast*", 4:5), which he claimed also because of his birthright, and he cannot overcome this bundle of pain, envy and rage. He invites Abel to go into the fields and there kills him. This is the great turning point, the great silence of creation.

The grammar connecting and combining gifts, obligations, expectations of reciprocity and claims is essential in any discourse on human life. Death comes as a 'horizontal' response to the frustration growing out of a 'vertical' relationship: the un-received and missed appreciation by God for his gifts does not push Cain to rebel against Him (as was often the case in the myths of the nearby Ancient Greece), but triggers violence towards an innocent brother. We are all '*sick*' because of the vital need for recognition, esteem, gratitude; but the gentleness of a life is built by practicing day after day not to feel angry with and hurt by our peers (from brothers to work colleagues) that seem to get more even when this difference in treatment seems unfair and unjustified. When this fundamental exercise of human-ness fails (and we see it too many times), there is still the 'crime' of fraternity.

Death comes into the world by the hand of a brother. And when Cain returns, alone, from the fields he hears the question being asked of him "*Where is your brother?*". Since that day, this question will not leave history any more, and will always be the first radical question of all ethics and all responsibilities. Cain was not the guardian (*shomer*) and therefore was not responsible (he did not answer): "*I do not know. Am I my brother's keeper?*" So, this chapter does not speak only about the first fratricide: it also reveals the first law of all fraternity in *controluce*.

Cain continues to talk with God, to converse with him, even after the fratricide. Even a fratricidal remains the Adam. The last word of Cain is a plea for help so that he would not die: "*Today you are driving me from the land … and whoever finds me will kill me*". And God: "*Not so…and the Lord put a mark on Cain so that no one who found him would kill him*" (4:14). We do not know what the mark of Cain was like, what sign it was. In any case, it was a sign of life. Even a murderer is still an image of the *Adam* (5:3), of *Elohim* and of the people who created and generated them – how many times did it happen that the mothers of children who have become murderers had to press an old photo of their baby son to their chest, and it was with the help of that far-away but vivid image that they tried not to let that child die deep inside themselves. Even a murderer is someone's child. And so, they have to live. However, human history has disregarded the mark of Cain, and it has continued, and still continues to kill him, and practicing Lamech's law of vengeance instead. Therefore, the commandment of 'thou shall not kill' is addressed to the sons of Cain, but also to those who would avenge Abel. Only with the mark of Cain does the logic of "*retaliation*" break, and it puts the law of equivalence of justice and vengeance into a crisis: a life taken is not to be fixed by another death, but by another life. In fact, the chapter closes with a hymn to life, with another child: Seth. '*God*', says Eve, '*has granted me another child in place of Abel, since Cain killed him*' (4:25). And as Cain starts a race, also Seth, the new Abel, will have his legacy that will forever intertwine with that of Cain. Lamech will descend from Cain – he is the first bigamist and murderer of children; but Noah the righteous will also arrive from Seth.

So we are descendants of Cain, but also the children and descendants of Seth. But most importantly, we are all Abel's descendants. The first murdered brother is still alive. This is also the power of the Scriptures. Every time we encounter, embody and re-live this fourth chapter, we can and must feel the temptation of Cain again. But, stronger than that, in us and in the world, there lives, in fact, Abel. The great power of the Word revives a thousand times.

Abel is still alive in the victims of history and he comes back to life every time an innocent or meek or non-violent person is killed. And he dies again, and we continue to feel all the pain of the innocent death. But above all, Abel comes back to life whenever we choose meekness in the face of our violence and that of others, and when we prefer to succumb as the righteous do instead of turning into killers: "*Even if you extend your hand to kill me, I am not extending my hand to kill you.*" These are the words that, in the Qur'anic version of the story, Abel says to Cain when he realizes that his brother is about to strike him down (Sura 5:28).

The earth is full of 'places of Abel'. Their redemption and their diminution measure the degree of human and spiritual development of every civilization and the world as a whole. Let us ask ourselves: throughout the two and a half millennia that separate us from that ancient Chapter 4 of Genesis: have the 'places of Abel' increased or decreased in number? It is not an easy calculation to do. Some were definitely eliminated, but new ones are born: the sidewalks or the five-star hotels where the '*slave trade*' is being practiced, the arcades and video-lottery, the many centres for the first '*reception*' of immigrants, the prison cells of those who ended up there as victims, the still too many refugee camps and the places of detention in forgotten wars, the death factories where children work in order not to die, the sad homes for the elderly where, left alone, they are waiting for death.

We should train ourselves to be able to watch the world by positioning ourselves on the side of the victims, and observe it from the perspective of Abel and his places. By visiting them and loving them we would learn things that are very different from those seen by the people who position themselves in the perspective of Cain and his many places. We would realize, for example, that it is not true that Cain is the one who wins, and that it is not true that the violent and the murderers are always destined to win. There is a victory for Cain, but there is also the triumph of Abel the non-fratricidal. History shows us violent people that kill and meek people that succumb, but the really fertile seed is the blood of Abel, giving rise to the many Noahs who have saved the world for us, and keep saving it for us every day. The world that has been saved and populated by the sons of Seth, which is the same world where the children of Cain live, who continue to strike Abel down, and still receive the 'mark' not to die.

Chapter 5
And Noah Rebuilt the Rainbow

There were two completely strange creatures among those that found refuge in the ark. Among those who sought asylum with Noah, there was Falsehood, which was rejected because it did not have a companion: in fact, the animals were only allowed to come into the ark in pairs. So he went in search of a mate and met Loss, who joined him on a condition of getting all the other would earn from then on. So the two were allowed in the ark. When they left the ark, Falsehood saw that everything he could scrape together disappeared at once, and went to ask for an explanation to his mate. But in response Loss said to him: "Didn't we agree that all your earnings would be mine?" So Falsehood remained empty-handed.

(Louis Ginzberg, *The Legends of the Jews*).

Abstract The first major work, the first enterprise narrated by Genesis is not the Tower of Babel, but a great ark of salvation and covenant built by a "righteous man". The roots of the dignity and value of every civil and ethical technique, every economy and every human endeavour are deeply rooted in the righteousness of Noah. The story of Noah is one of the most beautiful, popular and longest stories of the book of Genesis, extending through six chapters, from 5 to 10. His figure appears when humanity, already out of Eden, had departed from the original vocation of Adam, and the sons of Cain and Lamech had prevailed over those of Seth. God sends "floodwaters". Along with the human beings, animals and plants are also mysteriously destroyed – they share in the sad fate of mankind. As if the Creator, having seen human corruption, could no longer "see" his creation beautiful and good, as if the land could not be "beautiful and good" any more if that "very beautiful and very good" thing (the Adam) gets corrupted, lost and loses his vocation. This way the entire creation dies, too, to be reborn in the hope and expectation of a new Adam that would be still worthy to cultivate it and look after it in terms of a law of reciprocity.

L. Bruni, *The Economy of Salvation*, Virtues and Economics 4,
https://doi.org/10.1007/978-3-030-04082-6_5

The first major work, the first enterprise narrated by Genesis is not the Tower of Babel, but a great ark of salvation and covenant built by a "*righteous man*" (6:9). The roots of the dignity and value of every civil and ethical technique, every economy and every human endeavour are deeply rooted in the righteousness of Noah.

The story of Noah, the heir of Seth (the third son of Adam and Eve, the new Abel), is one of the most beautiful, popular and longest stories of the book of Genesis (extending through six chapters, from 5 to 10). His figure appears when humanity, already out of Eden, had departed from the original vocation of Adam, and the sons of Cain and Lamech had prevailed over those of Seth. God (YHWH) "*saw how great the wickedness of the human race had become on the earth, and that every inclination of the thoughts of the human heart was only evil all the time*" (6:5). So "*the Lord regretted that he had made human beings on the earth, and his heart was deeply troubled*" (6:6).

Therefore, God sends "floodwaters" (6,17). Along with the human beings, animals and plants are also mysteriously destroyed – they share in the sad fate of mankind. As if the Creator, having seen human corruption, could no longer "see" his creation beautiful and good, as if the land could not be "*beautiful and good*" any more if that "*very beautiful and very good*" thing (Adam) gets corrupted, lost and loses his vocation. This way the entire creation dies, too, to be reborn in the hope and expectation of a new Adam that would be still worthy to cultivate it and look after it in terms of a law of reciprocity. As for the ark of the Covenant (it is worth noting that the word ark (*teba*) means 'basket', the one in which Moses was saved from death: yet another instance of alliance and salvation from the "*waters*"), Noah receives the order to let in a couple of each species of animals, birds and reptiles, apart from himself, his wife, his three sons and their wives – the salvation of the ark is also for its builders. It is beautiful and important that it's is a raven and a dove – the latter one sits tamely on Noah's arm – to appear as the first allies of the human being in the new land, where the alliance is established with the family and descendants of Noah, but also "*with every living creature that was with you—the birds, the livestock and all the wild animals*" (9:10). In a context of perversion and corruption, the last word is not death: at the centre of the scene we find a righteous man, the only righteous man left on earth (7:1). And it is with this righteous man that God enters into a contract, a "*Covenant*" (6:18), a word that enters the world with Noah, never to leave it again.

In the story of Noah we find the first grammar of every authentic vocation: there is a person who receives a call; then there is an answer; therefore an ark; and finally there is a non-hero. This call is addressed to a "*you*", with a name. This "*you*" is a righteous man, *therefore* he responds to the call. When the call comes, especially if it is the decisive call of life, the righteous give an answer, and they answer in any context, at any age: at 20, 50 and also at 80, what's more, even at 600 (the "years" of Noah, cf.: Gen 7:6). Noah does not respond by words; he does not talk to God, but he "walked faithfully with Him" (6:9). Simply walking is what the righteous ones often do: they do not talk, but they do things, they love and give life, and their words become their work, they "*talk*" by building an ark of salvation. Vocation is not a psychological thing, not a feeling but a being, a saving edifice.

So the first sign of Noah's righteousness is his answer to the call. But the second, really decisive sign is the building of an ark, which gives content and truth to that personal call. When the call to build an ark is not felt inside a call, you should always question the authenticity of that call: without a task of "*building, construction*" a vocation is reduced to the mere experience of "*consumption*", and therefore does not save anybody, not even the one who received the call. Many self-deceptions and not infrequently neurosis has also been hiding behind "*calls without arks of salvation*". Human communities, businesses and the world are saved every day from situations of degradation, failure and from radical crises only because there are people who feel a call of salvation and answer it. *Because there is at least one such person.* A single person can be enough for a story of salvation. Instances of salvation come because someone feels a call to save themselves and to save all and, above all, because this someone builds an ark. Someone creates a work of art, founds a cooperative, a company, a union, an association, a political movement. Someone forms and takes care of a family, a child, a job or manages to carry a fruit-bearing cross for very long.

In all the stories of individual and collective salvation there is a "righteous man" and there is "an ark". One of the most amazing spiritual, moral and aesthetic phenomena on earth is the presence of people who have received a vocation and that of the works arising from these (sometimes completely "*mute*") vocations. The earth is full of people who build "*arks*" to save their own generation. These works, these arks are clearly distinguishable from other works, large and small, that also populate the earth and the economy. The conclusion of the story of Noah reveals a distinctive sign of the arks of salvation for us. His task completed, Noah returns to being a common man. Unlike Gilgamesh and the many protagonists of the numerous Sumerian and Akkadian accounts of the flood, Noah is not a hero or demi-god: he is simply a man, an ordinary man, but a righteous man. After having accomplished his work, Genesis shows him as a farmer: he plants the first vineyard on earth, gets drunk with the wine (the ambivalence of wine and life), lies naked in the tent (9:20–21), and is mocked by Ham, one of his sons (9:22). Noah, then, serves also as the paradigm of all the bearers of authentic charisma, who build an ark and do not feel a hero but a simple "*pencil*" (Mother Teresa), and who know when their task ends.

There are many righteous people who, at one point in their lives feel the call to build an ark of salvation for themselves and for many. This call comes in various forms, but if life grows and matures in justice, one day the crucial event arrives, when the "*righteous man*" realizes that if he does not build an ark he won't save his people, and neither will he save himself. In other, not less important cases, however, there is a person who becomes righteous because at a crucial moment of their life they recognize a call in a voice and they respond and build an ark, and the process of building itself becomes the salvation of the builder (and then of many). It is the ark that "*builds*" Noah. In other cases still, an ark is sought to save the seeker and many others, but no calling voice is heard (or it is not recognized). The building of something starts, almost always in response to the pain of the world, however without a clear idea of the purpose of the work. Still, work is done, and a voice is expected. Sometimes this sense-making voice arrives during the construction work, at other times the work is continued throughout life only waiting for it. In such cases the ark becomes the voice and the call, and this "*voiceless*" Noah is no less righteous. There may be, and there are some arks built with no call, but there must be no calls without an ark built.

The story of Noah closes in a cosmic horizon, in a celebration of the land: "*I have set my rainbow in the clouds, and it will be the sign of the covenant between me and the earth*" (9:13). Every time a righteous man builds an ark that first covenant is renewed. We are still saving ourselves, and with us the world is being saved. Noah the righteous continues to live among us, the whole earth is in celebration and we are given a new rainbow.

Chapter 6
Heaven Is Not Above Babel

Many, many years were passed in building the tower. It reached so great a height that it took a year to mount to the top. A brick was, therefore, more precious in the sight of the builders than a human being. If a man fell down, and met his death, none took notice of it, but if a brick dropped, they wept, because it would take a year to replace it. So intent were they upon accomplishing their purpose that they would not permit a woman to interrupt herself in her work of brick-making when the hour of travail came upon her. Moulding bricks she gave birth to her child, and, tying it round her body in a sheet, she went on moulding bricks.

(L. Ginzberg, *The Legends of the Jews*).

Abstract After the Ark the people built Babel, a fortified town with a tall tower in the centre. The Book of Genesis tells us the size of Noah's Ark, 132 meters in length, 22 in width, 13 in depth, while it only says about Babel that the top of the tower was supposed to reach the heavens. Based on this indication, some traditions have imagined great heights for the tower, perhaps based on memories of the pyramids of Egypt, or the giant ziggurat of Babylon, much larger than those of the ark that had saved the fathers and mothers of the builders of Babel. The companies of those who build in response to a call and to save themselves and others are not, in general, greater and more powerful than the companies of those who build to create empires. There are many meanings that have, over time, layered on Babel and should be traced into the Babylonian exile (Babel) and into the memories of the "building blocks" of the slavery of Egypt, and into the eternal critique of idolatry. The myth of Babel tells that blessing and fruitfulness lies in the popular new worlds, and in the variety and biodiversity of languages, and so cultures, talents and vocations. The corolla of the flower is only fruitful if it disperses its spores.

L. Bruni, *The Economy of Salvation*, Virtues and Economics 4,
https://doi.org/10.1007/978-3-030-04082-6_6

After the Ark the people built Babel, a fortified town with a tall tower in the centre. The Book of Genesis (6:15) tells us the size of Noah's Ark (132 meters in length, 22 in width, 13 in depth), while it only says about Babel that the top of the tower was supposed to reach the heavens (11,4). Based on this indication, some traditions have imagined great heights for the tower (perhaps based on memories of the pyramids of Egypt, or the giant ziggurat of Babylon), much larger than those of the ark that had saved the fathers and mothers of the builders of Babel. The companies of those who build in response to a call and to save themselves and others are not, in general, greater and more powerful than the companies of those who build to create empires.

There are many meanings that have, over time, layered on Babel and should be traced into the Babylonian exile (Babel) and into the memories of the "building blocks" of the slavery of Egypt ("*Let us make bricks*", 11:3), and into the eternal critique of idolatry ("*let's make a name for ourselves*", 11:4).

The story of Babel contains a radical critique of every empire, and so of power. As regards the founder of Babel (Nimrod), Genesis says: *he was the first "who became a mighty warrior on the earth"* (10:8). Babel is a symbol of the fortified city, but most importantly it is a symbol of the empire. It is not a radical critique of all types of power (also Adam and Noah have power), but the power that is not used to save. The saving power of Noah and that of the empires of Babel still live next to each other, and are intertwined in our cities and institutions. There are those who use for salvation the power they received from citizens or shareholders in a contract – alliance (whether it be political, economic, familial or educational), and also those, who use it to dominate and to extract gains and privileges – the empire. There is a type of power that saves and another that kills; and we find them often, almost always, cohabiting in the same organization, institution, company, sometimes in the same department and even in the same office where the builders of arks are seated next to the builders of Babel.

The Noah-Babel comparison gives us, however, other words and other messages of life. First of all, the message regarding work. The builders of both the ark and the city-tower were workers, and they were united with each other – without a form of work solidarity neither the right nor the wrong sort of work can start. This solidarity appears strongly in the story of Babel, because there is an explicit collective action, the work of a group, a community of work: "*Then they said to one another, "Come, let us build ourselves a city, with a tower*"" (11,4). There is a '*come*', a 'let's go', which is a mutual encouragement and exhortation for the construction of a work. Not all types of solidarity and cooperation are good, and not all works are good things: the work of the bricklayers and engineers of Babel is not a blessed work, and it gets dispersed. There are some works for which it is better if it is dispersed. Jobs created today by the powerful empires of the mafia, pornography, gamble, companies that are poisoning us, wars and prostitution are not blessed works, and we should disperse them. The works of the empires are works of slaves yesterday and today: forms of slavery and empires may be changed, but their signs and their fruits remain the same.

The fundamental error of Babel was to seek salvation by closing into a group of only the similar ones: they all had "*one language and a common speech*" (11,1). The city-tower was built in order not to "*be scattered over the face of the whole earth*" (11:4). To be scattered was exactly the command issued to those who were saved from the flood: "*multiply on the earth and increase upon it*" (9:7). But moving eastward the human community arrived in a valley and stopped there (11:2): they sought salvation not in a 'going', but in a 'staying' away from the risk of diversity and the teeming of life. That human community made a tower – empire (11:4) since it spoke one language and they all had the same words (11:1): it is the single language – the single "*lip*" – which produces the fortification of Babel. *The construction of empires is the ultimate act of human groups that lose biodiversity* and are flattened by having just one language, when language and thought are impoverished and become a "one" not after but before being manifold, a unit denying diversity.

So, the major fault of Babel was thinking that salvation is found in the creation of high walls, in giving life to a *cum-moenia* (common walls) type of community that loses the *cum-munus* (reciprocal gifts-and-obligations). Our history has always been an alternation and an intersection of cities-of-walls and cities-of-gifts, but when the walls killed the gifts it did not bring happy days for civilization.

So, God intervenes to save the inhabitants of Babel by a pseudo-salvation. For Babel, too, is a story of salvation: JHWJ continues obstinately to save humanity that stubbornly continues to want to save itself in the wrong manner and places.

In the case of the ark, salvation came with a building process, in Babel it was born from destruction, by dispersion. The first saving dispersion happens in the families that save their children when they send them out to "*disperse*" in the world and make them 'fly' free. This way they do not get "*consumed*" in "*incestuous*" relationships. Many communities (and many companies, too) are saved when their leaders do not fall into the temptation of surrounding themselves with only the similar ones in language and words, thereby expelling the speakers of other languages; or when they realize in time that they do not have to continue to grow in "height" and power, and have the wisdom and the courage to "scatter" the pieces of empire. And all this in order to start again, free and blessed to walk towards a land. The great message of the myth of Babel is then an invitation not to fall into the trap of pathology of the community (that becomes a giant ego), locked inside the protective walls of non-diversity.

The blessing and fruitfulness lies in the popular new worlds, and in the variety and biodiversity of languages, and so cultures, talents and vocations. The corolla of the flower is only fruitful if it disperses its spores. The temptation of Babel arrives promptly as soon as mankind has escaped a flood or is fearing another one. Instead of getting dispersed, leaving, looking ahead with hope, instead of looking for allies among the different ones for exchanges and encounters of mutual benefit, the tent is abandoned and the building of a tower is started. But in such towers no children are born. The tent is the right home for the human. Today in Europe and in world, in the post (or pre?) flood era, the temptation of Babel is about to return. And still, we must hope for a saving type of dispersion. In the valley of Babel people did not understand that “*the heavens*” to reach were not above them but in front of them, on the road towards multiples. They did not understand that a humble nomadic tent is more resistant than a sky-high tower.

Out of Eden, in the garden of history, a single language is not enough to utter words of life. The need for unity and the *saudade* of “home” cannot be answered by rejecting dispersions in multiples, but by meeting them and welcoming them. We shall not find the new language of Adam if we keep turning back or trapping our history inside the towers of the similar ones; we will only be able to retrieve it if we walk following a voice, a rainbow, a star, a wandering Aramean.

Chapter 7
Towards the Land of the Children

> *There was he who was great through his strength, and he who was great through his wisdom, and he who was great through his hopes, and he who was great through his love; but Abraham was greater than all of these.*
>
> (Søren Kierkegaard, *Fear and Trembling*).

Abstract After the flood and after Babel, the fortified city in which humanity had sought the wrong type of salvation without diversity and dispersion on the fertile land, the covenant and salvation are continued with the calling of Abram, who leaves his father's house and starts out on a journey, trusting a voice that is calling him. Faith and trust: because every faith is trust in a promise. Noah had saved us by building an ark, remaining in detention in the company of his family and the animals, waiting for the withdrawal of the waters. Abram, however, responds to the call of that same voice by starting a journey to a promised land. Even in the call of Abram we can find a universal grammar of religious as well as civil, professional, artistic, and entrepreneurial vocations. Abram arrives in the land of Canaan and finds the Canaanites there: the promised land is populated by others.

After the flood and after Babel, the fortified city in which humanity had sought the wrong type of salvation without diversity and dispersion on the fertile land, the covenant and salvation are continued with Abram, who leaves his father's house and starts out on a journey, trusting a voice that is calling him.

Faith and trust: because every faith is trust in a promise. Noah had saved us by building an ark, remaining in detention in the company of his family and the animals, waiting for the withdrawal of the waters. Abram, however, responds to the call of that same voice by starting a journey to a promised land: "*Go from your country, your people and your father's household to the land I will show you*." (12:1). At the beginning of his story he is not asked to build any ark, nor is he – like Moses – to free his people from slavery. In response, Abram has '*only*' to believe a promise of a land, and start a journey to reach it; he must leave the house of his father Terah and

L. Bruni, *The Economy of Salvation*, Virtues and Economics 4,
https://doi.org/10.1007/978-3-030-04082-6_7

move to a land that is described to him as a place of blessings and happiness, but unknown as yet. With Abram – the first Jew of the Bible – there appears a call to happiness, fertility, flourishing: "*I will make you into a great nation, and I will bless you; I will make your name great, and you will be a blessing. and all peoples on earth will be blessed through you*" (12:2). In this there lies a call to life, a promise of the future: hence it includes Adam, Eden and the continuation of Noah's rainbow. With him there is a wife, Sarai and together they reach not the safe land of the fathers but the unknown land of the children. The first calling of Abram lies entirely in believing a promise unconditionally, and setting out on a journey. This is his first righteousness.

Noah was "righteous" and because of his righteousness he was given a decisive role. It is not said about Abram that he had been righteous before the call, but his righteousness comes from having believed the promise: "*Abram believed the Lord, and he credited it to him as righteousness.*" (15:6). Noah was righteous and therefore he believed; Abram believed and became righteous.

There are people who receive a call to perform a task of salvation, to build an ark: they build it and so they save many and by saving others they save themselves. But there are others to whom that same voice makes a promise of happiness and fulfilment, and their righteousness lies in believing that promise wholeheartedly and obstinately throughout their life. These 'called ones' make their way to a land not to save someone or something, but because they can see or at least suspect blessing, happiness, fruits and as many 'children' as the stars in the sky in that promise. In these vocations the arks to be built arrive later (and if the call is real, they always arrive, too), but in believing and setting off there is no altruism or sacrifice; there are no gifts to make but only to receive. The fulfilment of these vocations starts by a twofold act of trust: trust is placed in a good '*voice*' that's calling, and it is believed that the fulfilment of that promise is the best happiness.

In every vocation there is always a radical act of trust in a 'voice' that is calling, even if you do not know whose that calling voice could be. The righteousness and goodness of Abram are not primarily the result of virtue: it is found in believing a promise, and continuing to believe and to walk. Many spiritual and then community diseases arise when blessing and salvation are turned into ethical perfectionism or the promise of a moral, when, instead of continuing to walk you stop to observe the virtues (of your own) and vices (of others).

Even in the call of Abram we can find a universal grammar of religious as well as civil, professional, artistic, and entrepreneurial vocations. Abram arrives in the land of *Canaan* and finds the Canaanites there: the promised land is populated by others. He does not find fruits and abundance, but famine that makes him migrate to Egypt. He stays in Canaan "*as a foreigner*" (17:8), the children promised to him in numbers of the stars in the sky do not come, instead, he and his wife inescapably get to old age.

The land promised by the calling voice appears always different from how we imagined it to be. A vocation is not a contract (but a pact or covenant), and so there are surprises, disappointments, trials, discomfort, sometimes even despair and, always, forgiveness, and the possibility to start over. The good fatigue of those who have received a vocation (and they are many more than we think) is to keep walking when the promised land looks dry and populated by others, and when your family and goods are taken from you in that land (14:12). The righteousness of Abram is found in his responding to the first call and, above all, in his persistence when that promise seemed to be very distant and perhaps even a self-deception. It was in continuing to believe that the earth and the dry womb of Saray could still generate and flourish in blessings. Abram found a land that was different from what he had thought at the time of the call, but he was righteous and the greatest of all people because he continued to believe that the land YHWH would show him was the promised land, and no other.

To be righteous is, in every vocation, to be able to recognize the promised land even in a dry land and see future children in a barren womb. I know many righteous business owners who set out on a journey following a voice; they believed in a promise, and then found, and still find, a dry land and see neither children nor grandchildren. Those, who were able to see the first fruits in the drought of the promised land were the ones that were saved and saved others, too; but especially those, who continued their journey and kept moving their tent forward, without constructing another land for themselves having been disappointed about the promise that is not arriving.

Abram received the first call when he was 75 years old (the number of years in the Bible carry many hidden meanings, all important and generally positive), but he only becomes Abraham when he is 99 years old: "*walk before me faithfully and be blameless. ... No longer will you be called Abram; your name will be Abraham, for I have made you a father of many nations. I will make you very fruitful*" (17:1–6). There had been a call already, but now something new is happening: Abram becomes Abraham, and Sarai becomes Sarah (17:15). After 14 years, the call to happiness and to the promised land becomes a covenant between JHWH and an entire people in sight of a universal blessing (reading and studying these early chapters of Genesis I am overwhelmed by the blessings originating from such a good look on the world and humans; a gaze that loves me and nurtures me). That new encounter reveals the calling; it renews and qualifies that first promise. But above all, it changes the name and thus reveals the true meaning of the first vocation. Abram had not been blameless (just read Chap. 13 about Sarai in Egypt), Abraham would become so.

There is a crucial moment in the (successful) development of any (real) vocation. One day there is a departure because after having listened to a voice of blessing, then the arrival in an unknown land, the fighting of a good battle, but still a lack of the deep meaning of the promise. And here comes a second vocation in the first vocation: Abram dies and Abraham is born. It is understood that the first land, the bountiful herds and rivers were not the true promise. And he also becomes '*blameless*', but not through a search for ethical perfection, because blamelessness is a gift and a profound seeking of truth in the service of the promise. Abram was a family man, Abraham becomes the father of a people, of many, of '*all the families of the earth*'. And yet the journey must be continued, even when the road goes up and it seems to become a silent procession with a child-victim to a mountain-altar, when the rainbow disappears and the countless stars go out. To be saved and to remain righteous, not to stop on the way, still looking forward, until the eyes go weary of gazing at the horizon.

Chapter 8
Hagar and Her Many Sisters

The first time in history that a woman used a belt was when Ishmael's mother started wearing one to conceal her pregnancy from Sarai.

(*The Book of Sayings About the Prophets*).

Abstract The first angel of the Bible was sent to comfort a slave-mother, Hagar, who was chased away by her mistress. Having realised her infertility and the crisis of the Promise, Sarai looks for a solution of her own, and invites Abram to sleep with her slave Hagar, and Ishmael was born. But when Hagar knew she was pregnant, she began to despise her mistress. Something did not work in this solution that had seemed simple: that baby will not be 'Sarai's son', but will always be only Hagar's. Then Sarai mistreated Hagar; so she fled from her. Hagar runs away into the desert and it is there, in the place that is always loaded with symbols, that an announcement is made to her. The message of this chapter is very important: the whole Bible is filled with the tension between law and prophecy, obligations and freedom, institution and charisma. The laws-and-institutions of primogeniture and patriarchy are recognised and it is on these foundations that the people and the Law are constituted. At the same time, they are re-dimensioned, blurred and sometimes even rejected by preference given to non-firstborns (Abel, Jacob, Joseph, David…), to slave women who talk to God or a patriarch who is obeying his wife.

The first angel of the Bible was sent to comfort a slave-mother, Hagar, who was chased away by her mistress. Having realised her infertility and the crisis of the Promise, Sarai looks for a solution of her own: "*so she said to Abram, "The Lord has kept me from having children. Go, sleep with my slave; perhaps I can build a family through her.*" (16:2) Therefore Sarai "*took her Egyptian slave Hagar and gave her to her husband*" (16:3).

As she is getting to old age, Sarai cannot believe in the reality of the call and finds a way out provided by the law (which is there also in Hammurabi's code in

L. Bruni, *The Economy of Salvation*, Virtues and Economics 4,
https://doi.org/10.1007/978-3-030-04082-6_8

Babylon), which, however, is a diversion from the promise. But when Hagar "*knew she was pregnant, she began to despise her mistress.*" (16:4). Something did not work in this solution that had seemed simple: that baby will not be '*Sarai's son*', but will always be only Hagar's (and Abram's). Every child is a gift and a mystery, a promise coming true. "*Then Sarai mistreated Hagar; so she fled from her.*" (16:6) Hagar runs away into the desert and it is there, in the place that is always loaded with symbols, that an announcement is made to her: "*I will increase your descendants so much that they will be too numerous to count.*" "*...you will give birth to a son. You shall name him Ishmael, for the Lord has heard of your misery.*" (16,10–11). Hagar returns to Abram's house and the humiliations continue. And when Sarai (who, in the meantime becomes Sarah) gives birth to Isaac from her already dried womb, she will say to her husband: "*Get rid of that slave woman and her son*". Abraham obeys Sarah, and the choice "*distressed Abraham greatly*". (21:11)

After this she is chased away for the second time, Hagar does not return. She leaves the scene but never the book of life where the many Hagars still cry out loud for being chased away and yet they talk to God. He "...then sent her off with the boy. She went on her way and wandered in the Desert of Beersheba. When the water in the skin was gone, she put the boy under one of the bushes. Then she went off and sat down about a bowshot away, for she thought, "*I cannot watch the boy die.*" And as she sat there, she began to sob". (21:14–16) In this desperate crying all the cries can be included of the slave women of the world of yesterday and today, of all the women who are humiliated by other men and other powerful women, the tears and silences of the victims, of all the migrating people and the refugees across the deserts and the seas. But in that desert Hagar meets YHWH again: "*God heard the boy crying, and the angel of God called to Hagar from heaven and said to her, "What is the matter, Hagar? Do not be afraid; God has heard the boy crying as he lies there*"". (21:17)

There are many messages that reach us from these chapters, so full of beauty, humanity and pain. The first one is about conflicts and the ways of resolution. Sarah never recognises Hagar as a 'you': according to the text she does not call her by her name but always only '*slave woman*'; it is only JHWH that calls her Hagar. Without recognising the other person there is no way out from any conflict. Sarah's status, her being a matriarch and a mistress, here wins over the solidarity among women that is born many times and is realized surpassing differences in status. The conflict is interrupted (but not resolved) by the use of mere power and so with the expulsion of the weaker one who becomes a victim. Sarah's non-solution is still very commonly practiced in our institutions and companies. But it is not the only way these episodes of Genesis talk to us. Once they reach Canaan, on return from Egypt, Abram enters into conflict with his nephew, Lot: "*But the land could not support them while they stayed together, for their possessions were so great that they were not able to stay together*" (13:6). Goods and abundance, that is, the promise of JHWH become the basis for a family conflict. But Abram finds a solution: "*Let's not have any quarrelling between you and me...for we are close relatives. Let's part company. If you go to the left, I'll go to the right; if you go to the right, I'll go to the left*" (13:8–10). Here Abram avoids the conflict by a generous move: he lets Lot choose the better land (13:10). It isn't a rare thing that the goods we are given by our vocation (the task, the land, the success, the talent…) become the reason for conflict and rivalry with others who accompany us on our journey. And when the territory (the company, the project, the community…) is too small compared to the abundance of goods and talents, salvation may come from a separation, from taking two different roads.

But the difficult, paradoxical and tragic questions of these narratives are not exhausted at this point. Sarah means princess. The name of Hagar, however, reminds us of the movement of migration. Hagar is Egyptian, perhaps (according to a certain *midrash*) daughter of the Pharaoh, and Egypt is not only the image of exile and slavery – it is also the place where Sarai emigrated with Abram after they found famine in the promised land, where she was entered into the harem of the pharaoh who, once he discovered the plot against him (she was not the sister but the wife of Abram) sent them away (12:19). Then Sarai was also a migrant, slave woman, victim and someone who was sent away. Hagar, as far as she is concerned, is a slave woman and a victim, but she is also the one to whom the first angel is sent, and, just like the great kings and prophets, she gets to talk to God, and a great descendance is announced to her. Sarah and Hagar swap roles at this point, one appears in the position of the other. Victims and slave women are still there, just like masters and powerful people, but these wonderful chapters of Genesis want to tell us something more profound.

In the comedy-or-tragedy of life the masks worn by personalities are always many, and every person hides more than one personality. But most importantly, Hagar's story tells us that if we want to capture some of the mystery of the Bible and life, it is indispensable to read salvation history not only from the perspective of Sarah and Isaac, but also from that of Hagar and Ishmael. They will only open up if and while we read them, and this way we may be given the '*intelligence of the Scriptures*' (i.e. the episode of the disciples of Emmaus in the Gospel).

The book of Genesis, and in a certain sense the whole Bible is filled with the tension between law and prophecy, obligations and freedom, institution and charisma. The laws-and-institutions of primogeniture and patriarchy are recognised and it is on these foundations that the people and the Law are constituted. At the same time, they are re-dimensioned, blurred and sometimes even rejected by preference given to non-firstborns (Abel, Jacob, Joseph, David…), to slave women who talk to God or a patriarch who is obeying his wife. The horizontal plot of the patriarchs and kings is interwoven by the vertical warp of the cast-off of yesterday, today and always. It is in their spaces that the '*needle*' of history passes through, creating the texture of life. The book of history can be read from the perspective of the fathers and ancestors, but everything is given a greater truth if we try to place ourselves also in the position of those who were defeated, if we look at the interrupted paths with attention and pietas.

The exercise to be done for recognising this inextricable and vital weave of Sarah-Hagar and Isaac- Ishmael, however, should not keep us from another, more important spiritual exercise: to try to make a choice and decide which aspect we want to give the first place. It always does matter if the first take on our lives and cities is that of Hagar or Sarah. If Hagar's eyes are the first to take a look it will be easy to see that the most fertile perspective of the world is not that of the princesses and the powerful, but the one that originates from the biblical and existential peripheries. The ones inhabited by Hagar, Noemi, Dinah, Mary and their many sisters yesterday, today and always.

Chapter 9
Faithfulness Throughout the Unexpected

> *After he had laid the wood in order, and bound Isaac on the altar, upon the wood, Abraham braced his arms, rolled up his garments, and leaned his knees upon Isaac with all his strength. And God, sitting upon His throne, high and exalted, saw how the hearts of the two were the same, and tears were rolling down from the eyes of Abraham upon Isaac, and from Isaac down upon the wood, so that it was submerged in tears.*
>
> (Louis Ginzberg, *The Legends of the Jews*, Vol. I).

Abstract "Your wife Sarah will bear you a son". Abraham laughed and said to himself, "Will Sarah bear a child at the age of ninety?". He could not believe a promise that would go against the laws of nature (which the very same Voice had given to the world and to life). Sarah, too, laughs near the great trees of Mamre. And Elohim will also be laughing when he utters the name of the son: Isaac, Jishaq, meaning 'God is laughing'. Abraham and Sarah knew that Isaac was only and entirely the gift of that first Voice. They realise all the rest through their life's experiences. It is only us, readers and re-readers of these texts that know about the 'test' of Mount Moriah, the angel and the ram. Not them: Abraham, Isaac, the servants, Sarah did not know what would happen to them one step further from the one just taken. If we do not take the actual humanity of these far-away narratives and their heroes, we inevitably end up thinking that they are just nice, educational fairy tales or stories with a moral message, and so we empty them of all their anthropological, social and spiritual power.

Every son and daughter hides in themselves the mystery of gratuitousness. It is true for Isaac, too, albeit in a unique and extraordinary way: "your wife Sarah will bear you a son" (17:19). Abraham 'laughed and said to himself, "Will Sarah bear a child at the age of ninety?"' (17:17). He could not believe a promise that would go against the laws of nature (which the very same Voice had given to the world and to life). Sarah, too, laughs near the great trees of Mamre: "After I am worn out and my lord is old, will I now have this pleasure?" (18:12). And Elohim will also be laughing when he utters the name of the son: "Isaac" (17:19), Jishaq, meaning "(God) is laughing".

L. Bruni, *The Economy of Salvation*, Virtues and Economics 4,
https://doi.org/10.1007/978-3-030-04082-6_9

Abraham and Sarah knew that Isaac was only and entirely the gift of that first Voice. They realise all the rest through their life's experiences. It is only us, readers and re-readers of these texts that know about the 'test' of Mount Moriah, the angel and the ram. Not them: Abraham, Isaac, the servants, Sarah did not know what would happen to them one step further from the one just taken. If we do not take the actual humanity of these far-away narratives and their heroes, we inevitably end up thinking that they are just nice, educational fairy tales or stories with a moral message, and so we empty them of all their anthropological, social and spiritual power. Taking them seriously, however, means that we follow Abraham and share in his experiences as he lives through them, 'unknowingly', just like him, offering our son as he did and gaining him back as he did. False consolations and ideologies can only be defeated through an 'incarnated' reading of the Bible. This means that we faithfully follow a voice towards a promised land without knowing if and when we may reach it; we finally are given a son, but then realize that we will have to leave him to his fate in the desert; we are given another son and then we have to lose him, too; we go with Cain to the fields and are then killed by our brother; we carry a cross towards Golgotha, we are crucified and left breathless for the resurrection.

"“'*Abraham, Abraham'". 'Here I am', he replied. Then God said, 'Take your son, your only son, whom you love—Isaac—and go to the region of Moriah. Sacrifice him there as a burnt offering on a mountain I will show you*'". (22:1–2) Genesis reports no words of Abraham. We only read that he set out for the place God indicated '*early the next morning*' (22:3), just like he set out '*early the next morning*' (21:14), when he sent Hagar and Ishmael into the desert. And just like when he received that first call at Ur of the Chaldeans back in time, Abraham responds by setting out on a journey, following a voice. Abraham set out on a journey towards Mount Moriah with the same faith and trust he had when he left for the promised land. He who sets out on a journey at the daybreak and in the night-time of life is faithful to the voice and to himself. The faith-faithfulness-trust is found in believing that the voice that promised you happiness could be the same voice that has given you a son and now asks you to sacrifice that son.

Abraham, already old, sets out again because he recognises that first voice in those words. And if we want a son to be given to us again, if we want to continue a story of salvation we have to relive this narrative by doing everything as and with Abraham. At least once in a lifetime.

The entrepreneur called Giulio is re-experiencing this saving journey of Abraham, who, having believed in the company he inherited from his parents gets a request of a bribe to be paid in order to continue the business relationship with his most important client just when his enterprise is starting to bring some fruits and happier days seem to be arriving. Giulio does not accept it and on his return home from that indecent meeting he only knows that he was listening to that voice within saying: 'It is better to close down the business than to become corrupt and unjust.' He does not know anything else: it is already a lot to know, it is enough for continuing the ascent of life well – but he does not know anything more than this. He does not know about the angels that will arrive, nor does he know that it is '*only*' a test he is going through.

It is the silent climb of Abraham that the bartender Giovanna goes through, who is taking off from a downtown bar that she has liberated from slot machines driven by her love for the poor and the children of her town, even if she was losing two thousand Euros per month; and now that through much effort the bar is beginning to work well again, someone appears to ask for protection money. Giovanna says no, because a voice tells her: '*It is better to have a burnt shop than lose your soul.*' She can hear and she knows only these few words inside her, and she only wants to see this kind of moral accountability.

Anna, a young mother is also a friend of Abraham. She regained the gift of health after a long and exhausting cure, but during a check-up visit a new outbreak of the illness is discovered: she doesn't get angry with life but embraces it in a docile and tenacious way and returns home without knowing what is going to happen to her atop the mountain she is about to climb. In these authentic adventures of the soul and spirit the angel arrives – if it arrives – only when everything has been done without knowing that it would arrive. Angels don't tend to announce their arrival.

Abraham's story tells us that impossible and incredible things may – but don't have to – happen if one knows how to get to the last words uttered in our lives. After that, and only after that may one realise, every now and then, at least once in a lifetime, that what had seemed to be the last word was really the last-but-one. But before having uttered it we could not know this because it was a word given to us. The ethical and spiritual value of the one who walks with and like Abraham is in the arrival to the mountain with the son, fire wood and fire, in the preparing of the altar and then preparing oneself to '*die*' with that son on the same altar.

But Abraham is company and ally to all those as well to whom the angel never arrives: even if the child could not be saved, the enterprise failed, the bar was burnt, the illness won. Abraham loves us and accompanies us with his strong and obedient faith as we walk that part of the road taking us from Sarah's tent to the instant before hearing the voice of the angel stopping us from striking down. The angel's voice does not add anything valuable to Abraham's faith, even if it reveals much of the logic and nature of Elohim. If Abraham had known about the angel before, his experience would have been a '*fiction*', the son given back to him would not have been a award of his faith but a poor incentive to make him set out quicker early in the morning.

He who has had the gift of '*dying*' and '*rising from the dead*' in their life at least once has learnt that resurrection only arrives if before it comes we know how to die. While we are living through our winters we do not know if and when the springs arrive. We are like the peoples of the Antiquity that after each sunset were unsure if the sun was to rise again at the end of the night. Even after a thousand resurrections, ours and others', when another mountain is showing up with another climb that makes us move again '*unknowingly*' just like it happened for the first time, knowing only that we have to keep going. Not even God – at least the God of the Bible – could possibly know if Abraham were to get to the end of the climb and prepare the altar: he only realised it, was amazed and perhaps even moved by it when Abraham was already grabbing the knife. And the wonder is what makes every moment of life unique, this is what gives an immense value to time, history, our freedom and responsibility.

It was not Abraham's logic that we used for the construction of Europe, the West, modernity and capitalism. The domain of technology, economic utilitarianism, cost-benefit calculations are the children of Ulysses, the Greek and then the modern ones. Not of Abraham. If, however, the world does not die, if the good businesses and families continue to flourish it is because Abraham lives on in many, and perhaps his echo survives in all of us. We would feel more loved by life and less alone on the Moriah Mounts of our existence is we were more conscious of being the children of Abraham every time we remain faithful – at all costs – to a voice, a promise, a pact, our conscience, the better part in us. Let us tell each other the story of Mount Moriah, Elohim, Isaac, Sarah, the altar, the angel and the ram. But above all, let us never stop telling each other about Abraham.

Chapter 10
The Promise Has No Owners

I discovered later, and I'm still discovering up to this moment that it is only by living completely in this world that one learns to have faith.

(Dietrich Bonhoeffer, *Reality and Resistance*)

Abstract The first time that the word "market" appears in Genesis is in the selling and buying of a tomb, the down payment for the Promised Land. The first part of the land of Canaan to become Abraham's property is a field he buys to bury his wife Sarah. God had promised him property of the promised land, but the only land he manages to make his "property" is a tomb. It happens often to those who follow a voice and set out on a journey in good faith – and the promised land appears, they live on it, they even love it but it does not become their property. Sarah dies in the land of Canaan, but she dies as a stranger and guest in that land. This first sepulchral property is telling us a lot about Abraham's call, but also about the adventures of those who try to follow a voice, a call in their lives: being strangers, walking the lands of others, the mobile tent of the wandering Aramean are all essential parts of the condition of those who respond to a call or try to do so. It is very interesting and revealing about the entire ancient Middle Eastern culture and about its contractual practice (the signs of which are completely lost in the suq of Damascus or Teheran) to see the process of closing a contract between Abraham and the owner of the field.

The first time that the word "market" appears in Genesis (23:16) is in the selling and buying of a tomb, the down payment for the Promised Land. The first part of the land of Canaan to become Abraham's property is a field he buys to bury his wife Sarah. God had promised him "*property*" (*ahuzzà*: 17,8) of the promised land, but the only land he manages to make his "*property*" (*ahuzzà*: 23,4) is a tomb.

It happens often to those who follow a voice and set out on a journey in good faith – and the promised land appears, they live on it, they even love it but it does not become their property. Sarah dies in the land of Canaan, but she dies as a stranger

L. Bruni, *The Economy of Salvation*, Virtues and Economics 4,
https://doi.org/10.1007/978-3-030-04082-6_10

and guest in that land. "*I am a foreigner (ger) and stranger (tosab) among you*" (23:4), says Abraham when he starts negotiating with the Hittites for the land where he could bury his wife – it is into the same land, the field and cave of Machpelah, where Isaac, Rebeccah, Leah and Jacob will also be buried. This first sepulchral property is telling us a lot about Abraham's call, but also about the adventures of those who try to follow a voice, a call in their lives: being strangers, walking the lands of others, the mobile tent of the wandering Aramean are all essential parts of the condition of those who respond to a call or try to do so.

If Sarah and Abraham were the proprietors of only a tomb, then the promised land is inhabited, loved and enriched by them, but it is not possessed by them. This story not only tells us about the importance of burying the dead in that culture (and in general, in the Antiquity: it is enough to think of Antigone), but also that to cross through the promised lands without possessing them is a high expression of that gratuitousness which is the truest nature of every calling. By the acquisition of this land from the Hittites for Sarah's tomb, Abraham transforms that territory into a "place" that will become a sacred place eventually; but the deeper message in this deal is that Sarah's tomb does not make property or place out of the promised land which is always in front of us.

It is very interesting and revealing about the entire ancient Middle Eastern culture and about its contractual practice (the signs of which are completely lost in the suq of Damascus or Teheran) to see the process of closing a contract between Abraham and the owner of the field. The selling price is shown as an almost marginal detail inside a conversation in which generous offers, praises and recognitions of dignity and honour are exchanged by the counterparts: "*Sir, listen to us. You are a mighty prince among us. Bury your dead in the choicest of our tombs.*" (23:6) And Abraham replies: "*If you are willing to let me bury my dead ... intercede with Ephron son of Zohar on my behalf so he will sell me the cave of Machpelah ... Ask him to sell it to me for the full price.*" (23:8–9) Ephron seems to be willing to give him the piece of land even free of charge: "*No, my lord. (...) Listen to me; I give you the field, and I give you the cave that is in it. I give it to you in the presence of my people.*" (23:11) At this point Abraham '*bowed down before the people of the land*' and he said, "*Listen to me, if you will. I will pay the price of the field. Accept it from me...*" (23:13) The price itself only appears at this point of the dialogue: "*Listen to me, my lord; the land is worth four hundred shekels of silver, but what is that between you and me?*" (23:15) Abraham took the 400 '*shekels of silver, according to the weight current among the merchants*' (23:16), and so '*the field and the cave in it were deeded to Abraham by the Hittites*' (23:20) – *shekel* was the measure of weight, about 11 grams. It is a high price when compared with the one paid by Jeremiah for a field (17 shekels of silver: Jer 32:9), or with the silver coins paid for Judah's betrayal (that could be Roman dinars [3,9 grams] but shekels, too, as the latter were much more common in Jerusalem in that time).

This "economic themed" dialogue between Abraham and Ephron – notwithstanding its symbolic complexity, much of which seem way too distant to us – is very telling about the economic exchanges that are encounters of persons. In fact, they are authentically human encounters if we do not rid them of their human dimensions, especially that of words. '*The first merchandise to be exchanged at the market are words*', this is what an African friend of mine told me one day. In his land markets, undisturbed by the logic of our individualistic-financial capitalism still exist and resist while the world is being transformed into a hypermarket without persons, without encounters, without words, without honour and recognition of the other's face. Yes, due payments should be "*honoured*", but first of all, persons can and should be honoured in the markets. Otherwise economic life and we ourselves with it will be turned into sadness. But that ancient business encounter tells us that a contract with the "full price" paid can be – and normally is – a more adequate means than a donation to obtain important things from others with whom we are not in a relationship to be exchanging gifts. Gifts are good and relationally and morally superior to contracts only if there are good reasons to offer them and receive them, as Isaiah reminds us, too: '*Those who walk righteously and speak what is right, who reject gain from extortion and keep their hands from accepting bribes*' (33:15). Gifts without good reasons for them being given free of charge are none other but 'bribes' as Isaiah says, that is, donations, the gifts of the king-pharaoh without the sense of gratuitousness.

Starting from gamble to the exploitation of the earth, the world is full of gains "originating from abuse" that will eventually become "donations", which the non-profit sector should not accept and "wash their hands" – hands that are still too rarely "agitated". A contract, therefore, could be a good means even for acquiring the first patch through the *pawn* of the promised land for the worthy burying of a wife. The most innovative and poor-friendly economic and social experiences we have generated throughout history have always been and are the intertwining of gifts and contracts, of gratuitousness and musts, of monastic rules and grace, obligations and freedom – they were contracts in the service of gifts and gifts in the service of contracts.

But Genesis also suggests that a contract, just like a gift, is deeply ambivalent (let us not forget that ambivalence is an important key to the reading of the biblical texts and to life as well if we want to penetrate them). Three chapters later (25:29–34), in fact, we realise that the second "*contract*" of buying and selling in Genesis is the one through which Jacob gets hold of Esau's birthright in exchange for a '*pot of beans*'. The contract is considered legitimate also in the buying and selling of the beans-for-birthright (it will not be returned to Esau), but there is an explicit moral judgement for the extremely low price: '*So Esau despised his birthright.*' (25:34). Abraham had valued the field in which he would bury his wife and paid a high price for it; Esau was satisfied with too little which was telling about how little consideration he gave for his status. Prices should be indicative of values, and when they aren't, they are wrong, and this is equally valid for yesterday and today.

The world has always suffered because of prices that were too high and so have excluded the masses of the poor from the possession of important goods. However, our capitalism is also suffering because of the prices that are too low: primary materials of food exchanged for a price that is lower than the value of '*a pot of beans*', prices that do not show value or values because they are the outcome of speculations and egoistic or short-sighted visions whose calculations do not include the future use of these resources by our children and grandchildren, a future that our capitalism values for less than a '*pot of beans*'.

At the end of the amazing adventure of Abraham, the father of all – that I found a very lovable story the last word should go to all those who, emigrants like Abraham and Sarah, died and continue dying in a foreign land, but without having any "*shekels*" to buy a tomb for their departed spouse. Abraham bought the tomb of Machpelah also for them, the pawn for a land without owners, the promised land.

Chapter 11
The Word that's Irreplaceable

The security of faith is not accessible and cannot be made accessible to people today. If one takes it seriously he knows this, and should not at all be deceived. But the ability to open himself up to faith is not denied to him. He can accept it, embrace it with all his might and wait for what will happen to him, see if a new sincerity sprouts in him.

(Martin Buber, *Hebrew Humanism*)

Abstract In thc cycle on Isaac the nature and power of the words come from the tension between Rebekah's "subversive" plan and Isaac's will. The alliance of JHWH and Abraham continues with the story of the twins who are presented to us as rivals and being in conflict ever since they left their mother's womb. For understanding this complex episode we should suspend "ethical" judgement and resist political analysis as well as the psychological opining about Jacob and Rebekah's behaviour – and concentrate on Isaac mainly, and the logic of the Alliance and of the word. Isaac is Abraham's son who was given and then re-given. He is the one to continue the Alliance of his father and of Noah's rainbow, the inheritor of the Pact with the Voice that had created the world by uttering it, pronouncing it. The same Word that had called Abraham, talked to him and later also to Isaac. They had entered into dialogue with the God of the Creating Voice and believed the power of those words. The words that made a promise were forceful, they were words uttered for eternity.

Without the Book of Job, the Song of Songs, the Psalms, the Gospel of Luke or the Book of Genesis art and poetry would be very different from what it is, and certainly poorer in beauty and words. But at the foundations of the (also poetic) powerfulness of the Bible there is a radical, unconditional, absolute faithfulness to the word that is very difficult to understand for us, contemporary readers, but is of decisive importance for us, too.

L. Bruni, *The Economy of Salvation*, Virtues and Economics 4,
https://doi.org/10.1007/978-3-030-04082-6_11

In the cycle on Isaac the nature and power of the words come from the tension between Rebekah's "*subversive*" plan and Isaac's will. The alliance of JHWH and Abraham continues with the story of the twins who are presented to us as rivals and being in conflict ever since they left their mother's womb ('*The babies jostled each other within her*', 25:22) Esau '*became a skillful hunter, a man of the open country, while Jacob was content to stay at home among the tents'* (25:27). At the same time the personal preference of the parents is revealed to us: '*Isaac ... loved Esau*', while the mother '*Rebekah loved Jacob*' (25:28). When he feels his nearing death, Isaac asks Esau to catch a wild game for him, "*so that I may give you my blessing before I die*« (27:4). Rebekah '*was listening*' as the two were talking and she said to Jacob, »*Now, my son, listen carefully and do what I tell you: go out to the flock and bring me two choice young goats, so that I can prepare some tasty food for your father... so that he may give you his blessing before he dies*." (27:8–10) And Jacob said, "*But my brother Esau is a hairy man while I have smooth skin. What if my father touches me? I would ... bring down a curse on myself rather than a blessing*." (27:11–12). And Rebekah said, "*My son, let the curse fall on me*." (27:13) So Rebekah '*took the best clothes of her elder son Esau ... and put them on her younger son Jacob. She also covered his hands and the smooth part of his neck with the goatskins.*' (27:15–17) And Jacob went to his father and said, "*I am Esau your firstborn*." (27:19) Isaac then touches his son and says, "*The voice is the voice of Jacob, but the hands are the hands of Esau*." (27:22) But after having smelled the clothes of Esau ('*the smell of my son is like the smell of a field*' 27:27), he pronounces the words of blessing: "*May God give you heaven's dew and earth's richness – an abundance of grain and new wine.*" (27:28–29) After the blessing has been stolen, Esau returns from the hunt and offers the dish to his father. And Isaac says, "*Who are you?*" He answers, "*I am your son ... your firstborn, Esau*." (27:32). And this is where the narrative twist comes.

At this point the modern reader who does not know how the story goes on would expect that Isaac's sense of justice would make him call Jacob back and take his blessing off him, and perhaps even change it to a curse on him. But nothing like that happens: '*Isaac trembled violently and said, "Your brother came deceitfully and took your blessing."*' (27:35). Isaac realises that he had been deceived and feels sorry for his beloved son but does not take his blessing back: "*I blessed him and indeed he will be blessed!*" (27:33) '*Then Esau wept aloud.*' (27:38) And so Esau joins the invisible people of those who are cast-off but not abandoned, together with Ishmael, Cain and their many children.

In order to gain a deeper understanding of this complex episode we should suspend "ethical" judgement and resist political analysis (Esau becomes the forefather of the rival peoples of Israel) as well as the psychological opining about Jacob and Rebekah's behaviour – and concentrate on Isaac mainly, and the logic of the Alliance and of the word. Isaac is Abraham's son who was given and then re-given. He is the one to continue the Alliance of his father and of Noah's rainbow, the inheritor of the Pact with the Voice that had created the world by uttering it, pronouncing it. The same Word that had called Abraham, talked to him and later also to Isaac (26:2–6). They had entered into dialogue with the God of the Creating Voice and believed the power of those words. The words that made a promise were forceful, they were words uttered for eternity.

The safeguarding of and faithfulness to the Alliance, therefore, were also meant to be safeguarding of and faithfulness to the given word. But in order to safeguard the word and prevent its degeneration, the "*price*" to be paid was its irrevocability: if the word can create as it is being uttered, then it can always create and for eternity, even when uttered to a deceitful son. Isaac could not take his blessing back because the words he uttered were of a creative power, they had worked, they had changed things, they had made Jacob, their taker, a blessed one who '*indeed will be blessed*'.

Genesis and the entire Biblical culture have saved all the power of the Word by affirming and saving the irreversibility of words, too, and by assuming all their painful (and at times really painful) consequences – for an extreme case let us think of the scandalous episode of Jephthah's daughter (Judges 11:30–50). But it was thanks to this safeguarding of the word at any cost that one day someone could write: '*The Word became flesh*' (John 1:14).

Poets, writers, journalists, all the lovers and friends of words, their value and responsibility should all have respect for Isaac and Biblical humanism for having saved the creating power of the word. Our culture has lost this power and this eternal validity. We are flooded with words that don't say anything anymore. Words that multiply as if multiplication of written words could compensate for the death of the creating force of the uttered word. So, we fill contracts with numberless words that are written but never pronounced and that tell a lot about the distrust in and inefficiency of words that should be their foundation.

But the power of the written contracts may only come from the power of words. Contracts were born as part of the evolution of pacts that have always been and are still words with a creating power. Contracts are dead pieces of paper if behind the written words there is nothing creative and efficient – when the different civilisations decided to put pacts in writing, contracts and laws were made to give more power to the given word, not to substitute it.

Some of the old power of words survives today in the (very few) pacts that have not yet been turned into contracts. During the wedding ceremony, for example, it is the words of the bride and groom that create the new reality of becoming '*one flesh*', words that later are reinforced and ratified by their own and their witness' signatures: the performative power of word (J. L. Austin). If those creating words were not there first, the wedding signatures would not say anything or have a very frail message. It is the reciprocal promises uttered that make the family, it is the meeting of the voices that create it. We all know and we should not forget that when we want to say something important to a relative or a friend – to apologise, for example – it is not enough to write a letter, and it is even less efficient to send an e-mail. We must talk, to say '*forgive me*', we have to hear '*I forgive you*' uttered, it is not enough to see it written. It was true in the past and is still so: in order to start a relationship, a family or business we have to learn and re-learn to speak, we have to say our pacts, promises, alliances and we have to say them '*aloud*'. All this is also true for enterprises and markets: when they lose contact with the words uttered by persons they lose their very nature and leave the realm of the human. The power of the words '*I love you*' uttered to a person (and only to one) can only be fully understood inside a frame that suggests responsibility because of the creating power and irreversible nature of the word.

Our era seems to be in a dark night of the word, of words, and so our society is risking to die suffocating in a sea of small talk, chats and text-messages. We ought to get reconciled with and get back in touch with the word and words, with their seriousness and responsibility. We may find help for this new, great and decisive encounter in listening and in the appreciation of poets. Poets are essential for life because they create: they make words alive and defend them from death. Above all, they are essential for our times without the word and so without words. After Leopardi the 'places' of Recanati and the world are not the same any more in the Italian language and each people have their own masters to re-create things by the power of the word. Their poetry re-creates and changes things for ever.

Thank you, Father Isaac and thank you, Esau: you have paid a great price to safeguard the word for us. The responsibility not to under-estimate your valuable gift is ours.

Chapter 12
The Gate of Heaven Is a Voice

Samuel said to Saul, «Why have you disturbed me by bringing me up? I am in great distress, » Saul said, «...God has departed from me. He no longer answers me, either by prophets or by dreams. »

First Book of Samuel, 28:15

Abstract The Jacob Cycle, from chapters 27 to 37, is a beautiful fresco of human greatness and contradictions where all the colours of life and all the tones of social and family relationships are at work: starting from the splendid and auroral theophanies and blessings to the dark and nocturnal lies and deceits. Jacob obeys his mother once again; he sets out on a journey in order not to die, avoiding this way that his brotherhood should take the course of that of Cain – brotherhood in the Bible is never a romantic or sentimental thing. Salvation comes yet another time through "dispersion", like in Babel, like the one between Abraham and Lot. And he is awaited by a decisive encounter in the desert, in the form of a dream. This is the first time Jacob meets JHWH who issues a personal call to him. From that moment on JHWH will not merely be the God of the fathers. YHWH is not anymore the God of his father, but also his God, the Voice that calls him by his name. A grammar of every vocation, where the family name is not enough.

The Book of Genesis is not a moral treatise, nor is it a manual of family ethics. It is much more than that. The Jacob Cycle (chapters 27–37) is a beautiful fresco of human greatness and contradictions where all the colours of life and all the tones of social and family relationships are at work: starting from the splendid and auroral theophanies and blessings to the dark and nocturnal lies and deceits.

Esau, having been deceived and left at the bank of the River of Alliance together with the other "*defeated ones*", discovers the second deceit of his brother (the theft of the patriarchal blessing). From then on, '*Esau held a grudge against Jacob. (...) He said to himself, "The days of mourning for my father are near; then I will kill my brother Jacob.*"' (27:41) As soon as their mother Rebekah, who was the mastermind

L. Bruni, *The Economy of Salvation*, Virtues and Economics 4,
https://doi.org/10.1007/978-3-030-04082-6_12

behind the deceit, gets to know Esau's intention, she says to Jacob: '*Your brother Esau is planning to avenge himself by killing you. (...) do what I say: flee at once to my brother Laban*' (27:42–45) Every brotherhood that is rejected is an opening for the possibility of fratricide. Jacob obeys his mother once again; he sets out on a journey in order not to die, avoiding this way that his brotherhood should take the course of that of Cain – brotherhood in the Bible is never a romantic or sentimental thing. Salvation comes yet another time through "*dispersion*" (like in Babel, like the one between Abraham and Lot). And he is awaited by a decisive encounter in the desert, in the form of a dream. This is the first time Jacob meets JHWH who issues a personal call to him. From that moment on JHWH will not merely be the God of the fathers ("*JHWH, your God*" as Jacob said to Isaac in their dialogue of the deceit: 27:20), but also his God, the Voice that calls him by his name. When he reaches the desert, night falls and Jacob falls asleep. He has a dream: '*he saw a stairway resting on the earth, with its top reaching to heaven, and the angels of God were ascending and descending on it.*' (28:12) And JHWH speaks to him in his dream, too: '*I am the Lord, the God of your father Abraham and the God of Isaac Your descendants will be like the dust of the earth... All peoples on earth will be blessed through you*' (28:13–14). Jacob, the third of the patriarchs, the deceitful substitute enters in a personal encounter with the God of the Alliance of the fathers, and the promise becomes his. Upon awaking from his dream he exclaims: '*Surely the Lord is in this place, and I was not aware of it. ... this is the gate of heaven.*' (28:16–17).

In the Antiquity, dreams were always considered to be mysteries, they were very serious and important things. They are the places of real theophanies in the Bible too: people did not yet know about the existence of the subconscious and so they were free to dream and had more means to listen to and decipher the many different words of life.

Before this dream, Jacob had not received a calling. He was only the "*grandson*" of Abraham, the son of the Alliance and the promise, but he was a man of poor behaviour and a low ethical profile, neither better nor different from many men of his people. He was inside a story of Alliance and promise, one that had been re-occurring in the times of evening story-telling under his family's tent, and one that had been feeding his soul with hope. The inheritance of the Alliance and the promise do not get passed on through blood links; it is not a noble rank, nor is it transferred to you by your family name. Every alliance is connected to a name, it is a vocational thing, a personal encounter with the Voice that calls you and creates a task and a destiny for you.

It is not enough to be the children or family members of the founder of a business in order to collect its moral inheritance. A son may inherit the status, the prestige and the goods of his parents, but the family business dies (or is sold) unless at a certain point, at least for one member of the family, a personal calling arrives to become the prosecutor of that first human and moral adventure, in order to continue the dream and the pact that have generated it. That first pact dies if Gianna remains only the daughter of Bruno, the founder, and will not be alive again until a new dream arrives. Vocations do exist, even in our post-modern world that is so disenchanted that it seems not to be able to dream or listen to the deep voices of life any more. We may have different ideas about Who or what the voice calling is, but it is a fact proved by experience that vocations fill the earth, make it live and be reborn every day. We could not explain (or our explanation would be poor or wrong) the existence of artists, scientists, poets, missionaries, but also the presence of many social and civil entrepreneurs without taking the category of vocation into consideration. And we would never know the essential dimensions of life (among them, gratuitousness) if there weren't people who are "*driven from within*" and are not pulled along by incentives but follow a voice.

Noemi was an employee for 20 years in a public corporation. One day, on a certain day, she feels that she had to leave that secure job of hers in order to bring an enterprise to life with some partners in the alternative energy sector, and so make her ethical ideals take shape in a professional and social project. One day, on a certain day, Marco reads "*by chance*" a book of economics and feels like writing to its author: '*You have written this book for me.*' A few years later Marco changed his life and today he is a civil entrepreneur and follows the principles of communion. Passions, interests, preferences...of course; but in order to understand and tell these stories of yesterday, of all times, the word "*vocation*" is much stronger and more efficient (we should write a "*dictionary of vocations*" collected from the different realms of the human). The experience is truer and deeper for those who can hear this inside: '*You can become something you are not now, and something that is the better part of you*'. Every person has got a vocation, a way leading to their own excellence and to the common good, a "*not yet*" that is waiting to become "*already*". However, not all vocations get to flourish because without meeting the people and places of gratuitousness these voices are not heard, they remain suppressed by the noises of everyday life, the noise that is too loud in our civilisation. Every time a person discovers, follows and cherishes a vocation, there happens an encounter between past, present and future, between heaven and earth, and it forever changes the world and makes it better. At times this voice is heard at 12 years old, at others only at 80: one's age or health condition do not matter much. What matters is only to find the "*gate*" of heaven one day and to see the "*angels*" ascending and descending on the "*stairway*" connecting it to the earth and to our lives.

Lorenza is a writer, and when she composes her stories, she sees her grandmother Anna "*descend from heaven*" who in the very few years she could attend school had memorised some poems that she used to recite to her on festive occasions. Franco is an entrepreneur, and the day his own company's headquarters could finally be inaugurated he "*ascended to heaven*" and thanked his great-grandfather, Giovanni, who passed on to him the beauty and wisdom in creating something by your hands and heart when he was a little child.

Upon waking from the dream-encounter, Jacob took the stone he had slept on – and that, in this way, had "*participated*" in the dream – '*set it up as a pillar and poured oil on top of it. He called that place Bethel, though the city used to be called Luz.*' (28:18–19) In the stories of vocation, geography has the same weight as the story itself: it isn't only facts and documents that can speak, places can speak, too. All symbols are a crossing point of a story and geography, of words and places. We could not possibly understand who Mother Teresa and Gandhi were without India, or Etty Hillesum without the Nazi-occupied Holland, don Oreste Benzi without the dark streets of Rimini. Places have names, too (which means they have a calling and a destiny), they participate as heroes in our stories and vocations, because between heaven and earth there exists a mysterious but real law of reciprocity. The man of the Bible knew this very well. We – who have already wasted our symbolic capabilities – know it much less, but we haven't forgotten it completely. So, in times of weariness, we instinctively return to the symbolic places of our life – where on a certain day in a certain place we heard the decisive Voice – in order to be loved by them, to let them chose us again, to re-dream that first dream and hear being called by our name again.

The earth and the heavens continue to live and talk to us. And we, just like Jacob, continue to dream them and to search for "*the gate to heaven*" and a "*stairway*" to reach it for all our lives.

Chapter 13
The Way: To State and Cultivate the Alliance

When he (Laban) he saw that Jacob was unattended, he concluded that he carried great sums of money in his girdle, and he threw his arms about his waist to find out whether his supposition was true. (…) But Jacob said to him: "Thou thinkest I have money. Nay, thou art mistaken, I have but words."

(Louis Ginzberg, *The Legends of the Jews, Vol. I*)

Abstract The man of the Antiquity had more access to the mystery of life. He lived in a world where men and women and visible beings were but a small part of the population capable of speech. The world was full of messages and symbols that were perceived in a deep and clear way. Many of those words were alive and real, but we have forgotten them, just like it happens when we learn a new language as adults and forget the one acquired in our childhood. And so, we become poorer. When he arrived in the land of his uncle Laban, Jacob saw a well in the open country. The well is a great symbol in the nomadic cultures. It was and it still is a sign of life, of nature's regeneration, of the survival of the flocks and people, the place of relationships, communities, oases and meetings, the place of life. And in the Bible it is at the wells that many encounters between men and women take place: Isaac, Moses, Jesus and the Samaritan woman. There is, in fact, an ancient and widespread familiarity of the figure of the woman and water (sirens, nymphs). Jacob, too, meets his cousin Rachel at a well while she is tending the flock.

The man of the Antiquity had more access to the mystery of life. He lived in a world where men and women and "visible" beings were but a small part of the population capable of speech. The world was full of messages and symbols that were perceived in a deep and clear way. Many of those "words" were alive and real, but we have forgotten them, just like it happens when we learn a new language as adults and forget the one acquired in our childhood. And so, we become poorer.

L. Bruni, *The Economy of Salvation*, Virtues and Economics 4,
https://doi.org/10.1007/978-3-030-04082-6_13

When he arrived in the land of his uncle Laban, Jacob 'saw a well in the open country' (Genesis 29:2). The well is a great symbol in the nomadic cultures. It was and it still is a sign of life, of nature's regeneration, of the survival of the flocks and people, the place of relationships, communities, oases and meetings, the place of life. And in the Bible it is at the wells that many encounters between men and women take place (Isaac, Moses, Jesus and the Samaritan woman). There is, in fact, an ancient and widespread familiarity of the figure of the woman and water (sirens, nymphs). Jacob, too, meets his cousin Rachel at a well while she is tending the flock ('for she was a shepherd', 29:9), and was at once enchanted by her: '...Jacob kissed Rachel and began to weep aloud.' (29:11) It is during the long and complex time period spent by Jacob at Laban's house that the word "wage" appears for the first time in the Bible. '*Tell me what your wages should be.*' (29:15) The first payment is a wife: '*I'll work for you seven years in return for your younger daughter Rachel.*' (29:18) Of course there are some traces of the ancient world (that we do not like) in this wage as daughters were considered "*merchandise*" (31:14), but there is also one of the most beautiful definitions of human love hiding between the lines like a pearl: '*So Jacob served seven years to get Rachel, but they seemed like only a few days to him because of his love for her.*' (29:20) In these complex and engaging chapters Jacob, the wage earning man, was not a free man: he was a foreigner without property, a dependent worker who was in a social and legal condition that is similar to that of a servant (in the pre-modern world only the property of land could generate wealth and status). But at the end of the agreed 10 years, the contracted wage did not work out: Laban deceives him (a rather familiar move for Jacob) and does not give him Rachel who '*had a lovely figure and was beautiful*', but Leah, his first-born daughter who '*had weak eyes*' (29:17), and asks Jacob to stay in his service for another 7 years to get Rachel for his wife. Jacob stayed because '*his love for Rachel was greater than his love for Leah*' (29:30). Another 7 years passed and Jacob wanted to return to Canaan. Laban has to pay him his due: '*Name your wages, and I will pay them.*' (30:28) They make another agreement to determine the part of the flock that will belong to Jacob. It is a very tricky contract (30:31–43) that will eventually compromise their relationship (31:1–2). Therefore, this second contracted wage between Laban and Jacob produces conflicts and injustice.

Contracts may produce more and more inequalities and conflicts because they become the means for impoverishing the weaker party in the exchange. The weak and the strong do exist and will remain such even when they sign contracts "*freely*". It is also because of this that for biblical humanism, contracts are not enough (even though they are necessary and often indispensable): it calls for pacts instead.

This, too, is the message of the outcome of the conflict dialogue between Laban and Jacob. Laban catches up with Jacob who is fleeing and his nephew pours all the injustices on him that he had suffered from his uncle who '*changed my wages ten times*' (31:41). But at the end of that hard dialogue, Laban says: '*Come now, let's make a covenant, you and I*' (31:44). After the covenant with JHWH, and those with the foreign peoples, here is the first alliance between people of the same community, a pact between two people who finally appear as equals. The contracted wage did not prove to be a good instrument of peace and justice for them, the pact will be. In all pacts the symbols are essential: '*So Jacob took a stone and set it up as a pillar.*' (31:45) He set up the first pillar in Bethel (28:18) as an altar after the dream of the '*stairway*' to heaven; and now he erects a second one for a pact with another man. Inter-human pacts are not worth smaller pillars because they too celebrate the Alliance, life, love – perhaps it is also for this reason that the Catholic Church inserted marriage (celebrated by bride and groom) among the sacraments, next to the Eucharist.

But the symbols of this pact do not end here: Jacob then '*said to his relatives, »Gather some stones.« So they took stones and piled them in a heap, and they ate there by the heap.*' Laban said, '*This heap is a witness between you and me today.*' 31:52) Isaac, too, ate with Abimelek (26:30) after stipulating their alliance with each other. To eat together after pacts was and is still much more than a "*working lunch*" (even if there is an echo of those ancient pacts in all working lunches). To share the food is to share life, it is the communion becoming food, too. The wedding reception is also an important element of the pact, as it is the community expression of other important words of life. A reconciliation, a statement of love become more powerful if they are accompanied by a dinner, a celebration of conviviality, perhaps prepared together in chasteness – I don't think that these good pacts should be celebrated in private or hidden clubs (it is there, however, that the wrong type of pacts are celebrated, we can see that every day). Even after funerals in many cultures it was customary to eat together with the relatives of the deceased one because that shared food became shared pain and the renewal of a community pact – our funerals are sad, but the post-funeral meals consumed in solitude are even sadder.

Our era will be remembered for many wonderful things but also for the invention of fast food and the sandwich eaten alone during lunch break. We all know what a great difference there is in terms of joy and the quality of life between a lunch shared with colleagues and a lunch consumed alone. When we eat with a good colleague-friend, along with the calories we "*eat*" relational goods, too, that nourish us no less than food and make us do better at work, in our lives and in terms of our health (data prove it). A sign of the non-sustainability of our economic model is that there are too many sandwiches eaten in solitude.

In the really important deeds human words are essential but not sufficient. We want to hear nature, heavens, our ancestors, the angels, all the world talk to us. When there is nothing that really counts (a new enterprise, a school, a hospital...) behind a contract, a toast will not suffice. I have gotten to know civil entrepreneurs and co-operators who invited their newly hired employee for dinner. During that meal consumed together they shared the history of the company and its original values with them, thereby reviving and extending the founding pact. You cannot become travel mates without the *cum panis*, without the shared bread.

Contracts that bring about good life and endure in time are preceded or followed by pacts. An enterprise born solely of contracts will either become a pact – often after overcoming a crisis – or it will die. In traditional societies, pacts were implicit in the communities that produced contracts of businesses and co-operatives that, not by accident, were born out of families or shared political or spiritual belonging. Our democracy and institutions, too, were born out of pacts blooming from the tears and blood of wars and dictatorships. And for this reason, the contracts generated from those pacts have been strong and good, and they make us live still.

But what foundation are we giving our new contracts, the new banks, the new parties, the new enterprises? Where are our pacts, our symbols, our pillars, our cum panis? How much longer are we going to be happy with having mortgages and lawyers as "witnesses"? This "*lack of foundation*" is the most profound reason for the many crises of our time. Our generation is still placing its own pacts on an ethical, spiritual and symbolic heritage that was built throughout many centuries of civilisation. But we are running short of it. If we wish to start regenerating it, we should begin to give a symbolic foundation to our relationships by re-learning to share the good bread.

After the pact and the meal of peace, '*the angels of God met him*' (32,2).

Chapter 14
Forgiving Is a Blessing Struggle

On that day, the dawn was shorter than usual: the sun rose two hours before its usual time ... And the early appearing sun was of wondrous power: the same glory that shone during the six days of creation and will return to flaunt the end of time.

(*Greater Midrash of the Genesis*, LXVIII)

Abstract We have reached a key episode of the Genesis and to the whole Bible: Jacob and the angel in the river Jabbok. In contrast to the ways of our consumer society, in the Bible the names of people and places are very serious things. Thcy are always chosen to indicate, symbolically, a vocation or a destiny. But when the first name is changed by an event or a special encounter, the name becomes also a call to a special and universal task. This is how after the Alliance Sarai and Abram become Sarah and Abraham, and after his night struggle Jacob becomes Israel. Once reconciled with Laban, Jacob now knows that he is awaited by a more difficult encounter, with his deceived brother Esau. But Jacob did not know that before he can meet Esau again, another special encounter was waiting for him in the ford of the Jabbok, a tributary of the River Jordan. After 20 years of exile, Jacob is afraid to return to the land of his brother. The blessing stolen 20 years earlier has accompanied him during his exile, and now he fears that Esau has not forgotten the deceit.

In contrast to the ways of our consumer society, in the Bible the names of people (and places) are very serious things. They are always chosen to indicate, symbolically, a vocation or a destiny. But when the first name is changed by an event or a special encounter, the name becomes also a call to a special and universal task. This is how after the Alliance Sarai and Abram become Sarah and Abraham, and after his night struggle Jacob becomes Israel.

Once reconciled with Laban, Jacob now knows that he is awaited by a more difficult encounter, with his deceived brother Esau. But Jacob did not know that before he can meet Esau again, another special encounter was waiting for him in the ford of the Jabbok (a tributary of the River Jordan). After 20 years of exile, Jacob is

L. Bruni, *The Economy of Salvation*, Virtues and Economics 4,
https://doi.org/10.1007/978-3-030-04082-6_14

afraid to return to the land of his brother. The blessing stolen 20 years earlier has accompanied him during his exile, and now he fears that Esau has not forgotten the deceit. As a first step, he announces his arrival: '*Jacob sent messengers ahead of him to his brother Esau*' (32:3). However, he learns that his brother was advancing towards him with 400 men, and he was 'in great fear and distress' (32:7). He is afraid of Esau and, seeking reconciliation, sends abundant gifts to his brother to precede him and prepare their big meeting: '*two hundred female goats and twenty male goats ... ten bulls, and twenty female donkeys ...*' (32:15). And he hopes that, 'I will pacify him with these gifts I am sending on ahead' (32.20). Ancient practices: communities used to meet and re-meet using the gifts as first words. The preparation of the meeting between Jacob and Esau is thus one of the oldest stories that reveal the deep connection that exists between gift and forgiveness. Jacob sends gifts to Esau to ask for the gift of forgiveness. True forgiveness is never a unilateral act, but a meeting of gifts.

Between the preparation for the meeting with Esau and the meeting itself, the sacred writer, however, places a strong narrative discontinuity: he takes us to the ford of a river by night, and makes us experience one of the most extraordinary episodes of the Bible, when Jacob, who is "*blessed by deceit*", becomes "*blessed for the struggle*". Jacob arrives at this late-night encounter with a huge, complex and painful human-divine luggage. To that ford, along with the flocks, goods and his family, Jacob also brings his birthright, the dish of lentils, the theft of the blessing, the lies told to his old father Isaac (and YHWH), the deceits committed against and received from Laban, the pains that live in him together with the dream of the "*stairway*" and heaven, the angels, the promise, the call, the renewed Alliance. So, let us accompany Jacob up to the Jabbok, and follow him that night as if it was the first time we read this story (the first is the only fruitful reading of the Bible), and fight alongside him.

'*That night Jacob got up and took his two wives ... his eleven sons and crossed the ford of the Jabbok. ...So Jacob was left alone, and a man wrestled with him till daybreak.*' (32:22-24). A man ("*ish*") confronts him in the ford. We do not know the reason for this as it is presented as a real and proper ambush. The man looks like a creature of the night who must leave the fight at '*daybreak*'.

Their struggle is long, and the mysterious man cannot prevail over Jacob (Genesis shows us Jacob as a person of extraordinary strength several times, cf. 29:10), and to break him, he hits him on '*the socket of Jacob's hip*', dislocating it, but still not winning over him (32:25). His opponent asks Jacob: '*Let me go, for it is daybreak*' (32:26). It is at this point of the dialogue – struggle that Jacob returns to being a beggar of blessings: '*I will not let you go unless you bless me.*' (32:26). His opponent asks: '*What is your name?*' '*Jacob.*' '*Your name will no longer be Jacob, but Israel, because you have struggled with God and with humans and have overcome.*' (32:28). Jacob also asks for his opponent's name and as a response he gets the blessing he asked for: '"*Why do you ask my name?*" *Then he blessed him there.*' (32,30). In fact, the name of the mysterious wrestler had already been revealed: '*because you have struggled with God and with humans.*' His opponent was a man, it was Elohim. Jacob was blessed and wounded by the same (P)person. This is a great metaphor of faith (the one of the Bible, not the one of the sellers of emotional and psychological consumption), which is an experience that blesses us only through wounding us. This is a great image that is also true for human relationships (the opponent was also a man), where the blessing of otherness comes to us when we are willing to expose ourselves to the possibility of injury. But this fight is also a powerful image of human relations in our market society, in businesses and organizations where we are losing the blessing of the other because we are afraid of being injured by them. And so, we have entered a phase of famine of blessings and happiness.

Still limping '*Jacob looked up and there was Esau. he bowed down to the ground seven times*'.

But '*Esau ran to meet Jacob and embraced him; he threw his arms around his neck and kissed him.*' (33:4) We can generate endless processes and win a thousand causes, but true reconciliation comes only when we 'cry together'. Anyone who has received a great wrong, especially if by family members or loved ones, will know that the pain is much deeper than any sentence to be served or cash compensation: the only effective treatment for the wound is reconciliation, embrace. When you do not get to 'cry together', the differences between the pain and compensation are too large, and the wounds remain open and continue to bleed. The many tears shed for the killings of loved ones, for the deep injustices suffered, for slander, for the blessings stolen can be dried up only by mixing them with the tears of those who made ours fall, in an embrace. We know this; we also know that it's very difficult, but most of all we know that there is no other real way to try to heal the wounds of the primary relationships of our lives – criminal and civil proceedings should facilitate the realisation of these embraces.

One question – among a thousand others – remains open: why has God dealt and fought with Jacob on his way towards the re-composition of fraternity? Why did He place Himself between Jacob and His promise? We can discover in this battle one of the deepest and least explored laws of human nature. In a decisive moment of life, what actually fights the righteous is righteousness, the founder is wrestling with his work, the charismatic with his charisma, the poet with poetry, the entrepreneur with his business. And it is not because of a perversion or an intrinsic evil of life, or maybe God, but because when the person who has received a call and answered it reaches the culmination of his moral existence, he or she inevitably reaches the *stage of the new name*. He must fight with what had been the first mission and his blessing to be able to receive – after the injury of the struggle – others that are more true. Jabbok and Jacob are Jewish-sounding names, the one being almost an anagram of the other. During these battles, the main opponent wrestler is that which is more beautiful and larger than life, that does not want to 'die' inside, and fights and wounds the other: *deus contra deum*. But only when you pass this 'ford' does the flight to infinity start: it is then that Raymund Maximilian Kolbe becomes Father Kolbe, and becomes that forever.

At the end of the fight, '*Israel*' receives the blessing from '*Jacob*', as he understands and feels that his life task of yesterday was not an enemy to fight, but a friend who embraces us and blesses us, and with that wound an access was opened to the deepest and best part of us. Until that night at the ford, the blessing of Jacob was the one stolen from his brother. Now that he has received a new blessing that is completely his own, and will remain inscribed forever in the flesh – according to the rabbinic tradition Jacob limped for the rest of his life – he can bless Esau, too: '*Please accept my blessing*' (33:11). And the circle closes. We too, like Jacob, are beggars of blessings. But today we risk losing the ability to understand the spiritual blessings that are hidden inside the wounds carved into the flesh of our relationships. '*And Jacob came safely to the city of Shechem, which is in the land of Canaan.*' (33:18).

Chapter 15
Why the World Doesn't End

One of them, when he saw he was healed, came back, praising God in a loud voice. He threw himself at Jesus' feet and thanked him – and he was a Samaritan. Jesus asked, »Were not all ten cleansed? Where are the other nine?«.

(The Gospel of Luke, 17:15–17)

Abstract In reading the sad narrative of Dinah there is a strong temptation to skip the entire chapter and look for other stories instead. But this time we won't do that, and we will go through these pages of the human realm that are as distressing as frequent and common in history, but also hide messages of life between the lines. Much of the effort of those who want to penetrate some truth of the human condition from any perspective lies in trying to hold together Adam and Cain, Lamech and Noah, Sarah and Hagar, the embrace between Esau and Jacob as well as Dinah, her captors and her avenging brothers. While reading the Bible there is a fatal, recurring temptation to concentrate only on the bright pages and discard the dark ones; but when you fall into this error you end up offering ideological readings, where a part becomes the whole, thus losing sight of the mixed but truer human reality. Authentic biblical humanism is not a collection of "best practices", but a look of love and salvation at humanity as a whole.

Looking at the story of Dinah there is no other possible reaction but silence: '*Now Dinah, the daughter Leah had borne to Jacob, went out to visit the women of the land. When Shechem, son of Hamor the Hivite, the ruler of that area, saw her, he took her and raped her.*' (34:1).

In reading the sad events of this chapter of Genesis there is a strong temptation to skip the entire chapter and look for other stories instead. But this time we won't do that, and we will go through these pages of the human realm that are as distressing as frequent and common in history, but also hide messages of life between the lines. Much of the effort of those who want to penetrate some truth of the human condition from any perspective lies in trying to hold together Adam and Cain,

L. Bruni, *The Economy of Salvation*, Virtues and Economics 4,
https://doi.org/10.1007/978-3-030-04082-6_15

Lamech and Noah, Sarah and Hagar, the embrace between Esau and Jacob as well as Dinah, her captors and her avenging brothers. While reading the Bible there is a fatal, recurring temptation to concentrate only on the bright pages and discard the dark ones; but when you fall into this error you end up offering ideological readings, where a part becomes the whole, thus losing sight of the mixed but truer human reality. Authentic biblical humanism is not a collection of "best practices", but a look of love and salvation at humanity as a whole. It is a humanism that does not tell us of the primacy of Adam over Cain and the victory of blessing over evil, hiding the dark side of our human condition. Instead, looking deep into our soul and our body it tells us that the evil appearing in its devastating power is neither the first nor the last word for us.

Dinah, the only daughter of Jacob, leaves the camp and her mother's tents one day '*to visit the women of the land*'. Dinah was very young according to tradition, maybe still a maiden (Genesis 30:21 and 31:41, the Book of Jubilees [30:2] mentions 12 years), and so she was looking for companions. Even today in many places of war and conflict, children go over the visible and invisible barricades and boundaries put up by adults; they go beyond them, as they are incautious and curious about life. They go in search of mates, games to play and adventures. But yesterday just as now, the purity of children and young girls can be, and often is met by the wickedness and crimes of adults. Especially the girls, the young ones, who like their friend Dinah continue to be vulnerable and exposed to danger in their games and in their curious leaves from home. We have been striving for thousands of years, but we still haven't managed to make the games and the outings of our girls from the tents similar to those of their male siblings: the presence of a single Shechem in town, or the possibility that there is one is enough for a girl not to be able to go out when she wants to "*seek companions*", and for her freedom and opportunities to be less than those of her brothers. The civilization of a people is measured by its ability to create the conditions for the cultural and institutional "walks of Dinah" to be increasingly possible and safe.

After the kidnapping and rape, the community of the Hivites (Canaanites) asks Jacob and his sons to let Shechem the rapist marry Dinah (in a "shotgun wedding"), by offering a generous dowry: '*Make the price for the bride and the gift I am to bring as great as you like.*' (34:12). But when the negotiations already seemed to go through, Simeon and Levi, two of Dinah's brothers '*took their swords and attacked the unsuspecting city, killing every male.*' (34:25). In ancient literature we often find the image of war triggered by the rape of a woman (Helen, the Sabine women...). But this war, this violence here take the place of peaceful and good alliances with the Canaanite people we have met several times in the cycles of Abraham and Isaac. Jacob, himself a man of the Alliance, of the alliances and pacts – that remain mysteriously and ambiguously in the background of the story of Dinah – cannot approve of that murderous outcome (he says to his sons: '*You have brought trouble on me by making me obnoxious to the Canaanites and Perizzites*' (34:30), which suddenly pushed the people of the promise back to the violent times before Noah's ark.

With the return of Dinah in his family, Genesis picks up the story of Jacob, his epiphanies and his journey. Elohim, in fact, spoke to him again: '*Arise, go up to*

Bethel and dwell there. Make an altar there to the God who appeared to you when you fled from your brother Esau.' (35:1) At Bethel, fleeing to Laban, he had received a personal vocation in a dream (28:13), he had seen the *stairway to heaven*, and it was there that his real story began. When Jacob-Israel returns to Bethel he is certainly richer than when he had passed there for the first time: now he has numerous descendants, many goods, reconciliation with Esau, but above all he has a new name and the great blessing of the Jabbok. Here then is his gratitude for the blessings received throughout more than 20 years following the first one: 'let us arise and go up to Bethel, so that I may make there an altar to the God who answers me in the day of my distress and has been with me wherever I have gone' (35:3). Gratitude, all true gratitude is an expression of gratuitousness (the Greek root *charis*, is the same). The most valuable is the gratitude that "looks back", not the one that "looks ahead". For many human feelings and passions it is not good to look back (see how Lot's wife turned to a pillar of salt because of this: 19:26). Gratitude is an exception to this rule, because it is more genuine and effective when it is evoked by looking back, without considering the future. You can thank a customer or a supplier with gifts and "altars", because good entrepreneurs that we are look ahead and know that thanking is a very good investment for the future of business relationships. There is nothing wrong with that, in fact it is very well to do so. But the thanks of those who pronounce it as if the world were to end with that thanks is very different, higher and purer. The gratitude that looks back is all-gratuitous thanks, and this is worth a lot, because its only reason is intrinsic to that relationship. It is the same gratitude, for example, lived by those who practice the art of "*closing circles of relationships*", and after a meeting or an event (which will not be repeated) write to people just to say thank you to them.

For this same reason, the greatest gratitude is the one that we express to the poor and to the little ones, not the one towards the powerful (who are never thanked too much). It is above all this gratitude that we exercise, if we think about it, when we participate at the funeral of a friend, or the golden wedding anniversary of our parents. This is the gratitude we express to our colleagues in retirement parties (this dimension would be enough to take better care of them in our businesses), but also to the artists and philosophers of the past, or in respect of the saints (holiness can also be read as a large collective gratitude that, by looking back at the life of a person, helps everyone look forward and look up). It is this gratitude that we say – and we say it to one another – to our spouse on their deathbed, when all the pain and the beauty of the universe get concentrated in a single moment. These "gratitudes that look back" are not the only important thank you's of our lives, but when they are missing, all other thank you's lose some of their depth and value.

But this pilgrimage also reminds us that during the journey of authentic vocations, whether they be individual or collective, the "pilgrimage of Jacob" should be occasionally repeated, and we have to set out on a journey towards the site of our first vocation. These pilgrimages are always useful, but they are simply indispensable for the people and the communities that are born from listening to a "voice" and having believed in a "promise", including that special type of community called business. Repeating the "pilgrimage" of Jacob is invaluable in times of crisis, when you have just lived through a conflict or a "war". Setting out towards an "altar" becomes a great and effective way to start over and find the ethical and spiritual foundations of a relationship, of a community, of ourselves. Setting out together, in order to find reasons for giving thanks and thanking each other sooner or later on our way. After her sad story is told, Dinah disappears from the Bible. But Dinah is still alive in many women and girls (and children) kidnapped and raped, yesterday, today, tomorrow, in Italy, in India, anywhere. And if the Bible chose to present us the only daughter of the three patriarchs as a young girl who is kidnapped and abused, then even this absurd pain is looked upon by God, who continues to suffer every time the sisters of Dinah shed the same tears as she did, to be collected and to remain forever in his '*wineskin*' (Psalm 51). '*And Jacob came to Luz (that is, Bethel), ... he and all the people who were with him and there he built an altar and called the place El-bethel.*' (35:6).

Chapter 16
Full of Days but not Fulfilled Any More

Only one thing grieved him, and that was that he was beginning to get old, and he had to leave the earth there behind him. This was an injustice on God's part, that after having slaved one's life away getting property together, when you've got it, and you'd like some more, you have to leave it behind you. (...) So that when they told him it was time for him to be turning away from his property, and thinking of his soul, he rushed out into the courtyard like a madman, staggering, and went round killing his own ducks and turkeys, hitting them with his stick and screaming: "You're my own property, you come along with me!".

(Giovanni Verga, *La Roba*)

Abstract After the sad story of Dinah, we witness the death of Deborah, Rebekah's nurse, who was buried under an oak of tears. She is followed by Rachel, the beloved wife of Jacob, who died in giving birth to her second child. And as she was dying, she called his name Ben-oni [son of my sorrow but his father called him Benjamin [son of prosperity]. Jacob continues to move, a pilgrim and an exile, through the promised land. And so, still as a traveller, he buries Rachel in Bethlehem, the 'house of bread', along the road that was bringing him back to the land of his father Isaac. On the grave, once again, he erected a pillar, to mark his wife's life and that land forever. Women still beget us through labour, and for all the progress medicine has made, childbirth remains a crucial moment in the lives of mothers, which gives them a unique value and dignity in the universe. But there are still too many women dying in giving birth, even in the most technologically advanced countries.

Is it not true that progress is a set of vectors oriented in the same direction. For many dimensions of life, modernity has brought great improvements, but not for the art of aging and dying, which is undergoing a rapid and strong recession. The final stage of the "Jacob Cycle" is streaked with pain and death, particularly of women.

L. Bruni, *The Economy of Salvation*, Virtues and Economics 4,
https://doi.org/10.1007/978-3-030-04082-6_16

After the sad story of Dinah, we witness the death of Deborah, '*Rebekah's nurse*' (35:8), who was buried under an "*oak*" of tears. She is followed by Rachel, the beloved wife of Jacob, who died in giving birth to her second child: '*And when her labour was at its hardest, the midwife said to her, "Do not fear, for you have another son". And as her soul was departing (for she was dying), she called his name Ben-oni [son of my sorrow]; but his father called him Benjamin [son of prosperity]*' (35:17–18). Jacob continues to move, a pilgrim and an exile, through the promised land. And so, still as a traveller, he buries Rachel in Bethlehem (the 'house of bread'), along the road that was bringing him back to the land of his father Isaac (Hebron). On the grave, once again, he erected a pillar, to mark his wife's life and that land forever.

Women still beget us through labour, and for all the progress medicine has made, childbirth remains a crucial moment in the lives of mothers, which gives them a unique value and dignity in the universe. But there are still too many women dying in giving birth (about a thousand every day), even in the most technologically advanced countries. Sometimes, in these encounters of life and death the alchemy of Rachel is repeated: the newborn who is a '*child of sorrow*' and death takes a new name and becomes a '*child of prosperity*' and life. And in these transformations and genuine resurrections, it is usually the father to give his son the new name, and then to always see in their son, like in every child of theirs (and more), the face of the mother, his spouse.

And finally, Isaac dies, too: '*And Jacob came to his father Isaac at Mamre ... where Abraham and Isaac had sojourned. Now the days of Isaac were 180 years. And Isaac breathed his last, and he died and was gathered to his people, old and full of days. And his sons Esau and Jacob buried him.*' (35:27–29) The death of Isaac repeats almost literally that of his father Abraham: '*These are the days of the years of Abraham's life, 175 years. Abraham breathed his last and died in a good old age, an old man and full of days, and was gathered to his people. Isaac and Ishmael his sons buried him in the cave of Machpelah*' (25:8–9). Both Abraham and Isaac die after a long life, '*full of years*', '*in a good old age*', and the father's death is an opportunity for the meeting of the children who had been in conflict with each other – a wonderful scene that is revived every now and then even in our everyday stories. In both of these beautiful deaths, we find the expression '*breathed his last*': when we die we return the '*breath of life*' that Adam had received at the time of creation, and that every man coming into the world receives. Life is not our artefact, but it's all the mystery that lies between the first breath given to us and the last breath we give back.

The contemplation of the beautiful death of the Patriarchs should not make us forget that not all deaths of past times and the present are good. In case of children and young people, death comes like a thief, an enemy that is to take what is not his due. But there are so many other deaths – in fact, most of them – that could be good if only we had the spiritual and moral resources to live them well. Religions, popular piety, family ethics and spirituality, the traditional non-western civilizations, had created a good management of pain and death, because they developed a culture of aging and end-of-life that was much more sustainable than the one emerging in our consumer society. There have been many (though not all) old people of past times who died '*full of years*' and '*in a good old age*' – my grandfather Domenico is one of them. But today, understanding less and less of it all and therefore not accepting the age of the decline of the body and life, we create "*markets of youth*" as its surrogates that are more and more flourishing; and we forget that however much we can delay it by expensive beauty treatments, gyms and extreme metropolitan clothing, the age of the sunset is sure to come. Without the preparation of physical decay the final meeting is devastating, because we perceive of death as the death of everything: ourselves, our loves, our '*property*', the past and the world. And not honouring and not loving our old age and that of others, we do not value and do not like the elderly, who have become a big "*periphery*" of our era – and so a highly valuable asset is being squandered by society and the economy.

We have a vital need of new "charismas" to teach us again the art of fulfilled years and good old age, and ones that have the eyes to see this great poverty of our time in a different way, and love it. Without a docile reconciliation with it, old age ends up, paradoxically, to dominate the years of youth, too, that are spent quickly and in the fear of them ending soon. If, however, we are able to love it and accept it, old age reveals its delicate, hidden beauties that are not little at all. Beauty has always been a spiritual issue that is a lot more ethical than aesthetic. I met Rita Levi Montalcini, Mother Teresa, Nelson Mandela when they were already late in life, and I always found them beautiful, not less beautiful than my grandchildren and the young people at my university.

Therefore it is a great injustice that today too many elderly people spend their last years of life without children and grandchildren around, who are essential to make old age joyful and our gray hair beautiful. The culture that is increasingly causing its elderly to die alone or in the "*company*" of other elderly people is shameful and deeply ungrateful. Today in Italy, 62.5% of elderly women live alone (compared with 30% of men); it is a very serious fact, especially considering that these women have spent the best years of their lives taking care of their old, giving up (more or less freely) entertainment and often professional fulfilment. There is a whole generation of women who are dying with a huge "*credit of care*": what they get in their old age is infinitely less than what they donated when they were young. Tomorrow we will find a new balance between generations and between the sexes (hopefully it will be better), and the credits will be reduced, but this does not change the unjust pain of a whole generation that suffered a real "*exodus of care*".

The happiness and wisdom of a civilization is measured primarily by how it handles aging and dying. When a young man sees a parent or a grandmother die badly, it is his own life that is saddened, even if he does not realize it. An old man who is able to grow old and die in '*good old age*' makes for a great act of hope and love for young people, for his children, and so for everyone. Then it may also happen that a righteous man grows old and dies badly and desperately, and he remains righteous nevertheless, but it is part of the job of living fighting '*all night*' and finally tearing even the blessing from the angel of death.

The '*good old age*' and '*fullness of days*' of Abraham and Isaac (and then of Jacob: 49:33) touch us and move us more when we consider that in that phase of history for the people of Israel, life after death was a very vague concept, it was vague and dark (the so-called Sheol). The God of the Alliance and the Promise was the '*God of the living*', not the god of the dead. They believed that YHWH acted and spoke to them on earth. For many biblical characters grief for the approaching death is above all that which arises from the thought of no longer being able to see the Lord, known as the Lord of life, who is met, heard, and followed while living in the world. Biblical faith is about encounter, covenant, discipleship, history. Religious experience is historical fact, it happens in time and space, it is a fundamental dimension of life. This, and no other, is the faith that gave us Abraham, Isaac and Jacob. It is located in the deep roots of their true laity: the place of faith is history, the promised land is our land. And as long as there is history and land, that same voice that they met may meet us, too, taking us by surprise: '*Surely the Lord is in this place, and I did not know it.*' (28:16). This is their greatest legacy.

After Jacob and his brother Esau buried their father Isaac, '*Jacob lived in the land of his father's sojournings, in the land of Canaan*' (37:1).

Chapter 17
The Gift of the Dreamy Brother

> *The splendid veil so perfectly matched his face that it would have proved difficult to offer any critically sober argument to counter his popular fame. It made him so handsome and beautiful that it was almost eerie, indeed bordered on the divine. The worst part was that his resemblance to his mother – the forehead, the eyebrows, the contours of the mouth, the eyes – had never been so patently evident before as it was thanks to this attire – and was so evident to Jacob's eyes that they welled with tears, for he could believe only that he beheld Rachel there before him in Laban's hall on the day of fulfillment.*
>
> (Thomas Mann, *Joseph and his brothers*)

Abstract Joseph, the hero of the last great cycle of Genesis, is not remembered as the fourth patriarch ("The God of Abraham, Isaac and Jacob", that's how it will always be said instead). Joseph is the son of Jacob and Rachel, but, above all, Joseph is one of the brothers, and his story is a great lesson on the grammar of Biblical brotherhood (and ours). Jacob-Israel begot Joseph from Rachel, the woman with whom he fell in love at the well. His father had a special love for Joseph, an explicit and known preference. The text is not afraid to tell us, that Israel loved Joseph more than any other of his sons. For this reason he made him a robe of many colours. This coat was special and different from those of the other brothers. It was long, with sleeves that covered the palm of the hand, and maybe colourful and embroidered, too. For Thomas Mann – who will guide us in this last cycle of the Genesis – the coat was Rachel's robe that her father Laban had given her for her wedding, and that had been bought from merchants and thought to have belonged to a king's daughter once. Joseph was a dreamer and a teller of dreams: in this lies vocation his tragedy together with his resurrection.

L. Bruni, *The Economy of Salvation*, Virtues and Economics 4,
https://doi.org/10.1007/978-3-030-04082-6_17

Biblical characters are not masks in a play. They are not there to interpret a role (good or bad, traitor or betrayed etc.). They are human beings, with all the colours and traits of the human as a whole.

Some of these characters have received a particular calling in view of a task of collective salvation, but they have never ceased to be men and women in the full sense. So, goodness, purity, cheating, theft, blessings, hugs, fraternity, fratricides intersect and give rise to a true story of salvation for all. The protagonists of Genesis are close to us and speak to us because they appear in the nakedness of their emotions and ambiguities, without fear to be presented even in the pettiness and contradictions of the human condition. And so, they build up a salvation that is possible for all and a great cure for any ideology, including many ideologies of fraternity.

Joseph, the hero of the last great cycle of Genesis, is not remembered as the fourth patriarch ("*The God of Abraham, Isaac and Jacob*", that's how it will always be said instead). Joseph is the son of Jacob and Rachel, but, above all, Joseph is one of the brothers, and his story is a great lesson on the grammar of Biblical brotherhood (and ours).

Jacob-Israel begot Joseph from Rachel, the woman with whom he fell in love at the well. His father had a special love for Joseph, an explicit and known preference. The text is not afraid to tell us, '*Now Israel loved Joseph more than any other of his sons*' (37:3). For this reason '*he made him a robe of many colours.*' (37:3). This coat (*ketônet passîm*) was special and different from those of the other brothers. It was long, with sleeves that covered the palm of the hand, and maybe colourful and embroidered, too – for Thomas Mann the coat was Rachel's robe that her father Laban had given her for her wedding, and that had been bought from merchants and thought to have belonged to a king's daughter once.

It was certainly a luxurious robe, and therefore not suitable for those who have to do physical work. It was a message of preference and status within the clan that came loud and clear to the other siblings: '*when his brothers saw that their father loved him more than all his brothers, they hated him*' (37:4). In this complex family situation – sons by his wives loved differently by Jacob, sons by his slave women, a favourite son – it just adds another element to further complicate the story. *Joseph is a dreamer*, but above all he is a public story-teller who keeps sharing his dreams. Joseph, unlike his father, does not dream of Heaven, nor does he hear the words of YHWH (in the whole cycle of Joseph, God remains very much in the background, the scene is taken completely by inter-human relationships). The protagonist of his dreams is he himself: '*Hear this dream that I have dreamed: Behold, we were binding sheaves in the field, and behold, my sheaf arose and stood upright. And behold, your sheaves gathered around it and bowed down to my sheaf.*' (37:6–7). So, his brothers '*hated him even more for his dreams and for his words*' (37:8). He then had another dream: '*the sun, the moon, and eleven stars were bowing down to me*' (37:9). After the second dream, Jacob (who was recognized as the '*sun*' of the dream) rebuked him (37:10), and his brothers ('*the eleven stars*') '*were jealous of him*' (37:11). Joseph, the son with the royal robe, already unloved by his brothers because beloved by his father, foolishly, naively, with the beautiful impetuosity and immaturity of youth, but also because of his temperament-task (dreams are part of the calling of Joseph), tells those dreams that ultimately transform the feeling of envy-jealousy of his brothers in real hatred and then into a plan of action to eliminate him. In fact, when Joseph joins his brothers who are pasturing their flock near Shechem, sent (unwisely) by his father to see if they were doing well (*shalom*), as soon as they catch sight of him from afar they cry: '*Here comes this dreamer. [the master of dreams]*' (37:19). And so, they deliberate to kill him ('*Come now, let us kill him*' (37:20). Then, following the intervention of Reuben, the eldest, they change their minds and decide to throw him in a pit in the desert ('*Shed no blood; throw him into this pit*'; 37:22). Finally, as suggested by Judah, they sell him to a caravan of merchants passing by ('*let us sell him to the Ishmaelites*' (37:27).

This tragic end of Joseph – that we later discover to be of a saving effect, too, but now we do not know, and *we should not know* – depends on one crucial element: the brothers *believe* the dreams of Joseph. They are the interpreters, and they read the contents of those dreams as a true revelation or prophecy. It is the power of the truth of his dreams and his words that condemn Joseph. If the brothers had not seen the potential in Joseph to become the 'first sheaf' of the family, they would have only derided him as a self-important, vain youngster. Instead, they recognize that the predilection of the father may be at the service of a divine plan and a natural talent that elevates Joseph above them.

With Joseph, then, a new type of intra-family conflict makes its first appearance. Until now, the conflicts in the house of Abraham were dualistic: Cain/Abel, Sarai/Hagar, Jacob/Esau, Leah/Rachel. Now the conflict is between a brother and his other brothers. We are facing *community* discrimination, for collective envy-jealousy that results in a violent persecution and, finally, expulsion, which is very close to fratricide.

Collective envy towards an individual is a serious and widespread social, organizational and community illness. We see it every time a group creates a certain perverse solidarity within itself through the process of envy-jealousy towards a person that turns into ostracism and persecution of that person by all the others. It happens (almost) always that, in order to justify themselves, the persecutors find reasons for the guilt of the persecuted, thereby covering up from themselves and all others the only real reason: jealousy-envy (even in the biblical text we find a passage where the narrator, on the basis of ancient traditions, leaves the possibility of a partial shared responsibility of Joseph open (37:2, 10)).

Furthermore, it is not uncommon that the first reason for the persecution arises from the "dreams" of the persecuted. A member of a group that was already standing out for some reason, communicates – to colleagues, community members, ... – a life plan, a plan for reform, a greater vision. The audience interprets the "dream", and knowing the quality of the dreamer, they believe that those projects that are larger than theirs will probably come true. The envy-jealousy kicks off (they are twin sisters), and not infrequently the plan, too, to eliminate the "master of dreams". This particular type of envy – *the envy for the dreams of others* – is particularly insidious and harmful, and it is activated by the presence of a talent in a member of the same group (all jealousies develop between peers), because it is his ability to dream of great things and implement them. This envy- jealousy towards the other arises from the lack of dreams in us that could be just as great and beautiful. In such relational processes, the presence of privilege (the clothes and dreams) is real, it is not invented by the envious, it is only interpreted as a threat instead of being seen as a common good. For this reason, this envy (especially when it develops within our primary communities) can only be cured through reconciliation with the talent of the other, until it feels like ours, everyone's – it is emblematic that before they threw Joseph in the pit, his brothers '*stripped him of his robe*' (37:23).

In similar community dynamics, the great temptation of the dreamer is to give up dreaming, and stop telling the dreams to friends. But if we do not tell our wildest dreams and vocations to anyone anymore, soon the day will come when we can no longer dream: we close our eyes to see more, and nothing happens. As long as we have someone to tell our dreams to, we still have friends (friendship is also the "place" where we can tell our biggest dreams to each other, reciprocally). Joseph told his dreams to his brothers because he considered them his friends; he was young and he trusted them (which younger brother does not trust the elder brothers?). Betraying or perverting a dream told by a friend-brother is the first crime against friendship and brotherhood (that thus remains only a matter of blood). When the envy of others snatches the colourful coat from us and kills our dreams within us, communities begin an inexorable moral and spiritual decline. And the dreamer is turned off, gets saddened, is lost.

Joseph did not stop to tell his dreams – and eventually those dreams he had told saved his brothers, too.

Chapter 18
The Word that Upturns the World

> *The journey was continued until they came to Ephrath, the place of Rachel's sepulchre. Joseph hastened to his mother's grave, and throwing himself across it, he groaned and cried, saying: "O mother, mother, that didst bear me, arise, come forth and see how thy son hath been sold into slavery, with none to take pity upon him ... Arise, O mother, awake from thy sleep, see how my father is with me in his soul and in his spirit, and comfort him and ease his heavy heart.*
>
> (Louis Ginzberg, *The Legends of the Jews*. vol. 2)

Abstract The word profit, bèça', makes its first appearance in the Bible when a brother is sold. After they had cast Joseph in the pit, the brothers gave heed to Judah and sold him for 20 shekels of silver to the merchants travelling through those parts. It was the price of a slave or a pair of sandals, 20 times less than the price Abraham paid to the Hittites for the tomb for Sarah. Thus Joseph, the younger brother was sold as a slave to the Ishmaelites, descendants of the son of Abraham and Hagar, the boy who was also refused and expelled to the desert by Sarah. Money and profit are presented to us as closely related to death. They come into play as a means to avoid it, but in reality they continue to stay very close to it. The great civilizations knew very well that the territory of profit shares a border with love and life, but on the other side also with death and sin; and that the stakes are mobile with border crossings in both directions that are very easy and frequent. Our civilisation, however, is the first that has entirely forgotten the existence of the left side border of the land of profit. After that horrible sale, Judah went down from his brothers and turned aside, and went into the land of Canaan, where, together with his daughter in law Tamar he becomes the protagonist of one of the most beautiful stories of Genesis.

L. Bruni, *The Economy of Salvation*, Virtues and Economics 4,
https://doi.org/10.1007/978-3-030-04082-6_18

The word profit (*bèça'*) makes its first appearance in the Bible when a brother is sold: 'What profit is it if we kill our brother (...)?' (37:26). So, after they had cast him in the pit, the brothers gave heed to Judah and 'sold him ... for twenty shekels of silver' (37:28) to the merchants travelling through those parts.

It was the price of a slave or a pair of sandals, 20 times less than the price Abraham paid to the Hittites for the tomb for Sarah. Thus Joseph, the younger brother was sold as a slave to the Ishmaelites, descendants of the son of Abraham and Hagar, the boy who was also refused and expelled to the desert by Sarah. Money and profit are presented to us as closely related to death. They come into play as a means to avoid it, but in reality they continue to stay very close to it. The great civilizations knew very well that the territory of profit shares a border with love and life, but on the other side also with death and sin; and that the stakes are mobile with border crossings in both directions that are very easy and frequent. Our civilisation, however, is the first that has *entirely* forgotten the existence of the left side border of the land of profit; and so, it has forgotten that 'The wage of the righteous leads to life, the gain of the wicked to sin.' (*Proverbs*, 10:16). There have always been – yesterday and today – merchants who buy and sell only 'gum, balm, and myrrh' (37:25); but there are others, often mingling on the same squares, that, apart from the goods also buy and sell "brothers", for 20 shekels or less.

After the caravan of merchants of goods and children drove off in the direction of Egypt, the brothers '*took Joseph's robe and slaughtered a goat and dipped the robe in the blood. And they sent the robe of many colours and brought it to their father ... And he identified it and said, »It is my son's robe. A fierce animal has devoured him. Joseph is without doubt torn to pieces.«*' (37:31–33). We are reading one of the most intense passages of Genesis: '*Then Jacob tore his garments and put sackcloth on his loins and mourned for his son many days. ...and (he) said, "I shall go down to Sheol (the kingdom of the dead) to my son, mourning."*' (37,34–35) They are verses of immense beauty and humanity that make this special kind of paternal pain eternal and sacred that make this, for which – unlike orphanage and widowhood – there is no specific word, perhaps because it is unspeakable. Heaven must exist, if only to do justice to these pains without a name, to return the immaculate long and colorful robes of our children.

Then Judah '*went down from his brothers and turned aside*' (38:1), and – perhaps to get away from the coat and the blood – went into the land of Canaan, where, together with his daughter in law Tamar he becomes the protagonist of one of the most beautiful stories of Genesis. Tamar, the Canaanite woman, is widowed after marrying Er, the firstborn of Judah. According to the so-called *levirate law*, Judah asks his second son Onan to give offspring to Tamar. But Onan, too, after he refuses to fulfil his duty to Tamar, dies (38:6–9). At this point, the thought creeps in Judah's mind that Tamar may be the cause of the death of his two sons (38:11) – it was common in many ancient cultures, and even today in some regions of India or Africa, to believe that widows bring bad luck and curses, and to discriminate against them and abuse them because of this. And so, he says to her: '*Remain a widow in your father's house, till Shelah my son grows up*' (38:11). Time passes, Shelah grows up, but Judah does not keep his word and does not respect the levirate law, and Tamar remains single and childless. At this point there comes a twist. Tamar hears that Judah is passing through her parts, away from his tribe. She removes the widow's clothes (38:14), covers her face with a veil so as not to be recognized by her father in law, and waits for him at a crossroads. When Judah saw her, '*he thought she was a prostitute*' (38:15), and as a price for her services he promises Tamar sending her a young goat. But in order to give in to Judah, the daughter in law wants a pledge: '*Your signet and your cord and your staff that is in your hand.*' (38:18), the "identity card" of the lords of those parts. Tamar gets pregnant. And when 3 months later Judah learns that his daughter in law is expecting a baby (actually, she will be having twins: Perez and Zerah: 38:29–30), he sentences her to death. While they lead her out to the stake, Tamar brings her plan to completion: '*By the man to whom these [the signet, the cord and the staff] belong, I am pregnant.*' (38:25). '*Then Judah identified them and said, "She is more righteous than I, since I did not give her to my son Shelah."*' (38:26) With this last act of responsibility Judah also redeems himself: he could have exercised his power of a man and the head of the clan to deny Tamar, a helpless woman. But he did not, and, at least in this action, he was a righteous man.

So ends the story of Tamar. From its conclusion we understand whose side Genesis takes: it is on the side of Tamar, who is presented as a positive and righteous figure ('She is more righteous than I'), with traits that are similar to the great women of the Bible (Judith, Ruth). And if we suspend the moralistic reading of these episodes (and we should always do if we hope to have a bit of "understanding of the scriptures"), we may discover many messages of life in the story of Tamar. First of all, Genesis, by blaming Judah and praising Tamar, reminds us that there is a wrong type of caution and also a saving type of transgression. Fearing that he might also lose his third son ('*he feared that he would die, like his brothers*': 38:11), Judah does not serve life and denies descendants to his daughter in law and her family. This risk avoiding caution is often the enemy of life and the future; hence it is not a virtue but a vice and a sin. In the story of Judah and Tamar there is a strong counterpoint that returns and accompanies the entire biblical act: the predilection and the redemption of the last and the least. Only by putting together the "*voice*" of the patriarchs, kings and the Law with that of the exalted humble can the Bible resonate in all its beauty and salvation. A more fruitful and true reading of the Word of God then is one that makes us upend orders and hierarchies of our human time, and exalts the humble and humbles the mighty, it is the one that shakes us and undermines our well-rooted ethical beliefs about what morality, sin, guilt or innocence is. A Bible without the presence of injured humanity and even that of the sinner would be a book that would not offer any benefit to real men and real women.

But in this episode of Genesis we can trace a hidden but not invisible additional message too, aimed primarily at males and the powerful: *the women you look for at the "cross-roads"* and the women that, like Judas, you "*mistake for prostitutes*", may be people from your own house. And they really are. You do not recognise them, you consider them strangers and faceless people, but Elohim can see through their veil, and the day will come when you have to render justice on behalf of the "*signets*" that you left in pledge with them.

We have to thank the author of these stories, and those who have kept them dearly over the millennia, for having had the courage to tell us about naked and wounded humanity, in an uncensored way and without shame. And if all of humanity is a gift, then every human being can find a life of redemption and salvation in these texts, yesterday, today and forever.

Only if we get into this "upturned" logic are we not amazed when we read in the genealogy of Jesus of Nazareth: '*Abraham was the father of Isaac, and Isaac the father of Jacob, and Jacob the father of Judah and his brothers, and Judah the father of Perez and Zerah by Tamar (...)*' (Matthew 1:2). Yes, between Abraham and Jesus there is Tamar and there is Judah, too.

At the roadside at the spring, Tamar not only met his father in law; she did not know it, but the real meeting on that road was another one, one that has given an eternal place for her, like a rare gem, in the great history of salvation.

A brother is not to be sold to the merchants for 20 copper coins, you are not supposed to send the long and colorful coat of a son to his father dipped in the blood of a young goat, a widowed daughter in law should not be humiliated and abandoned. But as long as there are people who continue to commit these crimes and generate victims, there will be at least one "place" (the Bible) in the world to find an identity in, to feel guided, loved, comforted by, to be taken by the hand and raised back to our feet, even in the most dramatic and dark moments of our existence and that of others. And also to find the strength to start walking again, in order not to die, and in order not to let people die, to really hope in a promised land, a resurrection, in the paradise of Abel, Ishmael, Hagar, Dinah, Joseph and Tamar.

'Now Joseph had been brought down to Egypt, and Potiphar (...) had bought him from the Ishmaelites' (39:1).

Chapter 19
Without Price or Clamour

Nekhludoff awoke next morning feeling as if he had been guilty of some iniquity the day before. He began considering. He could not remember having done anything wrong; he had committed no evil act, but he had had evil thoughts. (...) An evil action may not be repeated, and can be repented of; but evil thoughts generate all evil actions.

(Leo Tolstoy, *Resurrection*)

Abstract The story of Joseph in the house of Potiphar, the Egyptian official, is a great lesson on the grammar of loyalty. Loyalty is not a virtue of our time. For centuries, companies and institutions have resorted to living with a legacy of loyalty that was generated by the values of hard work and practices of families, churches, communities, and fuelled by the grand narratives, by art and literature. For some decades, we have intentionally stopped creating these values and practices, but the need for loyalty still remains and grows. So, a few decades ago we thought we could replace loyalty with incentives, paying and controlling workers and managers, hoping to make them "loyal" also in the cases when 'none of the men of the house was there in the house' to see them and control them. Too bad that now we have to realise, that this substitution only works for simple things but it is harmful when handling important or crucial situations. The radical fragility of our economic and social system derives from a severe deficiency of the virtue of loyalty.

The story of Joseph in the house of Potiphar, the Egyptian official, is a great lesson on the grammar of loyalty. Loyalty is not a virtue of our time. For centuries, companies and institutions have resorted to living with a legacy of loyalty that was generated by the values of hard work and practices of families, churches, communities, and fuelled by the grand narratives, by art and literature. For some decades, we have intentionally stopped creating these values and practices, but the need for loyalty still remains and grows. So, a few decades ago we thought we could replace loyalty

L. Bruni, *The Economy of Salvation*, Virtues and Economics 4,
https://doi.org/10.1007/978-3-030-04082-6_19

with incentives, paying and controlling workers and managers, hoping to make them "*loyal*" also in the cases when '*none of the men of the house was there in the house*' (39:13) to see them and control them. Too bad that now we have to realise, that this substitution only works for simple things but it is harmful when handling important or crucial situations. The radical fragility of our economic and social system derives from a severe deficiency of the virtue of loyalty – it would already be a great gift if we all became aware of it.

Joseph arrives in Egypt, sold as a slave to Potiphar, an officer of the Pharaoh. Genesis shows us Joseph as a person of great value: he is no longer the naive boy who narrated his dreams/prophecies to his envious brothers, but a perfect administrator, who did everything well: '*The Lord was with Joseph, and he became a successful man, and he was in the house of his Egyptian master.*' (39:2) Joseph wins the esteem and unconditional trust of Potiphar, who '*left all that he had in Joseph's charge, and because of him he had no concern about anything but the food he ate*' (39:6). And so '*the Lord blessed the Egyptian's house for Joseph's sake; the blessing of the Lord was on all that he had, in house and field*' (39:5). The blessing of Joseph, the heir of the first great blessing of Abraham, extends to the whole of the house where he lived and for which he worked. Good things exceed the goodness of the person performing them. If there is a just and good person working in a community or a business, the goodness-blessing infects everything he or she touches, and so this person becomes a common good. The first blessing of every human enterprise is the people in it, sometimes only one person: '*you [Abraham] will be a blessing*' (12:2).

The loyalty of Joseph that is at the heart of this story emerges in full strength in the way he handles the conflict with his master's wife (Genesis leaves her nameless). Joseph is presented as a young man who is '*handsome in form and appearance*' (39:6), just like his mother Rachel was (29:17). He is also a display of the moral beauty typical of righteous and honest people, which is not less fascinating than physical beauty. The wife of Potiphar '*cast her eyes*' on him '*and said: "Lie with me"*' (39:7). Joseph answered: '*Behold, because of me my master has no concern about anything in the house, and he has put everything that he has in my charge [he] has [not] kept back anything from me except you... How then can I do this great wickedness and sin against God?*' (39:9) Potiphar, in fact, had asked him to account only for '*the food he ate*' and in that culture the '*food*' was also an image or euphemism for spousal intimacy. And so even though '*she spoke to Joseph day after day, he would not listen to her*' (39:10).

The "*test*" Joseph is put to is the paradigm of all those situations in which a person is given the chance to become loyal. In loyalty, in fact, a typical dimension of all the virtues can be seen in its pure form; of the virtues that are, in fact, not a matter of preference or values, but of actions. Therefore, they constitute experiential goods, because the only way to become loyal (just, prudent, strong ...) is when our principles translate into concrete action. You can sincerely *believe* in the value of loyalty, but to *be* loyal it is necessary to prove it in the field. Good intentions or good thoughts are not enough – even if the person who manages to be loyal cultivates good thoughts and drives out bad ones before and during the action itself. And as for all the experiential goods, we cannot know if this "good" is really in our "basket" until we are inside a concrete experience where we find out whether we only *thought* to be loyal or we *really* are. Therefore, you can only become loyal, even after being disloyal for some time. How can it happen that in the face of new experiences we discover – and are surprised and moved to do so – to have a moral force in us that we thought we did not possess? Martyrdom must be something like this, and therefore before becoming a gift given to others there is a gift you receive. Joseph, who was already righteous, did not know that he was also loyal until that gaze of his master's wife found him. Not even a single moment before.

Here then we find an essential feature of loyalty. Its existence and its value is measured on the basis of an actual cost that the person who wants to be loyal must pay saying no to one (or more) unfair action(s) that would have saved the cost. Therefore, loyalty always costs a lot and often results in a "*don't*" – and it is also because of this that it is difficult to see. Without this costly alternative that comes '*one day*' when '*none of the men of the house was there in the house*', loyalty does not make an appearance. The price that Joseph had to pay be loyal to Potiphar was not so much the rejection of sexual pleasure as the likely consequences associated with the rejection, given the radical asymmetry of power that existed between him and his master's wife. It was a cost that manifested itself soon.

In the aftermath of this episode of the great cycle of Joseph, there is a lesson taught to us on another dimension of loyalty that is not a necessary one, but very common. If he wants to be loyal, Joseph should say no to an offer that comes from the same part where the person-institution with which he wants to be loyal stands. '*But one day, when he went into the house to do his work and none of the men of the house was there in the house, she caught him by his garment, saying, "Lie with me". But he left his garment in her hand and fled and got out of the house.*' After that the woman '*called to the men of her household and said to them, "See, he has brought among us a Hebrew to laugh at us. He came in to me to lie with me, and I cried out with a loud voice"*' (39:11–14). The woman then told the same false and upturned version of the story to her husband (39:17) who took Joseph and '*put him into the prison*' (39:19).

Yet another time his "*coat*" is taken from him, once again he is thrown violently into a "*pit*" (40:15). And Joseph is "quiet as a lamb"; he does not defend himself. The Bible tells us nothing about the reasons for his silence. That unsaid word can reveal to us another fundamental dimension of loyalty, perhaps the most typical one. Loyalty should be lived, not told about, especially when, to stay loyal, one had to say a big "no" to someone of the same intimate "home". Even these silences can be an expression of loyalty, but only when those who remain quiet take upon themselves the costly consequences of that loyal silence (sometimes it may happen that this loyalty enters into conflict with other virtues, such as justice: it is in conflicts between virtues that we exercise our moral responsibility).

Loyalty is a silent and invisible virtue in its most profound and true form; consequently, you cannot rely on the typical awards and gratitude that support and reinforce many of the '*public*' virtues. The reward for the price paid to be and to remain loyal is completely intrinsic, and therefore those who have no inner life from where this sole reward flows may not become or remain loyal. If we want the world and the institutions of tomorrow to be more loyal, we need to give life to a new era of inner life and spirituality. Without loyalty, you cannot remain faithful to the pacts and primary promises of life, and neither to the contracts that follow right after these.

Finally, if loyalty by its nature is difficult to observe, there is much more loyalty in the world than we are able to see. If we could see more deeply into our friends, our wives, our husbands, we would realize that behind their faithful love and their good eyes, invisibly and silently, there are many acts of loyalty hiding that are the very foundation of these strong relationships. Some of these decisive instances of loyalty/faithfulness are shared with our beloved in the final moments of life, as our most precious inheritance; others, perhaps even more beautiful and certainly more painful ones, we cannot or do not manage to tell and so these die with us; but they all bear much fruit, and make our world more beautiful and more worthy. 'And Joseph's master took him and put him into the prison... But the Lord was with Joseph' (39:21).

Chapter 20
The Honest Eyes of the Prophet

> *'God will also predict something good for Pharaoh.' 'You say God,' Amenhotep investigated. 'You've said that several times. Which God do you mean? Because you come from Zahi and Amu I suppose that you mean the bull of the fields, the one that is called Baal, the Lord in the East.' Joseph's smile became more reserved; he shook his head. 'My ancestors, the dreamers of God,' he said, 'made their pact with another Lord.' "Then it can only be Adonai, the Groom,' the king said quickly, 'for whom the flute cries in the ravines, the god who rises again."*
>
> (Thomas Mann, *Joseph and His Brothers*)

Abstract Although innocent, the young Joseph found himself in prison, thrown again to the bottom of a pit. That prison, however, also became the site of the full bloom of his vocation, the one that had been announced to him by the prophetic dreams of his boyhood. Those early dreams got him to Egypt as a slave; the dreams that he interprets now in the land of the Nile will be the road that will make his great youthful dreams come true, and they will help him find his brothers who sold him and his father. It is in a prison where a new phase in the life of Joseph begins, the decisive one for himself and for his people. In that pit, from the teller of his own dreams Joseph becomes the interpreter of the dreams of others. As a boy he only told the story of his dreams, but did not interpret them. The pain he felt over being hated and sold by his brothers, becoming a slave and then being imprisoned helped him mature and discover his own self. And in the crucible of suffering and injustice he discovered his vocation: he became a servant of the dreams of others. And it was his salvation.

There are many different types of famine. We are passing through the greatest famine of dreams that human history has ever known. It is the famine of dreams produced by this solitary and individualistic capitalism which is a very serious form of poverty, because while the lack of bread does not exhaust hunger, if we deprive

L. Bruni, *The Economy of Salvation*, Virtues and Economics 4,
https://doi.org/10.1007/978-3-030-04082-6_20

ourselves of the dreams we end up not feeling their absence anymore; we get used to a world of wishes that are more and more choked by goods, and soon become so poor that we become unaware of this poverty. How is it possible to dream of angels, heaven, the great rivers of Egypt, when we fall asleep in front of the TV? For big dreams, you should fall sleep with a prayer on your lips, or wake up with a book of poems open on your chest that watched over your sleep.

Although innocent, the young Joseph found himself in prison, thrown again to the bottom of a "*pit*" (40:15). That prison, however, also became the site of the full bloom of his vocation, the one that had been announced to him by the prophetic dreams of his boyhood. Those early dreams got him to Egypt as a slave; the dreams that he interprets now in the land of the Nile will be the road that will make his great youthful dreams come true, and they will help him find his brothers who sold him and his father. It is in a prison where a new phase in the life of Joseph begins, the decisive one for himself and for his people (it is not uncommon for a "prison" to become the place of the beginning of a new life). In that "*pit*", from the teller of his own dreams Joseph becomes the interpreter of the dreams of others. As a boy he only told the story of his dreams, but did not interpret them. The pain he felt over being hated and sold by his brothers, becoming a slave and then being imprisoned helped him mature and discover his own self. And in the crucible of suffering and injustice he discovered his vocation: he became a servant of the dreams of others.

In that prison there were two senior officers of the court with him: the cupbearer and the baker of the pharaoh (40:1). And '*they both dreamed*' (40:5). The next morning 'Joseph came to them (...) he saw that they were troubled. So he asked (them): "*Why are your faces downcast today?*" They said to him, "*We have had dreams, and there is no one to interpret them.*"' (40:7–8). The two officers tell their dreams to Joseph and he interprets them. Only those who have dreamed and had the courage to tell their dreams can decipher the dreams of others. Because of a paradoxical law that is at the heart of many high things of life, the best interpreters of dreams of others are those who have suffered the most because of their own dreams.

To have dreams and not to find somebody who can interpret them is a great cause of unhappiness for those who, despite the famine, dream on – there are still many, especially in the countries with the lowest GDP and the richest dreams, dreams that soon will also produce wealth. Dreams are always serious things, but the decisive ones are our "*daydreams*", those that we call projects, aspirations, desire for liberation and justice, desire for the future and for happiness, the ones that make us glimpse our place in the world. The dreams of yesterday and today, however, need interpreters, someone who knows how to decipher the contents – or else, those dreams will die away. These interpreters are always important, but they are fundamentally so for young people, living the age of great dreams.

Joseph begins to interpret dreams as a gift to his two fellow prisoners: '*Joseph said to them, »Do not interpretations belong to God? Please tell them to me.«*' (40:8). The "*good*" interpretation of dreams is that which arises from gratuitousness, and not the one made for profit ('*Do not interpretations belong to God?*'). The reason for the scarcity of good interpreters of our dreams lies in the essential need of this gratuitousness. They are a rare gift, but not extremely rare. "Spiritual guides" belong to this precious human category, they are the people who listen to and interpret our dreams and signs. The good interpretation of dreams is requested and given free of charge, as a gift. It's not a job, and if it becomes a job it is not good.

The interpretations that Joseph gives those two dreams are very different: for the chief cupbearer he predicts liberation, for the chief of the bakers he announces death – as it later happens, too. The moral value of an interpreter of dreams is measured by his honesty, that is, the ability and the courage to tell even those interpretations that we do not want to hear. There have been and there are still too many fawning interpreters who tell us only the interpretations that we like to hear. Sometimes misinterpretations may also come from honest interpreters who do not have enough courage and love in themselves for this – even if the charisma of interpretation of dreams dies out if it is not nourished by the suffering of difficult interpretations. I have met young people whose lives were made very difficult, at times even wrecked by bad interpreters of their dreams, who, facing the obvious signs of a vocation different from that which the young man thought he had did not have either the honesty or the courage for a true interpretation; and so instead of exposing them to the pain of that hard truth, they manipulated the dreams and fed illusions, disappointments, frustrations, unhappiness to those young people. Trusting a manipulator of dreams is more damaging than the death of a dream for lack of interpreters.

After 2 years, the pharaoh, too, had a dream. '*(...) he was standing by the Nile, and behold, there came up out of the Nile seven cows attractive and plump, and they fed in the reed grass. And behold, seven other cows, ugly and thin, came up out of the Nile after them ... And the ugly, thin cows ate up the seven attractive, plump cows.*' (41:1–4) And Pharaoh woke up troubled; went back to sleep and he had another dream: '*(...) seven ears of grain, plump and good, were growing on one stalk. And behold, after them sprouted seven ears, thin and blighted by the east wind. And the thin ears swallowed up the seven plump, full ears.*' (41:5–7). *The two dreams disturbed the pharaoh's mind so much that he "called for all the magicians of Egypt and all its wise men. Pharaoh told them his dreams, but there was none who could interpret them to Pharaoh"* (41:8).

At this point, there comes a narrative turn in the story. The chief cupbearer, to whom Joseph had interpreted the dream 2 years before, remembered him. He spoke to the pharaoh, who in turn sent him for Joseph. Joseph immediately reveals the key to the understanding of what is going to happen, and the nature of his task: "*It is not in me; God will give Pharaoh a favourable answer.*" (41:16) We are facing a crucial time and era: the end of the age of diviners, soothsayers, magicians, and the start of the time of prophecy. Here Joseph becomes the first prophet of Israel. In fact, in this reading of the dream of the pharaoh we find the essential features that distinguish an authentic prophetic interpretation from the products of diviners and false prophets of all times. This prophetic interpretation is given as a gift and freely, because it is an exercise of the charisma that the "*prophet*" receives, it is not his artefact nor a technique learned in any school. It is a gift that must be accepted and believed in by its recipient in order to perform his function. It always leads to action and change.

Our society is full of for-profit advisors and it is increasingly inundated by magicians and horoscopes, but it desperately lacks good interpreters of dreams – and those few that we have are neither sought nor listened to, and thus they are at risk of extinction due to the lack of demand. That pharaoh, however, believed the interpretation/prophecy by Joseph, and acted accordingly. '*There will come seven years of great plenty throughout all the land of Egypt, but after them there will arise seven years of famine, and all the plenty will be forgotten in the land of Egypt. The famine will consume the land [the thin cows and ears that eat up the fat ones]*' (41:29–30). And so, Joseph continued, '*Now therefore let Pharaoh select a discerning and wise man, and set him over the land of Egypt ... (to) take one-fifth of the produce of the land of Egypt during the seven plentiful years.*' (41:33–34).

Famines of the "*thin cows*" do happen. These famines, sooner or later, end of course, although sometimes at a great cost. The famines of dreams, however, do not end by themselves. They end only if, we decide to learn to dream again. It is not impossible. We have been able to do it after endless and unspeakable times of misery: after the wars and dictatorships, after the fratricides, after the death of children. We wanted to begin to dream again, together. So, we listened to the poets, saints and artists who were able to interpret our new dreams. We prayed and cried together, recited their poems – our poems – and sang their songs – our songs. This is the only way individuals and peoples are reborn and resurrected.

Chapter 21
Brotherhood Cannot Be Bought

> *Accept my offer. Take me instead of him to be your servant: ... I want atonement, atonement for all. Here, before you, strange man, I take the frightful oath we brothers swore – with both hands I take that oath and break it in two across my knee. Our eleventh brother, the father's ewe lamb, first son of the true wife, him the beast did not rend; but we, his brothers sold him into the world.*
>
> (Thomas Mann, *Joseph and his brothers*)

Abstract The second part of the cycle of Joseph is a wonderful lesson on the process of the reconstruction of denied fraternity, especially of the broken brotherhoods where there is a victim, an innocent man who succeeds in reaching forgiveness and reconciliation after a long and painful journey. After the first 7 years of abundance, the 'fat cows', there came a harsh famine, but in all the land of Egypt there was bread. The famine reached Canaan, too. Jacob-Israel learned that there was grain for sale in Egypt, and he sent his sons to the land of the Nile. The sons left, except Benjamin, his last born by Rachel. Jacob kept him home, because he feared that harm might happen to him. The same harm that had happened years before to Joseph who now awaited them, having become "visir" in Egypt. It is not uncommon that it is a "famine" that makes us reconcile after many years of conflict. Joseph, still as a young boy, was sold into slavery by those brothers whom now, as an adult, he is saving by giving them grain.

For the healing of the deep wounds of the primary relationships of our lives (fraternity), there is a vital need of time. We never really get reconciled if we do not let the pain/love penetrate to the core of the wounded relationship, to be absorbed there and to slowly heal it. But what is most needed are the actions as they communicate in the language of behaviour that we want, really, to start over.

The second part of the cycle of Joseph is a wonderful lesson on the process of the reconstruction of denied fraternity, especially of the broken brotherhoods where

L. Bruni, *The Economy of Salvation*, Virtues and Economics 4,
https://doi.org/10.1007/978-3-030-04082-6_21

there is a victim, an innocent man who succeeds in reaching forgiveness and reconciliation after a long and painful journey. After the first 7 years of abundance (of the 'fat cows'), there came a harsh famine, '*but in all the land of Egypt there was bread.*' (Genesis 41:54).

The famine reached Canaan, too. Jacob-Israel '*learned that there was grain for sale in Egypt*' (42:1), and he sent his sons to the land of the Nile. The sons left, except Benjamin, his last born by Rachel. Jacob kept him home, because '*he feared that harm might happen to him*' (42:4). The same harm that had happened years before to Joseph who now awaited them, having become "visir", in Egypt (41:40). It is not uncommon that it is a "famine" that makes us reconcile after many years of conflict. Joseph, still as a young boy, was sold into slavery by those brothers whom now, as an adult, he is saving by giving them grain.

With the arrival of Joseph's brothers in Egypt, a narrative masterpiece of the Bible begins. Joseph immediately recognized his brothers, but '*they did not recognize him*' (42:8).

Genesis does not tell us much about the emotions of Joseph in that meeting. It says only that '*he treated them like strangers*', that he '*spoke roughly to them*' (42:7), and that '*he remembered the dreams that he had dreamed of them*' (42:9). He accuses them of being spies, and sends them into prison. As a price for their release, he asks them to return home and bring their '*youngest brother*' (42:15), Benjamin to him. In the meantime, he holds one of them (Simeon) hostage, earnest of their return (42:24). The nine brothers depart for Canaan, and Joseph sets up a test to verify the actual change in the hearts of his brothers. Along with the grain he orders (unbeknownst to them) that the money they had paid for the grain should also be put in their sacks (42:25). When they open the bags – he probably pondered – will they take the money and not return to liberate Simeon (in short, will they sell him for money, as they had done to him), or will they go back to redeem him? 'What was the real reason why my brothers sold me to the merchants?', Joseph surely kept asking himself over the years in Egypt. 'Was it only for those twenty pieces of silver? And now, will they do the same to another brother? Or have they changed?'

In many serious conflicts with our "brothers", sooner or later the question emerges: but have they done this for the money? For the inheritance? For the house? But was it really for so little that we hurt each other, broke the bond of our brotherhood, and made our parents "die"? All this pain for just 20 pieces of silver?

The brothers find the money in the sacks (42:28), however, after a difficult time persuading their father Jacob (43:6–12) they return to Egypt, bringing Benjamin, the money found in the sacks to return and many gifts. Joseph now changes his ways towards them, he invites them for lunch (43:41), and, seeing Benjamin '*his compassion grew warm for his brother, and he sought a place to weep. And he entered his chamber and wept there.*' (43:30).

Joseph has not yet revealed himself as their brother, because the process of the reconstruction of fraternity has not yet been completed. And here, in fact, is another twist: Joseph orders his steward to put a sacred cup into Benjamin's bag (44:2). So, the 11 brothers leave for home, but the steward reaches them and accuses them of having stolen the cup. They deny it, and, being sure of their innocence they state, '*Whichever of your servants is found with it* [the cup] *shall die*' (44:9).

But then the cup was found in Benjamin's sack, and '*they tore their clothes*.' Heartbroken, they go back to Joseph, where the second test of repentance and conversion takes place, which touches the heart of the relationship of brotherhood.

Judas – who was the inventor of the selling of Joseph – speaks to his brother Joseph: '*...please let your servant remain instead of the boy as a servant to my lord, and let the boy go back with his brothers*' (44:33). The brothers have already shown that they are not willing to exchange money for Simon, and now Judas proves that his heart has changed, offering himself in exchange for Benjamin: "*Accept my offer. Take me instead of him to be your servant: ... I want atonement, atonement for all. Here, before you, strange man, I take the frightful oath we brothers swore – with both hands I take that oath and break it in two across my knee. Our eleventh brother, the father's ewe lamb, first son of the true wife, him the beast did not rend; but we, his brothers sold him into the world*" (Thomas Mann, Joseph and his brothers).

After certain wounds, to be able to really start over again, words are not enough, not even in the biblical culture founded on and by the Word. Joseph could have interrogated his brothers and verified their repentance.

Instead, he wanted to see their reactions, secretly. After a marital betrayal, a great deception of a brother or a partner, the words "*forgive me*", or "*sorry*" are just not enough. They are necessary, but not sufficient: we need facts, acts, atonement and penance. This is not about revenge or retaliation, but their opposite: it's all about love. If you have intentionally betrayed our marriage covenant, if we really want to reinvest in our family and start over, words are not enough, neither is a gift nor a dinner. It is important that you show me with some "*costly*" and unequivocal acts that you really want to start over, you really want to believe in our relationship again, you want to heal that wound that you have procured to our relationship together. Biblical forgiveness is the *for-give-ness* that evokes resurrection, it is not the "*forgetting*" of the past, but the remembering of the pain in order to rebuild a new future. It is forgiving aimed at reconciliation.

Every family, every brotherhood, every community knows what the concrete necessary actions are, and without these acts, reconciliation is not there, or it is too fragile. Human relationships are actually "*embodied*", they are not just feelings or good intentions.

Our relationships are "*third parties*" who are in front of us, they are alive with us and they are like us.

Just as our children, they are our "*flesh and blood*", and when a relationship is denied or betrayed it is this "body" that is hurt, and what needs to be healed, with time and actions. This is a great teaching of biblical humanism that reveals the logic of the sacrament of penance (you do not understand "sacrament" without having an idea of the "*embodied*" nature of relationships and life), and one that has made it possible that one day a relationship (the Spirit) could be called a Person.

Joseph also suggests that many instances of reconciliation after great betrayals have not proved durable because there was no time for a journey of reconciliation, because these ways are very costly for everyone (Joseph cries many times in these chapters). The virtue of fortitude is especially important to those who must accept repentance and forgive, as there is a great temptation to stop too soon (perhaps out of pity), and therefore not to allow enough time for the cure of the relationship by reaching to the bottom of the wound.

When you have the force to resist, every involved person's feelings get purified (even those of Joseph) – the forgiveness of the innocent ones is one of the few actions that can touch the sky. We live only in history, and all the crucial events of life have an essential need of time: to return to Canaan, 9 months in a womb, 3 days in a tomb.

Finally, in this fresco of reconciliation, money is given a special role. In that money slipped into the bags and then returned, there is not only a test of repentance and conversion. Joseph, in fact, puts the money back in the sacks in the second voyage, too (44:1), when the first 'economic' test of the brothers had been over. Therefore, in that return of money a treasure may be hiding. When an engagement is (or was) broken off, it is customary to return the gifts, because in the absence of love those objects aren't "good" anymore: they become "bad". The story of Joseph tells us that when brotherhood is denied, the contractual payment should also be returned. The fees we pay to lawyers because we fight over inheritance, or those paid for conflicts in family businesses do not produce any good. Money is always a bad coin to heal relationships, but it is even worse when we have to deal with brotherhood. Without a new covenant of reconciliation, our hunger for grain in the famines of fraternity cannot be satisfied by any contract: "*They shall return and dwell beneath my shadow; they shall flourish like the grain; they shall blossom like the vine; their fame shall be like the wine of Lebanon.*" (Hosea 14:8).

Chapter 22
Brothers, But Never Without Their Father

'It is me. It is me, your brother Joseph.'
'But of course it's him!', shouted Benjamin, almost suffocating from joy and rushed forward, up the steps to the upside, where he fell on his knees and clasped the knees of the Newly Found One vehemently.
'Yashub, Joseph-el, Jehosiph', he sobbed looking at him, raising his head. 'It is you, it is you, of course it is you. You are not dead.'

(Thomas Mann, *Joseph and His Brothers*)

Abstract Joseph received the announcement of his vocation as a boy in a dream in Canaan, he saw his sheaf standing straight in the middle of the field and the other 11 sheaves (his brothers) prostrate in front of it. Only after many years and after a lot of pain does Joseph manage to interpret the dreams of his boyhood. Sometimes it takes a lifetime and mountains of suffering to decipher our dreams and those of others, to understand that the talents of a brother (or a colleague, a member of our community...), that had first appeared to us only as a threat were salvation for all instead. 'I am Joseph! Is my father still alive? ...I am your brother, Joseph, whom you sold into Egypt.' The culmination of the cycle of Joseph is entrusted to a few, very human and wonderful verses. Up to this cry-out Joseph was a brother only as the son of the same father; now he becomes a brother again through a new bond of brotherhood generated by pain and love.

To follow the development and fulfillment of a vocation is one of the most amazing human experiences. It is a precious gift especially in times of famine of "voices" and dreams, when we long for gratuitousness, and feel nostalgic for those stories of pure *charis* that only those who receive a vocation can live and make us live through it.

Every true vocation – artistic, religious or civil – is therefore a public good, just as, and even more than a fountain, a forest or an ocean, because the presence of vocations that reach maturity makes the earth a better place; this earth where we all

L. Bruni, *The Economy of Salvation*, Virtues and Economics 4,
https://doi.org/10.1007/978-3-030-04082-6_22

live, die, give birth and raise children. The Bible is also a treasure chest where many great stories of vocations have been kept through the ages. Just for us. To relive them, incarnate them, make them our stories, and so improve our life and the lives of all.

Joseph received the announcement of his vocation as a boy in a dream in Canaan, he saw his sheaf standing straight in the middle of the field and the other 11 sheaves (his brothers) prostrate in front of it (37:7). Only after many years and after a lot of pain does Joseph – and do we with him, now – manage to interpret the dreams of his boyhood. Sometimes it takes a lifetime and mountains of suffering to decipher our dreams and those of others, to understand that the talents of a brother (or a colleague, a member of our community...), that had first appeared to us only as a threat were salvation for all instead.

'*I am Joseph! Is my father still alive? ...I am your brother, Joseph, whom you sold into Egypt.*' (45:3–5) The culmination of the cycle of Joseph is entrusted to a few, very human and wonderful verses. Up to this cry-out Joseph was a brother only as the son of the same father; now he becomes a brother again through a new bond of brotherhood generated by pain and love. Brotherhood "by blood and nothing else" has never saved anyone, and it often becomes the cause of injustice, privilege, discrimination and violence. Joseph's first, natural brotherhood had died along with the goat in whose blood the brothers dipped his royal robes in order to simulate death to Jacob (37:31). Now, after the years in Egypt, Joseph and his brothers are reborn into a new brotherhood that rises from the dead of the one by blood.

In that cry, next to the word brother we also find the word father: '*Is my father still alive?*' Brotherhood and fatherhood. Throughout the cycle of Joseph, which is a great narrative on fraternity, his father Jacob and his mother Rachel are by no means absent. They are a constant presence, they are essential co-protagonists of that story, even if they are only in the background to make room for the process of metamorphosis of the brotherhood among their children.

Biblical fraternity, unlike that of the French Revolution, is not a brotherhood without or against fatherhood. Paternity and maternity tell about history and common destiny, and are the root and chord (*fides*) binding us to each other through time. Unlike the paternity of the great Greek myths (denied in Oedipus, or awaited by the sea in Telemachus), biblical paternity is at the service of fraternity, because it is the memory of the Covenant and the fulfillment of the Promise. Paternity/ maternity are also the place where fraternity gets reassembled: Isaac and Ishmael meet again at Abraham's bedside, Esau and Jacob next to Isaac. Genesis tells us that we can only truly be reconciled through a pact, mutually believing the same promise, a common journey again. This reconciliation takes place in Egypt, away from home, but under the sign of a father, even if a distant and not too authoritative one. '*Then he fell upon his brother Benjamin's neck and wept, and Benjamin wept upon his neck. And he kissed all his brothers and wept upon them. After that his brothers talked with him.*' (45:14–15) When Joseph was with them in Canaan, his brothers '*could not speak peacefully to him*' (37:4). Now the brothers speak with another type of peacefulness that is new and more beautiful. The most telling sign of broken relationships is not to talk to each other anymore. There are few nastier experiences than that of work colleagues or neighbors who do not talk to each other, not because they do not know each other, but because, as a result of conflicts, they stopped talking to each other. The word, the daily bread of our relationships, disappears, along with good life, joy, and often the enterprise itself, too. When we do not talk with our colleagues, or we do not talk to each other 'peacefully', we get up with a bad feeling in the morning, work hours never seem to end, and sometimes we even get ill. Silences in relationships are always very sad, but they become even more sad and inhumane when there is no more talk between brothers and sisters who live under the same roof. Here the word that dies out does not only take away the joy: it makes us "die", it takes the blessings off our work and lets our children grow up poorly (the first deed of love for a child is to try to give them recomposed primary relationships). When it happens that you start to 'speak peacefully' again after years of wrongful and terrible silence (and, thank God, it happens because the world is loved, even if it has forgotten about this), the first words are almost always tears and speechless kisses of peace ('*he kissed all his brothers and wept upon them*'). These are the first words that we manage to say to each other, especially when we have to be forgiven: '*But his brothers could not answer him...*' (45:3).

If we read between the lines of this reconciliation, we discover a new dimension of Joseph's vocation which becomes fundamental in the new fraternity. Until the revelation was given to him he had first dreamed, then told his dreams, and finally became an interpreter of the dreams of others. To rebuild the relationship with his brothers, Joseph does not interpret dreams anymore, but becomes the interpreter of a story, the story of their fraternity that was denied and then rebuilt. Now his gift is to offer a saving interpretation of the facts of the past. He does not blame anyone, he does not take revenge, he doesn't condemn them – instead, he pronounces the only words capable of bringing reconciliation: '*And now do not be distressed or angry with yourselves because you sold me here, for God sent me before you to preserve life.*' And he concludes: '*So it was not you who sent me here, but God.*' (45:5–8).

We are facing a masterpiece of the art of reconciliation after deep wounds. Joseph, the victim, takes upon himself the evil that his brothers had done to him and their father, and creates a more beautiful interpretation for it, the only form that has the capacity to heal and reconcile: '*It wasn't you, but God*'. There are no other words that could cure the betrayed brotherhood. We need words that help us take a different look at the past, words that love it and save it. To cure a great betrayal in depth, we should do everything to find a reading of the facts that show the good that was born from what was evil. These readings by the victims (and only the victims can do them) are neither simple nor painless, because they must be true, and it takes a lot of effort to find a good truth that is truer than that which appears to the eye. Without these transforming interpretations with the power of resurrecting dead relationships, reconciliations are fragile, and upon the first crisis there is a return to demands, accusations, guilt; and the old wound starts bleeding again. '*Your selfishness has caused many losses to our company and enormous suffering to our family. But over the years they made all of us mature, and thanks to that pain, we can now start a new life, an even more beautiful one*'. The evil done remains evil ('*...your brother, whom you sold into Egypt*'), but the chance to really start over depends on the interpretation of the fruits of life born out of the evil done and suffered. Even the morally high moments of the history of the peoples are the result of different interpretations of the past fratricides in order to resurrect them into a present of fraternity. We did that, and therefore we can, and we know how to do it. These difficult interpretations of the past are collective experiences, but they do not take place without the presence of at least one "Joseph", one or more concrete and great persons/victims who are capable of using different words.

The word creates and it is effective: this is one of the great gifts of Genesis. The story of Joseph tells us something new: the word is able to re-create our broken relationships, make them rise from their graves/pits where our wickedness keeps throwing them. It is possible to cure the wounds of our brotherhood through words, by providing interpretations of the stories that help to bring them back to life. It is the possibility of another fraternity, deeper and more universal than that of one blood, the greatest gift that Joseph continues to give us. If the Bible sought to place a fraternity that died and was resurrected into the heart of the history of the Covenant and the Promise, then the miracle of a fratricide turned into a new fraternity is possible; it is part of the human repertoire. And so, it can be repeated everywhere and every day – even today.

Chapter 23
Beggars of Blessings

> *"Who is the fairly thickset man," asked Jacob, "arrayed in all the splendor of this world... ..."That is your son Joseph, Father," replied Judah. ...he peered and searched with his tired old eyes...with love and sorrow painted on his own, and did not recognize his son. But it came to pass that Joseph's eyes slowly filled with tears under Jacob's gaze. Their blackness swam in moisture, they overflowed; and lo they were Rachel's eyes..."*
>
> (Thomas Mann, *Joseph and His Brothers*)

Abstract After the reconciliation with his brothers, Joseph sends them back to Canaan to bring Jacob and all the family clan to Egypt for there are yet 5 years of famine to come. He gives each of them 'a change of clothes'. To Benjamin, the brother of the same mother, Rachel, he gives 300 shekels of silver and five changes of clothes. The colorful royal robe with long sleeves, that his father Jacob gave him, was at the centre of the conflict between young Joseph and his brothers. The robe that was taken from him before throwing him into the pit in the desert and then returned to his father stained with the blood of a slaughtered goat, now becomes Joseph's gift to his brothers. Everyone gets new clothes; 11 spotless garments take the place of the one stained by their envy. Where blame abounded one day, charis abounds now. To read the end of the story of Jacob is important because it is there that one of the most precious treasures of the whole Bible is revealed: the promised land is not a territory to occupy – it is the following of a voice.

The best point of observation of existence is the last one. The true and full sense of an entire life is revealed at the end when the vocation is fulfilled and the original plan is revealed. Old age, for those who have the gift to reach it, is therefore a crucial stage of life because it is there that we can find, in the bright light of the sunset, the plot of our story.

So, when our earthly life seems to be nearing the end, it may happen that our spiritual life goes through a new, decisive time of spring (there are many springs in

L. Bruni, *The Economy of Salvation*, Virtues and Economics 4,
https://doi.org/10.1007/978-3-030-04082-6_23

the autumn of life, but we do not always have the eyes to recognize them even in people who live beside us). And the journey starts over, the adventure of the soul takes a new start, with the same initial enthusiasm of the child. This was the life of the patriarchs, this is the life of Jacob, who, as an old man, starts out on a journey to Egypt, following the same voice that had called him as a young man, at Bethel.

After the reconciliation with his brothers, Joseph sends them back to Canaan to bring Jacob and all the family clan to Egypt '*for there are yet five years of famine to come*' (45:11). He gives each of them '*a change of clothes*'. To Benjamin, the brother of the same mother, Rachel, he gives '*three hundred shekels of silver and five changes of clothes*' (45:22).

The colorful royal robe with long sleeves, that his father Jacob gave him (37:3), was at the centre of the conflict between young Joseph and his brothers. The robe that was taken from him before throwing him into the pit in the desert (37:23) and then returned to his father stained with the blood of a slaughtered goat (37:31), now becomes Joseph's gift to his brothers. Everyone gets new clothes; 11 spotless garments take the place of the one stained by their envy. Where blame abounded one day, *charis* abounds now.

'*Joseph is still alive*' (45:26), his sons bring the message to Jacob-Israel. Unlike them, Jacob (perhaps with Benjamin and the women of the family) was convinced that the blood on the dress was that of Joseph who had been killed by a wild beast. For many years he had lived with that pain in his heart. Having received the news of the "*resurrection*" of his son, after an initial moment of disbelief ('his heart became numb', 45:26), Jacob-Israel exclaims: '*Joseph my son is still alive. I will go and see him before I die*' (45:28).

He wants to go, but before his departure he must do something important: '*So Israel took his journey with all that he had and came to Beersheba, and offered sacrifices to the God of his father Isaac*' (46:1). Jacob leaves Hebron, the land of the promise, and goes to stay in the house where his father Isaac and his mother Rebekah had lived, when they were still migrants, in the desert of Beersheba, where Hagar, the servant-mother of Ishmael had fled. There, during a famine, Isaac had met YWHW in one of the decisive moments of his life. He had spoken to him, announced the promise and told him: '*Do not go down to Egypt; dwell in the land of which I shall tell you.*' (26:2). This time, however, because of another famine, Jacob is to leave the land of Canaan and go right to that Egypt that the Lord had forbidden for Isaac. Egypt had been forbidden to his father because the land promised by YHWH was another one, that of Canaan, now inhabited by Jacob. The first voice that had spoken to Isaac, promising a land that was other than Egypt, could not have the same strength of the voice of his fatherly heart that now wants to see his son again, who has been believed dead for decades. Voices are not all equal in biblical humanism, and salvation lies in identifying and following the truest voice which is not the most convenient one, nor that of the false prophets or the gods of wood, not even the simple voice of the heart. That is how Jacob returns to the land of Isaac – in the world of the Bible even places can have vocations – to understand, to pray, to listen, to discern the voices, to choose from them. And once again, '*God spoke to Israel in visions of the night and said, »Jacob, Jacob.« And he said, »Here I am.« Then he said, »I am God, the God of your father. Do not be afraid to go down to Egypt ... Joseph's hand shall close your eyes.«*' (46:2–4).

Jacob now knows that the voice that speaks to him and calls him again and again ('Jacob, Jacob') is that of the God of his father, that of YHWH; and if it is the same voice to send him to that Egypt that had been denied from Isaac, then he can and he should go.

To listen to the voice and to understand what it says, Jacob did not go to Bethel, the place where he had received his first vocation and where he had seen the angels and heaven (28:13–22).

Instead, he returns to the land of his fathers and wants to listen to the same God of Isaac, at his father and mother's place. He wants to hear being called by his name by the same true voice, the one that never cheated him, the one of the Alliance and the promise.

It often happens, very often, that those who try to live in truth return to the "*fathers*", on their land, in their places before they make an important and decisive choice. It is good to make a return, especially when you are about to make a choice that goes in the opposite direction of that which once formed the first covenant, the promise, the vocation. He returns to his mother's house for signs, hoping to hear a deeper voice again, in order to get truer certainties, to find the meaning of life, vocation and the promise. To hear himself called by his name again.

The family business was going through a long period of difficulties. Then there came the offer of a corporation that would have relieved it by paying a large sum. 'Am I to sell the company founded by my grandfather, which later became the life of my parents, the great story of the family, the most beautiful story that we could tell each other? Do I have to be the one to write the last word of this story?' As the expiration date is approaching, nights become long and tough. Luigi feels the urge to return to the first building that is now abandoned but where the pieces of history are still alive and real, and so are the relationships, words, pain, heart and flesh. And it was in that building that he had learned the trade from his dad. From there he goes up to the old farm of his grandfather, where, in the workshop, he had learned to work with wood, and where he had heard the stories, glorious ones, from the early days of the founding of the company, after their emigration to America, after the war, famine, hunger, the frontline, the terrible deaths of their children that can never be forgotten. And in that "inhabited silence" he tries to capture those age-old voices and identify those of his youth among them, when everything was clear and easy to see through, the voice that made him give up the fixed work place to continue that story. To find out if the voice that now seems to tell him 'sell it' is the same good voice that one day had told him to 'stay'. The authentic pilgrimages are those where we seek, perhaps without being aware of it, the blessing of the fathers for the difficult choices of today. Maybe we should do more, and not stop begging for blessings, especially when the good voices do not speak any more to us in our homes, in the time of the reforms of social pacts, during the seven lean years of Southern Europe economic crisis (2008–2015).

In the house of the fathers Jacob listened to the same voice again, and he realized that he had to leave, and so he took off. He will close his eyes in Egypt, not in the land of Canaan. As an old man ('*The days of the years of my sojourning are 130 years*', he will say to Pharaoh: 47:9) he was called to leave the promised land, and start on a journey again to a foreign land (47:4), and die there in exile. And the 'yes' he said in his old age was the decisive one, no less decisive than the first, because it was the fulfilment of his vocation.

To read the end of the story of Jacob is important because it is there that one of the most precious treasures of the whole Bible is revealed: the promised land is not a territory to occupy – it is the following of a voice. And so, every land, even the promised one, is foreign land, because the land is a gift, you live on it only temporarily, you do not possess it. Any man who follows a "*voice*" is a stranger over all the earth and for all life. The right house for the human is the nomadic tent.

'*...and they came into the land of Goshen. Then Joseph prepared his chariot and went up to meet Israel his father in Goshen. He presented himself to him and fell on his neck and wept on his neck a good while. Israel said to Joseph, "Now let me die, since I have seen your face (...).*"' (46:29–30).

Chapter 24
At the End of the Night – and After

So he spoke to them and they were laughing and crying at the same time, and they all stretched out their hands toward him who stood between them, kissed him, and he caressed them. And so endeth the beautiful story and God-invention of Joseph and His Brothers.

(Thomas Mann, *Joseph and His Brothers*)

Abstract The wonderful death of Jacob generated a new crisis in the fraternity. As in the first time of forgiving, Joseph uses the best words for all instances of reconciliation: It wasn't you, but God. In the curing of the wounded brotherhood, and when, just like in the case of Joseph and his brothers, forgiveness is not to forget the past but to invest in a new, resurrected relationship, the forgiveness of the victim is not enough: it is necessary that those who have committed the crime really believe in the forgiveness they have just received. We have reached the conclusion of the commentary of the Book of Genesis. During this journey we were flooded, inundated, overwhelmed and loved by the blessings that surpassed the many instances of ambiguity and malice and that come alive in our flesh when we hear them, even if we had met them before. Blessings that we have communicated to us a thousand times in a thousand ways that the last word on the world and man is not that of Cain, even if that is the one heard most all over the earth, yesterday, today and maybe tomorrow, too. Genesis has given us ears to hear other voices that are less noisy but more true: our first task is to try to detect them among the many noises of history if we want to remain human, spiritual beings capable of infinity.

'*What is your occupation?*', Pharaoh asked Joseph's brothers. '*Your servants are shepherds...*', they replied (47:3). The question about profession is the first one in adulthood. And if we do not have an answer to that first question, the one that suffers it most is not just our job but our place in the world. Our profession is the syntax we use in composing our social discourse.

L. Bruni, *The Economy of Salvation*, Virtues and Economics 4,
https://doi.org/10.1007/978-3-030-04082-6_24

So when a young person is not given a profession (which is a gift before being talent and effort: a profession is always learned from someone), he or she lacks the words to talk about themselves, to others and to themselves. The extreme lack of jobs in our times is also a consequence of a profound crisis of professions. Those generated by the artisan, maritime and farming culture, by the professions, from the factories to the offices, are rapidly diminishing, many have disappeared; and we, living in the time of this famine of promises and dreams, cannot generate enough of them.

Jacob '*lived in the land of Egypt seventeen years. So, the days of Jacob, the years of his life, were 147 years.*' (47:28) Feeling his nearing death, Jacob-Israel re-reads and re-summarizes his long life: '*God Almighty [El Shaddai] appeared to me at Luz in the land of Canaan and blessed me, and said to me, »Behold, I will make you fruitful and multiply you, (...)« As for me, when I came from Paddan, to my sorrow Rachel died in the land of Canaan..., and I buried her there on the way to Ephrath (that is, Bethlehem).*' (48:3–7) Vocation, the voice and Rachel. The Alliance, the promise, the struggles, the hugs, faithfulness. The people in this story are the loved ones, the places, God; everyone always present, always all protagonists. When you have the gift of living the last precious moments of life consciously (which is a true gift), the faces return and the places of love and pain, of good choices made and missed chances at the decisive intersections all come back to life; and it is not uncommon that the last look on a face or a place is that of full reconciliation with life, where we grab the final blessing from the angel of death. We are space and we are time, which eventually fade into one another: Rachel and Bethlehem, El Shaddai and Luz, Paola and the G. Leopardi High School where we met: they all come back to life and together they tell our last-first words.

Then Jacob laid his hands on the heads of his grandchildren Manasseh and Ephraim, and blessed them with the words of heaven (48:15–16). Then he called his sons and said, '*Gather yourselves together...Assemble and listen, O sons of Jacob*' (49:1–2). And so, he says his last words to each of his sons, '*blessing each with the blessing suitable to him*' (49:28), without hiding the errors and faults (of Reuben, Simeon and Levi). But once again the most beautiful blessing is the one that is given to Joseph, like in a psalm:

> '*Joseph is a fruitful bough,*
> *a fruitful bough by a spring; his branches run over the wall.*
> *The archers bitterly attacked him,*
> *shot at him, and harassed him severely, yet his bow remained unmoved; (...) blessings of heaven above,*
> *blessings of the deep that crouches beneath,*
> *blessings of the breasts and of the womb...*' (49:22–26).

As a last will, he asks his children to bury him in the cave of Machpelah (49:31), the one that Abraham bought for Sara from the Hittites, purchased '*to possess*' (49:30), with a regular contract (50:13). And when he finished speaking to his sons, Jacob '*drew up his feet into the bed and breathed his last and was gathered to his people.*' (49:33). He dies in Egypt, but will rest in the land of Canaan.

The wonderful death of Jacob – in these times of enmity with death, and so with limits, we should re-read the beautiful deaths of the patriarchs many times, to feel loved though them – generated a new crisis in the fraternity: '*When Joseph's brothers saw that their father was dead, they said, »It may be that Joseph will hate us and pay us back for all the evil that we did to him.«*' (50:15) Taken from this fear, they get a message to Joseph that (probably) contains a lie: '*Your father gave this command before he died: »Say to Joseph, "Please forgive the transgression of your brothers and their sin, because they did evil to you."«*' (50:16–17) But Joseph '*wept when they spoke to him*' and he said once more: '*As for you, you meant evil against me, but God meant it for good, (...) So do not fear*' (50:19–21). And as in the first time of forgiving, Joseph uses the best words for all instances of reconciliation: '*It wasn't you, but God*'.

In the curing of the wounded brotherhood, and when, just like in the case of Joseph and his brothers, forgiveness is not to forget the past but to invest in a new, "resurrected" relationship, the forgiveness of the victim is not enough: it is necessary that those who have committed the crime really believe in the forgiveness they have just received. The brothers, upon being given the first pardon, could have thought: '*Is he doing it for us, or for our father?*'. The death of Jacob reactivates that doubt and it makes it evolve into a new crisis: a new lie, new tears and a new forgiveness.

It is not uncommon that the death of a parent generates a crisis in the relationship of brotherhood or sisterhood. And not only, nor mainly, for reasons of heritage and interests. The death of the last parent, even when it occurs late in life (for the parent and the children alike) is always a decisive step in the relationship between brothers and sisters. It is then that they return, really, into a situation of orphanhood, and they feel that some deep roots are drying out inside them. The principle of unity of the family – that was also a "*place*", the mother's house that was the venue of meetings, celebrations and reconciliations – no longer exists, or it does but in a different way, and a new or renovated form of it must be found. And if the relationship was deeply wounded, sometimes it is necessary to forgive again, in order to give the forgiven one the time and space necessary to receive and accommodate our forgiveness: 'Thus he comforted them and spoke kindly to them.' (50:21) Forgiveness is not an act, it is a process: you forgive and forgive again, once, twice, seven times or seventy times seven. Then '*Joseph died, being 110 years old. They embalmed him, and he was put in a coffin in Egypt.*'

Here, my commentary on the Book of Genesis reaches its end.

We started this difficult and wonderful adventure of the soul aiming to look for new words for the economy. We found much more: travelling to the '*end of the night*' we glimpsed the tree of life.

We woke up, called into existence, in the garden of creation, and there, amazed by our being, we talked with God in the cool of the day, and witnessed the first crossing of two human eyes, seeing each other '*eye to eye*'. Then, in the fields, we witnessed the first fratricide/homicide and the smell of the blood of the first brother/man killed came down to us; and we also saw Lamech murder a child. Time was stopped, we all died with Abel and the children killed in all the wars in the world, and we still die these deaths today (it was painful to write commentaries on these last chapters while rockets were falling on the 'land of Canaan'). We got into an ark built by the only righteous man, and we were saved, men, women and animals.

After the flood, we stopped at Babel: there we felt the temptation of communitarianism(?), we overcame it, and we set off, dispersed and saved in the course of history.

And so we came to Ur of the Chaldeans where we met a wandering Aramean who had departed believing in a different voice that was truer than that of the gods of wood. We paid our respect to him and thanked him for having believed also for us, and we wished to be like him. We smiled to a son born to his parents in their old age, and then we fled, chased by Sara, in the desert along with Hagar and Ishmael. We climbed up Mount Moriah with Abraham and Isaac; and on that mountain, and in many other places, we lost and regained a son, but most importantly, we met the first voice again, listened to it and believed in its promise again. We fell in love with Rachel at a well, and then we died with her giving birth to Ben-Omi.

We forded a stream to return to our cheated brother, and there we were attacked, fought, wounded, blessed, and along with Jacob we became Israel. We saw heaven, dreamed of angels and God, the dream of dreams. Finally, we ended up in a pit/tomb with Joseph, and we rose from it to arrive in Egypt and become interpreters of dreams. There, accompanied by Thomas Mann, we re-learned fraternity, we realized that the promised land is the land of all, and we discovered the importance of dreams. But first and above all we were flooded, inundated, overwhelmed and loved by the blessings that surpassed the many instances of ambiguity and malice and that come alive in our flesh when we hear them, even if we had met them before. Blessings that we have communicated to us a thousand times in a thousand ways that the last word on the world and man is not that of Cain, even if that is the one heard most all over the earth, yesterday, today and maybe tomorrow, too. Genesis has given us ears to hear other voices that are less noisy but more true: our first task is to try to detect them among the many noises of history if we want to remain human, spiritual beings capable of infinity.

But most of all it left us with a question inside, which is also a commitment, a cry, a desire: when will we start to dream of God again?

References

Beretta P. (a cura di). 2006. *Genesi. Ebraico – Greco – Latino – Italiano. Versione interlineare*, Milan: San Paolo.

Bonhoeffer, D. 1951. *Widerstand und Ergebung*.

Boschi, B.G. 2007. *Genesi*. Bologna: ESD.

Brueggemann, W. 1973. *Interpretation: A Bible Commentary for Teaching and Preaching. Genesis*. Atlanta: John Knox Press.

Ginzberg, L. 1913. *The legends of the Jews*. 1st ed. Philadelphia: Jewish Publication Society of America.

Giuntoli, F. ed. 2013. *Genesi*. vol. 1 (cc. 1–11) e vol. 2 (cc. 12–50). Milan: San Paolo.

Hillesum, E., *Diary 1941–1943*.

Kierkegaard, S. 1843. *Frygt og Baeven*.

Mann, T. *Joseph and his brothers*, 2 voll. English translation: Helen Tracy Lowe-Porter. First German edition 1933–1943.

Nietzsche, F. 1891. *Also sprach Zarathustra. Ein Buch für Alle und Keinen*.

Pavese, C. 1951. *Verrà la morte e avrà i tuoi occhi*. Turin: Einaudi.

Quasimodo, S. 2003. Uomo del mio tempo. In *Tutte le poesie*. Milan: Mondadori.

———. 2008. *Un commento alla Bibbia*. Milan: Adelphi.

Quinzio, S. 1967. *Il cristianesimo dell'inizio e della fine*. Milan: Adelphi.

Stefani, P. 2013. *L'«invenzione» del peccato*. Brescia: Morcelliana.

Tolstoj, L., 1899. *Voskresenie*.

Turoldo, D.M. 1948. *Io non ho mani*. Milan: Bompiani.

Verga, G. 2011. La roba. In *Tutte le novelle*. Turin: Einaudi (original edition 1883).

Wénin, A. 1999. *Isaac ou l'épreuve d'Abraham. Approche narrative de Genèse 22. Coll. Le livre et le rouleau*. Lessius.

Wiesel, E. 1983. *Five Biblical portraits*. Notre Dame: University of Notre Dame Press.

Part II
Exodus

Chapter 25
Love Does Not Give in to Power

> *If ye are truly the ambassadors of God, then may He judge between us and Pharaoh. ... You are responsible for the widespread stench now issuing from the Israelitish corpses used as bricks for building when our tale was not complete. We are in the quandary of the poor sheep that has been dragged away by a wolf. The shepherd pursues the robber, catches up with him, and tries to snatch the sheep from his jaws, and the wretched victim, pulled this way by the wolf and that way by the shepherd, is torn to pieces.*
>
> (L. Ginzberg, *The Legends of the Jews, Vol. 2*)

Abstract The beginning of Exodus shows us a wonderful alliance between women, cooperating for life beyond social hierarchies, husbands and fathers, oppressors and oppressed. These alliances between women have saved many lives during the wars and dictatorships of men, by building 'baskets' of salvation with their hands. These are the covenants that we continue to see in our cities, and the ones that allow our children to live and grow up. Children should be saved: it is the law of midwives, women, the first law of the earth. In this first chapter we encounter the splendid figures of two midwives, Shiphrah and Puah. These two women tell us that children should not be killed, neither the children of the Egyptians, nor those of the Jews should ever be killed. Children should not be killed either in Egypt or in any place. Yesterday, today, ever. If we want to remain human, that is. And every time we do not do so, we do not 'fear God', we do not obey life and we deny the legacy of the midwives of Egypt. In Shiphrah and Puah, two workers, two human beings on the side of life, echoes of the Greek myth of Antigone may be heard, she disobeys the king to obey the more profound law of life: to bury his brother who died in battle.

L. Bruni, *The Economy of Salvation*, Virtues and Economics 4,
https://doi.org/10.1007/978-3-030-04082-6_25

The beginning of Exodus shows us a wonderful alliance between women, cooperating for life beyond social hierarchies, husbands and fathers, oppressors and oppressed. These alliances between women have saved many lives during the wars and dictatorships of men, by building '*baskets*' of salvation with their hands. These are the covenants that we continue to see in our cities, and the ones that allow our children to live and grow up. Children should be saved: it is the law of midwives, women, the first law of the earth.

Between Genesis and Exodus there is a direct continuity: '*Then Joseph died, and all his brothers and all that generation. But the people of Israel were fruitful and increased greatly; they multiplied and grew exceedingly strong, so that the land was filled with them. Now there arose a new king over Egypt, who did not know Joseph*' (1:6–8). The population growth of the Jews (Exodus 1:10) coupled with the fear that among the newborns there might be those who would have undermined his power (1:22) in Pharaoh's mind and he perceived it as a serious threat. And so, he exacerbates the conditions of the Jews – that is, the tangle of heterogeneous nomadic peoples who were foreigners in Egypt as slaves, and among whom the tribes of Israel also ended up. So, he '*made their lives bitter with hard service, in mortar and brick, and in all kinds of work in the field*' (1:14). But the hard labour for men was not enough for Pharaoh. He attempted a more drastic solution, one that opens one of the most beautiful pages of the Scriptures: '*Then the king of Egypt said to the Hebrew midwives, one of whom was named Shiphrah and the other Puah, »When you serve as midwife to the Hebrew women and see them on the birth-stool, if it is a son, you shall kill him, but if it is a daughter, she shall live.«*' (1:15–16).

The profession of midwives in Egypt was highly respected and developed. At Sais there was a school known throughout antiquity, and two midwives, Neferica-Ra and later Peseshet, are remembered as the first lady doctors in history. The midwives have always been regarded by the people as a "*common good*", women who help with the labour of mothers through their work, always fighting on the side of life, beloved by the whole community that is receiving its children from their expert, good hands ("Signora Germana", the last midwife of the place where I was born, is still a bright star among locals). In ancient times this craft was altogether and exclusively female: managing the last stage of pregnancy, that sacred moment in which women generate us and regenerate the world. In biblical culture, birth is given a central place. Rachel, one of the most beautiful and important characters of Genesis, dies while giving birth. And it is during that last birth that the word midwife first appears in the Bible: '*the midwife said to her, »Do not fear, for you have another son.«*' (Gen 35:17). That first midwife said, whispered, good words of hope (you do not talk to mothers in childbirth: you whisper to them, caress them, speak to them through hand gestures). But Benomì-Benjamin was born to the death of Rachel. We'll meet the midwife again when Tamar is giving birth, then she puts a 'scarlet thread' on the hand of her first twin born (Gen 38:28). And finally, there are the midwives of Egypt, and they are the last ones, because after the infinite words of Shiphrah and Puah all was said.

Those nomadic people, with difficult births in mobile tents, decided to put two midwives of Egypt to the origin of their great history of liberation. Of Shiphrah ('beautiful') and Puah ('splendor', 'light'), we know little. Almost certainly they were Egyptian, perhaps the heads of the midwives of the Jews or of the whole of Egypt. We know their names, but above all we know that they were the first conscientious objectors: '*But the midwives feared God and did not do as the king of Egypt commanded them, but let the male children live.*' (1:17). The first art of the earth is that of midwifery: 'letting the children live', our children and those of others, the children of all. When this first art is eclipsed, life loses the first place and civilizations mingle, become ill and, eventually, fall. In this "no" to Pharaoh, and "yes" to life, a great message for each job is hidden: the deepest and truest law of our professions and our crafts is not the one enacted by the many pharaohs who are dominated by old and new forms of greed for power and omnipotence. Their laws must be complied with only if and only when they serve the law of life. When we forget that the "law of the pharaohs" is always the second law, never the first one, we are all transformed into subjects of empires, and do not start any liberation of ourselves and others. Shiphrah and Puah tell us that 'children should not be killed', neither the children of the Egyptians, nor those of the Jews should ever be killed. Children should not be killed either in Egypt or in any place. Yesterday, today, ever. If we want to remain human, that is. And every time we do not do so, we do not 'fear God', we do not obey life and we deny the legacy of the midwives of Egypt.

In Shiphrah and Puah, two women, two workers, two human beings on the side of life, echoes of the Greek myth of Antigone may be heard (she disobeys the king to obey the more profound law of life: to bury his brother who died in battle). The women of Genesis and the other women of the Bible come back to life through them. Mary is announced by them, and all the women who beget children. The charismas and the "Marian image" of the earth come back to life through them.

The whole beginning of the Book of Exodus seems to be ordered under the sign of women who save lives. Moses' mother disobeyed the new order of Pharaoh, '*Every son that is born ... you shall cast into the Nile' (1:22),* and saved her baby boy. She first hid the baby, and when she could *'hide him no longer,*' she built a basket from papyrus, put him in it and trust him to the waters of the Nile (2:2–3). Another woman, the daughter of Pharaoh, found the basket in the river, and when she saw that it contained *'one of the Hebrews' children*' she "*took pity on him*" (2:5–7).

The whole scene of the discovery of the basket on the bank of the great river is accompanied by the gaze of the Moses's sister: '*And his sister stood at a distance to know what would be done to him.*' (2:4) It is wonderful how, running along the shore, the gaze of this woman-child accompanies the passing of the basket along the river. It is a benevolent gaze of innocent love that reminds us of Elohim who followed the passage of that other basket-boat on the water which contained Noah the righteous – it is not by coincidence that the Hebrew word tevah is used both for Moses' basket and Noah's ark. Moses' sister talked to Pharaoh's daughter, and offered to find a nurse for him among the Jews. Pharaoh's daughter accepted the offer and said: '*Take this child away and nurse him for me, and I will give you your wages.*' (2:9).

Another work of a woman with a saving effect, the most intimate one (milk exchanged between women for life), which here is being combined with another crucial word: *wage*. In a time when both work and wages suffer, and when the laws of the pharaohs do not want children to be born or turn them into merchandise, the beginning of Exodus should speak to us loudly and shake us strongly. Pharaoh wanted to use two types of work in order to eliminate the children of Israel: the forced labour with bricks and that of the midwives. But neither of the two was an ally of death. By vocation the midwives chose life, but forced labour could not win either, because '*the more they were oppressed, the more they multiplied and the more they spread abroad*' (1:12). Contrary to the pharaohs design, work remains an ally of life, and will not be easily used for purposes of death. Pharaohs are always tempted to manipulate our work, but we can save ourselves even in the worst jobs. Work is part of the human condition, and so we have the ability to befriend it in spite of powerful leaders and empires, and convert the "*work wolf*" into "*brother work*". In fact, in our days it is more difficult to save ourselves from "*forced non-labour*".

'*So God dealt well with the midwives ... And because the midwives feared God, he gave them families.*' (1:20–21) It is the numerous '*family*' of midwifery in the world, families of loving people, guardians of life, mothers of the baby girls and boys born to all.

Chapter 26
Enriching Cries

Awake! Why are you sleeping, O Lord?
Rouse yourself! Do not reject us forever!
Why do you hide your face?
Why do you forget our affliction and oppression?
For our soul is bowed down to the dust;
our belly clings to the ground.

Rise up (Psalm 44)

Abstract The first prayer that we find in the Bible is a cry, a cry that rises into the sky by an oppressed people. To have an experience of liberation one must first feel the need to be liberated, and then cry, believing or hoping that there, or up there, is someone to pick up the cry. If we do not feel oppressed by any pharaoh, or if we have lost hope that someone will listen to our cry, we have no reasons to cry out and we will not be freed. Moses begins his public life by killing a man. Moses, the announcer of the law 'Thou shalt not kill' becomes a murderer. In these opening words of the story of Moses, one of the most profound laws of the Bible returns in a mysterious and, for us, a bit disconcerting way. The patriarchs and prophets of the Bible are neither heroes nor models of virtue. They show themselves to us as women and men taken from life, so human in their repertoire to include even the murderous act of Cain. It's on the basis of being so fully human that their immense vocations come, and that is how they embark on and end their great spiritual experiences that are also always human. Only if we take upon ourselves the whole of their humanity may their stories of salvation, their hopes and their liberation become ours, too.

The first prayer that we find in the Bible is a cry, a cry that rises into the sky by an oppressed people. To have an experience of liberation one must first feel the need to be liberated, and then cry, believing or hoping that there, or up there, is someone to pick up the cry. If we do not feel oppressed by any pharaoh, or if we have lost hope that someone will listen to our cry, we have no reasons to cry out and we will not be freed.

L. Bruni, *The Economy of Salvation*, Virtues and Economics 4,
https://doi.org/10.1007/978-3-030-04082-6_26

Moses begins his public life by killing a man: '*One day, when Moses had grown up, he went out to his people and looked on their burdens, and he saw an Egyptian beating a Hebrew, one of his people. He looked this way and that, and seeing no one, he struck down the Egyptian and hid him in the sand.*' (2:11–12). Moses, the announcer of the law '*Thou shalt not kill*' becomes a murderer. In these opening words of the story of Moses, one of the most profound laws of the Bible returns in a mysterious and, for us, a bit disconcerting way. The patriarchs and prophets of the Bible are neither heroes nor models of virtue. They show themselves to us as women and men taken from life, so human in their repertoire to include even the murderous act of Cain. It's on the basis of being so fully human that their immense vocations come, and that is how they embark on and end their great spiritual experiences that are also always human. Only if we take upon ourselves the whole of their humanity may their stories of salvation, their hopes and their liberation become ours, too.

After the murder, Moses is taken by fear and he flees from Egypt and arrives in the land of Midian as a stranger (2:15). The years that Moses spends with the Midianites, separated from his people, are also the image of the eclipse of God that Israel is living in Egypt. The oppression of the people, the midwives of Egypt, Moses saved by the women and by the water all take place within a horizon of God's silence, during a night of the Covenant. God in Egypt is silent, as if he had forgotten his Covenant. The promise dimmed out, the people of the Covenant is oppressed and enslaved in a foreign land. But the oppressed people cannot find the strength to yell and scream, even though it is only their cry that can end this night: '*...and the people of Israel groaned because of their slavery and cried out for help. Their cry for rescue from slavery came up to God. And God heard their groaning, and God remembered his covenant with Abraham, with Isaac, and with Jacob. And God looked upon the children of Israel, and God took heed of them.*' (2:24–25).

Until this cry, in the prehistory and history of Israel we encountered stalks, altars and sacrifices that the patriarchs raised towards heaven to express their thanks. But to find the first prayer we had to go down into Egypt, and get as far as the forced labour camps. It is from there that the first prayer of Israel was raised towards the sky, which was the collective cry of a slave people. And just like when God heard Hagar's baby cry in the wilderness (Gen 21:17), he also listens now to the cry-prayer of the oppressed. And he answers. The God of the Bible is not the God of the philosophers: YWHW is moved, forgets about himself, he rages, has ears to hear the cry of the oppressed; he remembers and takes heed of them.

There is something valuable, hidden in this cry that goes up and is heard. If even God can "*forget*" about the covenant, and if the cries of the oppressed people succeeded in making him remember the promises made, then to cry out is very important. It is always important, but it is essential when a pact suffers an eclipse and we are abandoned by those who made a covenant with us, when someone with whom we have made promises to each other abandons us. If the screams of pain of the poor once ended the silence of heavens and then opened the sea, then we can and we must also cry out when those who are bound to us by a pact of reciprocity forget us and abandon us as slaves in Egypt.

If God forgot his covenant and the cry of the poor reminded him, then Marco can – and must – cry out to Giovanna, who, forgetting her marriage covenant, left the house and has not returned. We can and we must cry out to Franco, with whom we had made and built the dream of a co-operative with and for the poor, decided to follow the mirages of the many gains, and has left us. We can and we must cry out when those we have sent into parliament and in the government offices forget the political pact for the Common Good, and let the poor die under the oppression of the emperors of gambling or weapons.

When an alliance is broken and, though blameless, we end up with forced labour under the empires, the first thing we need to do is cry out, scream. These cries that rise to the one who has forgotten his covenant with us are the first step towards a possible reconciliation, because they say to ourselves and others that we are aware of us being unfairly in Egypt, that we suffer and we want to get out of these conditions of slavery.

To cry out, however, is not always easy. The first condition to be able to cry out is to believe that those who have abandoned us can be reached by our grief, moved by our tears, remember the covenant and be willing to continue the alliance. We cry out when we believe that the other one can still hear us and start over. The Jewish people cried out because they still believed in the Covenant and in the promise; they believed that the sky they cried out to was not empty. When, however, you lose the faith and hope that you can still start over, the cry goes out inside your throat, not screaming anymore, and the non-cry is the first sign that the faith-hope has died in that relationship.

People, communities and entire peoples have learned how to pray, crying out. It turns out that the sky is not empty when we call it hard, asking, begging to listen to us. When you have already looked ahead and around yourself with no success, it is then that you suddenly and with amazement realise that there is still one direction to try: your gaze is raised to the sky, your eyes and voice are directed upwards together. And that is when the time of true prayer begins.

There are many pacts that die and never rise because someone does not want or is not able to hear our cry of pain. We cry, we scream, and no one answers. The earth is full of these unheard cries. But there are other pacts that are not healed because we cannot scream. We do not succeed for a lack of faith and trust in that broken covenant, because of our pride or too much pain that cuts our breath. Because we did not cry out, no one heard it either; the deliverer did not arrive due to the lack of cries of pain. And so, we will never know if on the other side there was someone who was anxiously waiting to hear our cry to start over, and may still be waiting for it. We cannot repair our broken pacts if we lose the faith that those who have abandoned us (or seem to have done so) can still hear our cry, will be moved by it, and maybe start over. Then there are also those who are certain that the other will not listen and will not respond, but cry out nevertheless; and it is not uncommon that their faith-confidence returns to them after this desperate cry. Crying out can be a love song, even when it is a desperate prayer.

The poor continue to suffer. Sometimes they manage to cry out, every now and then someone picks up their cry, and liberation comes to them. To be freed and have the experience of liberation, one has to be poor first, to feel some form of poverty. Although it may seem paradoxical to those who only know the side of the pleasures of consumption in life, the absence of cries can be a serious form of poverty. The rich and powerful do not cry out, and so they cannot be freed: they remain slaves in their opulence, and do not have the experience of liberation, which is among the most sublime that this world knows. The great shortcoming of our society is liberation, because the fictitious wealth offered by goods is convincing us that we no longer need to be freed. We are slaves in another type of forced labour, but the new ideologies of the new pharaohs succeed in making us feel no need for liberation. There is no slavery that could be deeper than that of those who do not feel their condition of a slave. This slavery is worse than that of those who, feeling oppressed, do not cry anymore because they think no one will hear it and free them (although there are many such people in our muted cities). Today the poorest "peoples" are the opulent ones that do not cry out, do not see or do not recognize their Moses and do not assist in the miracle of a sea that opens to a land 'flowing with milk and honey'.

Forced labour and forced non-labour continue to grow in the world, but our labour camps do not raise their voice and cry out to heaven. It is only by returning to the state of indigence that we shall find the strength to cry out together, and then we will get a new Moses, and we will set out to walk across the sea.

Chapter 27
Thorn Bushes and Liberations

When King Solomon was seated on the throne of his kingship, his heart was exalted, and he rejoiced in his riches. The Lord's anger was unleashed against him. He took the ring from his finger so he had to go as a vagabond and wandering in the world. He went to the cities of the land of Israel crying and pleading, and he said: 'I am Qoheleth', because his name had been Solomon before.

(Targum, *Ecclesiastes 1,12*)

Abstract The decisive meeting in Moses' life takes place during an ordinary workday. Moses was a stranger in that land who worked for a living. Just like Jacob at Laban's, like many men of his time and ours. And it is during this humble and dependent work that the event that will change his story – and ours – occurs. Factories, offices, classrooms, fields and houses can be and are the site of the fundamental type of meetings in life, even of theophanies. The decisive events reach us in the places of our ordinary life, that is, while we are at work (work is also important because of this). We can participate in a thousand liturgies, pilgrimages, and do dozens of retreats and so have some wonderful experiences; but the events that truly change us happen in everyday life, when without looking for it or expecting it, a voice calls us by our name in humble places of living. While we are doing the dishes, correcting homework or driving a tram. Or as we are shepherding a flock, near the thorn bushes that are burning at the edge of the grasslands. The entire first part of the life of Moses is a story of normality. Biblical vocations are not spectacular, neither related to the extraordinary character or the merits of those who receive the call.

The decisive meeting in Moses' life takes place during an ordinary workday: '*Now Moses was keeping the flock of his father-in-law, Jethro, the priest of Midian, and he led his flock to the west side of the wilderness and came to Horeb, the mountain of God.*' (3:1) Moses was a stranger in that land who worked for a living. Just like

L. Bruni, *The Economy of Salvation*, Virtues and Economics 4,
https://doi.org/10.1007/978-3-030-04082-6_27

Jacob at Laban's, like many men of his time and ours. And it is during this humble and dependent work that the event that will change his story – and ours – occurs.

Factories, offices, classrooms, fields and houses can be and are the site of the fundamental type of meetings in life, even of theophanies. The decisive events reach us in the places of our ordinary life, that is, while we are at work (work is also important because of this). We can participate in a thousand liturgies, pilgrimages, and do dozens of retreats and so have some wonderful experiences; but the events that truly change us happen in everyday life, when without looking for it or expecting it, a voice calls us by our name in humble places of living. While we are doing the dishes, correcting homework or driving a tram. Or as we are shepherding a flock, near the thorn bushes that are burning at the edge of the grasslands.

The entire first part of the life of Moses is a story of normality. Biblical vocations are not spectacular, neither related to the extraordinary character or the merits of those who receive the call (the lovers of "meritocracy" will not find allies in the Bible). Moses is not chosen because he is good or better than others. Like Noah, he is called to build an ark of salvation: '*God called to him out of the bush, »Moses, Moses!«, And he said, »Here I am.« Then he said, »Do not come near; take your sandals off your feet, for the place on which you are standing is holy ground.« And he said, »I am the God of your father, the God of Abraham, the God of Isaac, and the God of Jacob.«*' (3:4–6).

Another cry, this time by God, which Moses knows how to listen to; a voice he believes in, recognizing it without knowing it. Moses, in fact, was not educated among his people. He grew up among the Egyptians (he even received his name from them), then he had lived among a foreign, idolatrous people. He did not get a chance to listen to the stories of the patriarchs during the long evenings under the tent. Perhaps the very names of Abraham, Isaac, Jacob, were telling him little or even nothing. Whose was then the voice speaking to him from the bush? How to distinguish it from the voice of the many gods who lived in the land of Midian? Unlike the patriarchs, Moses converses directly with God, he argues with him, he asks for his name (YHWH), he wants signs from him, he is looking for excuses but in the end he sets out on a journey: '*Come, I will send you to Pharaoh that you may bring my people, the children of Israel, out of Egypt.*' But Moses said to God, '*Who am I that I should go to Pharaoh and bring the children of Israel out of Egypt?...they will not believe me or listen to my voice*' (3:9–11; 4:1). And so, God gives him signs (4:2–9), but Moses is still not convinced: '*Oh, my Lord, I am not eloquent*' (4:10). Now Moses doubts his own capability of carrying out the task given to him. He is not a good speaker, perhaps he is a stammerer ('*I am slow of speech and of tongue*') and so he is lacking the primary skill of a prophet. God convinces him by telling him that the primary and real instrument of a prophet is not his speech but his person: the voice will be granted to him by his brother Aaron: '*You shall speak to him and put the words in his mouth*' (4:15). And so, Moses set out on the journey (4:18).

In this dialogue an essential dimension of every authentic prophetic vocation is revealed to us (every vocation is prophetic, given that it is authentic). The contents and power of prophecy is not provided by verbal means or techniques. There are prophets who have saved and still save many people without being skillful speakers or writers – they have spoken and written words of life. A prophecy is always a free gift, too, and its first expression is the recognition that the vocation received is a gift altogether and not a personal achievement. It is an overflow and whoever is being called is not the master of the voice. The only necessary word for a prophet is *Here I am*.

Eloquent speech is often the attribute of false prophets, the sophists who make use of their talents and techniques to manipulate others and the promises. They are but clanging cymbals. Subjective (and at times even objective) perception of one's own inadequacy to carry out the task for which one has been called is the very sign of the authenticity of a vocation. To doubt one's own voice is essential for believing in the truthfulness of the Voice calling us. Therefore, it is necessary to be suspecting about those who expect to be called to go out and save someone because that is what they have been made for, having taken up the "job of a prophet" and feeling ready to practice it.

Moses recognises that difficult voice as a good voice of salvation. In his entire dialogue with God he never questions the truthfulness of the voice calling him. To be able to recognise the good voice that talks to us in the decisive encounters of our life is a capacity we do have: it is part of the human repertoire. When it comes, this voice is unmistakable. We may choose not to respond or to reject it because it asks uncomfortable things from us. We may cover our ears and soul but we will always recognise it.

This dialogue also tells us a lot about the God of the Bible: he is not a sovereign giving orders to his subjects. He is the God of the Covenant who enters into a dialogue, gets angry and argues with people. He is a *logos*. And he needs that 'yes' by Moses in order to take an active part in history; just like in the time of the flood: to save his people he needs the response of a man. He needs to become a friend and companion of man – without the great biblical vocations, and without the vocations that continue to fill the earth, God would be too far away.

The great vocation of Moses then tells us that to regain freedom it is not enough to find the strength and faith to cry out our pain from the deep of our slavery. And if that cry of pain is received in Heaven (*'I've clearly seen my people oppressed in Egypt. I've heard their cry of injustice because of their slave masters'*, 3:7) it is still not enough. To escape from deep and collective slavery someone must answer '*yes*' to a vocation for the liberation of others.

Moses is the greatest example of those who are called to free others from slavery, without himself being a slave. Moses is not subjected to forced labour in Egypt, but is a migrant worker and a wage earner in the land of Midian. However, he is part of the oppressed people, one of its sons, a brother. He is standing just on the rim of the "pit" where the others have fallen, and so he can deliver them. He is not a slave, but suffers from his brothers' condition of slavery to the point of killing an Egyptian who hit one of them.

We won't be able to liberate anyone unless we feel the pain in our flesh of their suffering. Gandhi, Madre Teresa, Don Oreste and thousands of other "liberators" have been able to respond '*Here I am*' to a call that reached them one day and urged them to liberate others. They did so because before that call they had already suffered and felt pain over the situation of their enslaved "people". They were outside of the pit but suffered for and with those who were at the bottom of it: they felt themselves to be part of the same people and actually went through the same pain.

Our liberators from forced labour are not the pharaohs. The liberation of the oppressed comes from the oppressed: from the people, by one of its sons, by a '*brother*', whether by blood or by vocation for it is possible to become brothers. Without experiencing indignation, pain, heartache and tribulation over the fate of our brothers oppressed by any form of "*slavery*", without living in exile to escape from pharaohs, without risking to end up in court, reported by those in power (and often actually ending up there) you cannot save anyone – and at times you even realise that the "*liberators*" were actually on the payroll of the pharaohs. Those entrepreneurs and politicians who have really liberated and who really liberate the poor from the traps in which they have fallen are the ones that have gone through physical and spiritual pain themselves while meeting and embracing the inhabitants of the peripheries of the world. They have felt sympathetic, at times they have become their brothers, and when they heard a loud voice they had the strength to become someone else, to respond and to set out on a journey. Without these pains, embraces, without this attention and brotherhood all you may be able to do is some philanthropic deed or the launching of a media campaign. But the real liberations are born from a cry, from being heard, from pain, and from a '*Here I am*'.

We don't see enough liberations because we do not cry out enough or because we do not manage to cry out for those who do not have the strength to scream anymore. But the world is suffering mainly from the lack of the people able to suffer for their oppressed people, to listen to the good voice, let themselves be converted and then to respond. To suffer for the injustices that surround us is another form of the agape type of love, which is the precondition for every liberation.

There are many thorn bushes burning on the peripheries of our grasslands. They have been in flames for centuries and they do not burn up. It is from these that the calling voices originate, waiting for our '*Here I am*'.

Chapter 28
Where Real Freedom Begins

For all my life, I must confess, I have been pushed by two forces operating together. First of all by outrage, the impossibility to embrace the world as it is. ...the other force is the light. Perhaps today I'd call it transparency. I could say: it is faith."

(Paolo Dall'Oglio, *Outrage and Light*)

Abstract Empires have always tried to use work to black out the dreams of freedom, gratuitousness and celebration in the souls of the workers. Exactly for it being the number one friend of man, work lends itself to be manipulated and used against workers and so it can easily become an instance of "friendly fire". To be able to work has always been and still is one of the ways to freedom for many, while not to be able to work is still one of the main non-freedoms and a form of mass violence of our time. But next to work that liberates and makes us noble, there has always been also the idea of work used by the pharaohs as a means of oppressing the poor. Work is what opens Italian republic's constitution, but it once also opened the Nazi "work" camps: to understand and love work we have to keep both of these "entrances" together. Today, too, we live working and we still do not prosper and are blacked out because we cannot work; but we still live and die humiliated by too much work or the wrong type of work when the new pharaohs make us work all day and every day, when they do not allow us to think, pray and celebrate holidays and so they take us back to the brick factories of Egypt.

Empires have always tried to use work to black out the dreams of freedom, gratuitousness and celebration in the souls of the workers. Exactly for it being the number one friend of man, work lends itself to be manipulated and used against workers and so it can easily become an instance of "friendly fire". To be able to work has always been and still is one of the ways to freedom for many, while not to be able to work is still one of the main non-freedoms and a form of mass violence of our time. But next to work that liberates and makes us noble, there has always been also the idea of work used by the pharaohs as a means of oppressing the poor.

L. Bruni, *The Economy of Salvation*, Virtues and Economics 4,
https://doi.org/10.1007/978-3-030-04082-6_28

Work is what opens Italian republic's constitution, but it once also opened the Nazi "work" camps: to understand and love work we have to keep both of these "entrances" together. Today, too, we live working and we still do not prosper and are blacked out because we cannot work; but we still live and die humiliated by too much work or the wrong type of work when the new pharaohs make us work all day and every day, when they do not allow us to think, pray and celebrate holidays and so they take us back to the brick factories of Egypt.

Moses, after hearing the Voice speak from the bush, goes down from the mountain and has a mysterious encounter. Like Jacob who was attacked by God at Jabbok River while he was returning with his family to the land of his fathers, Moses, too, has to face God on his journey to Egypt with his wife and son. God who has just revealed his name (YHWH) to him now confronts and combats him: '*During their journey, as they camped overnight, the Lord met Moses and tried to kill him.*' (4:24) God who gives a task to the prophet and then fights him is a theme that is present all through the Bible, up until the Son sent to us to perform the greatest of all tasks, the one who ends up crucified, abandoned by Elohim (Mark 15:34). The voice that calls you and shows you the road of salvation to take becomes also the person who stops you and combats you along the same way that it opened up to you. Vocation and trust/faith are gifts; but they are also fights, a combat taking place at the border of life and death, known and loved only by those who have listened to a voice and followed it. In contrast to the episode at the Jabbok River that Genesis describes by a wealth of symbols and details, here the text does not dwell on the combat of Moses and God, but only describes the actions of Zipporah, Moses' wife. During the attack, Zipporah circumcises their son and Moses' salvation gets mysteriously connected to the blood of the son. (4:25–26) After the midwives of Egypt, Moses' mother and sister, the daughter of the pharaoh, Moses is again saved by women, by their special vocation for life as humble mediators between the divine and our flesh bodies.

Moses continues his journey to Egypt alone. His people gives credit to Aaron's words who acts as Moses' mouth (4:27), and they all '*bowed down and worshipped*' (4:30–31) immediately. The dialogue with the pharaoh, however, is much more complicated and disastrous: '*Afterward, Moses and Aaron went to Pharaoh and said, »This is what the Lord, Israel's God, says: "Let my people go so that they can hold a festival for me in the desert."« But Pharaoh said, »Who is this Lord whom I'm supposed to obey by letting Israel go? I don't know this Lord, and I certainly won't let Israel go.«*' (5:1–2) The pharaoh calls for the slave masters of the Israelites and takes immediate action to toughen up their working conditions: '*Don't supply the people with the straw they need to make bricks like you did before. Let them go out and gather the straw for themselves. But still make sure that they produce the same number of bricks as they made before. Don't reduce the number!*' (5:7–8).

The pharaoh's reaction to Moses' request offers us a powerful description of what work becomes under the emperors of yesterday and today. Pharaoh's first reaction regards God directly: '*Who is this Lord?*', which is as good as saying: '*Does anyone know him at all?*' All forms of oppression, be it that of peoples or workers, begins by not accepting any other god than that of the "pharaoh", by not recognising that there exists a heaven that is higher than the one touched by the pyramids. In

Egypt, the pharaoh was a divinity, the only mediator between the people and the divine. To recognise YHWH and listen to his request would have put the pharaoh's divine nature in doubt and it would have meant that the existence of other mediators (Moses and Aaron) is admitted. Emperors are not atheists: they are all idolaters. They do not negate the existence of God; they just make people, things (money, power) or ideas become gods, producing gods in their own image, gods with whom they can feel very comfortable.

In this episode, there is also a passage that is especially relevant for work. What Moses and Aaron asked of the pharaoh was the ultimate liberation of the people. In that first meeting, they only made a request to him to be able to '*go on a three-day journey into the desert*' (5:3) to offer sacrifices to their God, to pray, to make a celebration. The pharaoh rejects it without appeal, because if he lets them leave the work camps even for just one day of holiday and religious rites, he would recognise that they are a people and not merely slaves. You can pray anywhere, and the prayers directed to heaven from the camps of imprisonment are no doubt the most beautiful and truest ones. But to leave the work camps in order to pray and celebrate a holiday together is not just a prayer: it is a symbolic act that every now and then has triggered the downfall of even the greatest empires. If the pharaoh would have permitted the people to celebrate their holiday in the desert, he would have recognised not only another, different religion, but also their right to celebrations, to free gifts and to non-work, a right that only a free man can possess, not a slave (it is also because of the remembering of the people's slavehood in Egypt that Israel's Law extends the celebration of the Shabbat to all living beings). By saying no to this request of YHWH, the pharaoh actually simply confirmed that the sons of Israel were nothing more than slaves to do forced labour. The first and most natural act through which the emperors tell us that we are only forced labourers is to deny us the time for non-labour, for religious rites, for giving free gifts, for celebrations. All peoples' liberation was started by praying, singing and celebrating together. For the emperors, holidays are more fearful than protest marches because they contain the infinite powers of gratuitousness. And when they feel the "mood for celebration" among their workers, their reaction is to toughen up the forced labour.

Every time an entrepreneur makes a woman sign her "voluntary" resignation in case of maternity in advance, or when the present form of capitalism denies us the right to rest and observe a holiday and makes us work on Sundays, we return to the logic of that ancient pharaoh and all the empires. When the company asks us to work every hour and every day to reach the objectives set, or when it orders us to observe its own corporate holidays and denies us the holidays of everyone else, these companies become very similar to the brick factories of Egypt; and we become all too similar to the slaves of the ancient times, even if we signed our contract of our own accord and are paid well.

In all empires people die for the lack of work, but they also die for too much or awful work because the person is extinguished when he or she is reduced to being a mere labourer. Work without non- work is the forced work of slaves because it is freedom itself that puts a limit to work, thereby generating that anthropological variance between us and the world of things, between Marco and Engineer Bianchi.

This differentiation is essential to give dignity to things that we produce and to save the spiritual overflow of our life and that of others. We'd better not forget about this, especially in the present deep crisis of work. Today we will only learn to work and create work if we are able to ask the current pharaohs for time to dedicate to giving freely and celebrating holidays, even if these are words that they do not like to hear as they are subversive and useless in the production of their bricks.

Freedom of religion, gifts and holidays is the first form of the anthropological overflow and ethical dignity of every civilisation because it says to the pharaohs and to their descendants today: '*You are not god in my eyes, in our eyes and you are not god in anyone's eyes, not even your own. Your festivities that are oriented towards profit are not enough for us, we want other altars where to celebrate our freedom and our liberations.*'

Those three days of walk towards that different type of altar would have been the first steps towards the promised land, the end of slavery. The pharaoh did not want to and could not grant it to them. Yet they made it there.

The days of walking freely in order to celebrate and be merry together still happen throughout history, notwithstanding the emperors. Because those high pyramids do not manage to satisfy our desire for heavens which is always higher up than they are.

Chapter 29
Loyalty Makes Even the Sky Open

If ye are truly the ambassadors of God, then may He judge between us and Pharaoh. ... You are responsible for the widespread stench now issuing from the Israelitish corpses used as bricks for building when our tale was not complete. We are in the quandary of the poor sheep that has been dragged away by a wolf. The shepherd pursues the robber, catches up with him, and tries to snatch the sheep from his jaws, and the wretched victim, pulled this way by the wolf and that way by the shepherd, is torn to pieces.

(L. Ginzberg, *The Legends of the Jews, Vol. 2*)

Abstract It is typical of empires to consider their subjects weak and lazy, and make them work harder to prevent that in the gaps of non-work the desire for freedom or the desire for a different God than the Pharaoh should filter in. For the emperors, their workers only work when they feel the prod of the slave-masters on their back. Today in many (but not all) regions of the world, there are no emperors anymore, but it is very common to see leaders who multiply the tasks of workers and force them to spread all through the land of Egypt in search of the missing 'straw'. Stress and discomfort increase in the places of work, and it is still thought that work is not hard enough in the fields and incentives are not well designed. Nestled within this episode of Exodus, we also encounter the first protest of managers mentioned in the Bible, that of the 'foremen'. It is among the most beautiful protests and one of the most important ones of the entire Scripture, because it contains valuable messages for all managers of enterprises, institutions and communities, of all times.

The culture of the incentive is becoming the new ideology of our time, and it is migrating from the large capitalist enterprises towards health, culture and education. The main limitation and danger of this type of work culture is an impoverished vision of the human being, thought and described as an individual who works when

L. Bruni, *The Economy of Salvation*, Virtues and Economics 4,
https://doi.org/10.1007/978-3-030-04082-6_29

motivated by extrinsic and monetary rewards only, and as someone from whom you can get pretty much everything and in all areas of life if you pay them adequately.

Thank God, men and women are much richer and more beautiful than this caricature. We can do really great things, but we want a lot more money, because the most valuable "*coins*" are those of recognition, respect and gratitude. We are able to do our best if and when we feel valued and recognized, if we are "*seen*" and therefore thanked. The real big question at the heart of the culture of the incentive is that of freedom then.

'*They are lazy*'. These were the words that the king of Egypt said to his officials after his meeting with Moses and Aaron, who had asked him, in the name of YHWH, to liberate the people to celebrate for 3 days in the wilderness: '*They are weak and lazy, and that's why they cry, »Let's go and offer sacrifices to our God.« Make the men's work so hard that it's all they can do, and they can't focus on these empty lies*' (5:8–9). It is typical of empires to consider their subjects weak and lazy, and make them work harder to prevent that in the gaps of non-work the desire for freedom or the desire for a different God than the Pharaoh should filter in. For the emperors, their workers/subjects only work when they feel the prod of the "*slave masters*" on their back. Today in many (but not all) regions of the world, there are no emperors anymore, but it is very common to see leaders who multiply the tasks of workers and force them to spread '*all through the land of Egypt*' (5:12) in search of the missing '*straw*'. Stress and discomfort increase in the places of work, and it is still thought that work is not hard enough in the fields and incentives are not well designed. Weak and lazy people do exist, but they are much less than we think, because there is a scientifically proven and invincible tendency that makes us overestimate the laziness of others and underestimate our own.

Nestled within this episode of Exodus, we also encounter the first protest of "managers" mentioned in the Bible, that of the '*foremen*'. It is among the most beautiful protests and one of the most important ones of the entire Scripture, because it contains valuable messages for all managers of enterprises, institutions and communities, of all times.

The leaders of the labour camps were divided into two categories: the '*slave masters*' and the '*foremen*'. And their different and opposite reactions to the order of the pharaoh to tighten the working conditions of the oppressed people reveal to us two different and opposing cultures of responsibility and leadership. The new conditions of work and production imposed by the pharaoh (to manufacture the same amount of bricks as before but without having the straw made available for it) could not be met by the workers who were already subjected to extreme conditions (1:14). And such, in fact, was the case (5:14). The slave masters, who were Egyptians employed by the pharaoh, responded to this failure to achieve production goals by blaming the foremen of the labour camps, who were Jewish, brothers of the workers: '*The Israelite foremen, whom Pharaoh's slave masters had set over them, were also beaten and asked, »Why didn't you produce the same number of bricks yesterday and today as you did before?«*' (5:14) The foremen, however, did not beat the workers in the factories. Just like the midwives of Egypt, these people in charge of the workers made a deliberate and costly choice to stand with the people and the truth, and so they did not obey the orders of the pharaoh. They chose to be brothers of the oppressed, and therefore to share the same fate with them. And so, instead of raging at their companions they went to Pharaoh to complain: '*Why do you treat your servants like this? No straw is supplied to your servants, yet they say to us, »Make bricks!«*' (5:15–16). And, just as it happens still all too often, the pharaoh's response to the loyal protest of the foremen was none other than blaming them, too, of the same laziness of their workers: '*You are lazy bums, nothing but lazy bums. That's why you say, »Let us go and offer sacrifices to the Lord.« Go and get back to work*!' (5:17–18) At this point, '*the Israelite foremen saw how impossible their situation was when they were commanded*' (5:19).

This is, often, the '*worst case scenario*' in which you find those who, to be loyal to the weak, reject the orders of the powerful and are accused by the latter of being too lazy and undeserving. No middleman and no manager is a good '*foreman*' if they are not willing to take the risk of being associated with the defect given by the leaders to the people whom they are defending, or being '*beaten*' with and like them. Outside of this logic of solidarity and responsibility, there remains only the mercenary, who, unlike the '*good shepherd*', does not give his life for his flock, he does not share the same fate with them. Taking upon ourselves the '*beatings*' without passing it all on to those who are entrusted to us, is, among other things, a great and beautiful image of the vocation of all true fatherhood and parenting, whether it is natural or spiritual.

The foremen did not retaliate against their workers even after the failure of their protest to the pharaoh. They continued to exercise their loyalty, and went to confront Moses and Aaron directly. They went to meet them with hard words: '*You've made us stink in the opinion of Pharaoh and his servants. You've given them a reason to kill us.*' (5:21).

Moses took the harsh and loyal cry of the foremen very seriously, and he went through the first crisis of his mission in Egypt because of it. But, above all, as a result of this hearing he had another meeting with the voice that had called him. The costly and fraternal loyalty of those foremen produced a new *theophany*, a new encounter with their God, a new vocation: '*Then Moses turned to the Lord and said, »My Lord, why have you abused this people? Why did you send me for this?«*' (5:22) And God talked to him and called him again: '*I am the Lord. I'll bring you into the land that I promised to give to Abraham, Isaac, and Jacob. I'll give it to you as your possession. I am the Lord.*' (6:1–8).

We cannot know how far an act of true loyalty may get, or what can happen when we cannot obey the wrong orders of the pharaohs in our '*grasslands*' and chose to be faithful to the truth and to the dignity of those who work with us. Sometimes this faithfulness can open the roof of our offices and our buildings, or make Noah's rainbow grow back into the sky. It is this loyalty that makes it possible that among the executives and their workers there may be a relationship generated that some call brotherhood, and when it is born out of this quiet and costly loyalty it is free of all patina and moralistic rhetoric. We truly become brothers and sisters of those who work at our dependencies when we, standing between them and the pharaohs, turn our backs to the wrong orders.

If those foremen had not done all that was in their power in their loyal protest, if – out of fear or respect – they had stopped just a step before facing Moses and Aaron, they would not have reopened the sky and YWHW would not have renewed his promise. Many acts of true loyalty do not produce all their fruit because they do not come until the end of the process.

The most difficult challenge that those who respond to a vocation and agree to carry out a task of liberation must overcome is to keep their faith in the truth of their vocation, the task received, and the promise of the voice when they see the suffering of those who should be loved and liberated by them increase; when the people whom we were supposed to free from forced labour ends up in worse conditions, and the suffering of the innocent grows. From these tests that are always very painful and come mainly (though not exclusively) in the early stages of the processes of liberation, one manages to escape and return to the right path only if the first miracle of Mount Horeb is repeated, and so one can feel being called by the name again. A miracle that can be donated by the loyalty of another person, from their love or their protest – and these two are often the same thing.

In our businesses and organizations, the *slave masters* and the *foremen* continue to live together, next to each other. Executives who '*beat up*' their subordinates, ready to do anything to satisfy every request of the owners, and managers who prefer to be '*beaten*' in order to remain loyal to their companions. Many start as foremen and over time they become (perhaps due to delusions or unhappiness) slave masters, but the process rarely takes place in the reverse direction. We see it all, every day. But let us not forget that many workers do not die under the weight of the impossible production of bricks exactly because among us there are many descendants of the loyal foremen of Egypt, and they are certainly more than we are able to recognize around us.

Chapter 30
The Plagues of Our Invisible Empires

As long as salvation has not come, the expectation of salvation can only be a constant universal aggravation of tensions and sufferings for us today, just as it was for Israel in the time of Moses. The announcement of salvation, breaking the mundane balance, only reveals brutal power relations.

(Sergio Quinzio, A Commentary on the Bible)

Abstract Each generation should re-read the Exodus to discover and face their own pharaohs and slavehood, long for liberation, recognise the plagues of their own age and leave the land of empires, moving towards the new land of fraternity and justice. In the real passages towards liberation, there is always a moment of the plagues of Egypt, that are the great signs of times in the eras of empires that the pharaohs do not manage to interpret because their "hearts" are hardened. And so, they call for the "magicians" to divine some assuring answers. Exodus tells us, if we can and want to listen to it, that when the empires prove to be reluctant to do good (and they always are, otherwise they wouldn't be empires), the only salvation available for the oppressed people is flight: leaving behind the land of forced labour in order to make a decisive move towards another land.

Each generation should re-read the Exodus to discover and face their own pharaohs and slavehood, long for liberation, recognise the plagues of their own age and leave the land of empires, moving towards the new land of fraternity and justice. In the real passages towards liberation, there is always a moment of the "*plagues of Egypt*" – these are the great signs of times in the eras of empires that the pharaohs do not manage to interpret because their "*hearts*" are hardened.

And so, they call for the "*magicians*" to divine some assuring answers. Exodus tells us – if we can and want to listen to it – that when the empires prove to be reluctant to do good (and they always are, otherwise they wouldn't be empires), the only salvation available for the oppressed people is flight: leaving behind the land of forced labour in order to make a decisive move towards another land.

L. Bruni, *The Economy of Salvation*, Virtues and Economics 4,
https://doi.org/10.1007/978-3-030-04082-6_30

'Moses spoke thus to the people of Israel, but they did not listen to Moses, because of their broken spirit and harsh slavery.' (6:9) After the costly and fraternal loyalty of the *foremen*, Moses returned to the people to tell them again the promise of YHWH. But they did not listen to his words because of all the pain they suffered from, blocking their ears and souls.

There is a point after which the suffering becomes so deep and radical that it keeps people from listening to the prophets and their promises. When the great suffering of people and communities lasts long, the prophets, even the greatest ones, are not listened to because the overload of pain creates an invisible curtain that even the powerful words of the prophet cannot penetrate.

Every generation has been through these desperate forms of deafness, and mostly know how to fight and eliminate them. It is known to our age as well, but in addition to the deafening pain of the oppressed being produced and not healed, there is also the new type of deafness of the spiritual and moral peripheries of the wealthy where the voice of the prophets is not heard and no efforts for liberation are made even though they would be as necessary there as in the peripheries of misery.

The story of the plagues in Egypt tells us that there is a threshold of pain for the peoples and for persons beyond which the only credible language of liberation is actually made up of facts because only facts can get into the great depths reached by the wounds of pain. It is deep down there that the origin of the promise can still be found and is still active, even inside their oppression. The words of YHWH and Moses become history, they penetrate the flesh of the peoples, they wound them and bless them. Only this incarnate word can reach the depths of certain types of human pain. Only certain facts, certain embodied words – in a gesture, in a last caress, in a thousand nights spent sleeping on a couch in a hospital's corridor, in the finding of the door of the house open even after a hundred betrayals... – can speak of that pain that words cannot capture anymore, not even to ask for or grant forgiveness. This also pertains to the dignity of human suffering, the only thing that can be stronger than words (it was to compensate for the dignity of human pain that one day the verb incarnate had to die nailed to wood).

The first light that the people immersed in darkness glimpsed was dim but enough to break up the shadows for the dawn of resurrection. What actually gave back hope and faith in the promise for those poor ones, is inside the paradox of the plagues of Egypt – and it is quite common even today that our hopes are resurrected by the plagues hitting us or others, when we manage to see in them, while going through them, a light of dawn. And the ears of the soul open up in a collective, liberating *effatà*.

The plagues are but the beginning of Easter, the precondition and presumption of the crossing of the Red Sea. There is a dominant dynamic in the development of plagues. While the given plague is still in action, the pharaoh promises Moses to let the people go so they can honour their God in the desert, Moses believes or hopes that the new plague will finally convert the pharaoh and asks YHWH to put an end to it. But as soon as the plague ends, the pharaoh feels '*that there was a respite*' (8:15) and takes his promise of liberation back. The message is clear: these empires and these pharaohs are inconvertible and their promises are but chatter because their only interest is the increase in the production of bricks to construct the pyramids in honour of their idolatrous divinity.

In the first plagues (the waters of the Nile turned into blood and was invaded by frogs) the magicians and soothsayers of the pharaoh re-appear. We have already come across them in the Cycle of Joseph in Genesis (41:8) – Egypt is not only a place of slavery in Israel's memory, it is also the fertile land of fraternity rediscovered. These magicians repeat the same mysterious deeds as Moses (*'But the magicians of Egypt did the same by their secret arts'*: Exodus 7:22; 8:3) to demonstrate that the presence of the plagues could be explained without appealing to the actions of the God of Israel. However, upon the third plague, that of the gnats, *'the magicians tried by their secret arts to produce gnats, but they could not.'* (8:14) It is the beginning of a decline that culminates in the sixth plague (of the boils), when *'the magicians could not stand before Moses because of the boils, for the boils came upon the magicians...'*. (9:11).

When the empires start to vacillate, the rulers call for the magicians, the oracles and the soothsayers. They ask them for confirmation that whatever painful is what is happening in their empire, it is nothing to really worry about, and it may be explained by the very logic of the empire itself. For years, we have been assisting to the succession of divinations and horoscopes of the magicians of the world of finance and economy who wanted (and still want) to convince us that the "*plagues*" that we were (and are) suffering through were (are) not a powerful sign of the great necessity of conversion and change in the deep logic of our empire, but merely natural oscillations of the economic cycle or internal errors and disturbances of the system that may be overcome "*in the long run*". For decades, we have been suffering the consequences of climate change, we see people, rivers, animals, plants, insects die, but the magicians of the empire keep denying the evidence and still want to demonstrate to us that these phenomena are only natural and therefore explainable through their secret arts. But the plagues grow and the empires are about to fall. The simulations of the soothsayers do not work anymore because the evidence is of such great power that it can scatter even the best and most sophisticated magicians – and some of them even contract the same illness they have been trying to deny before.

Our economic system, deeply intertwined with the environmental and climate issues, is still at the stage of the "*plague of the frogs*" where the pharaoh calls and generously pays his magicians to convince him and all the people that what is happening is nothing really new and there is nothing to really worry about. But there are signs suggesting that we are perhaps entering the third plague. Because simulations and persuasion are becoming more and more tiresome. However, we should still hope that it won't be like what happened to the pharaoh, and, this time, we will be able to convert after the first plagues and not wait for the "*death of the firstborn*" (the tenth plague) in order to finally free the poor and save the world.

This rich, complex and colourful story of the plagues contains a great teaching about conflict resolution, above all the resolution of the conflict between an oppressor, appearing unequivocally and unjustly as the oppressor, and the oppressed, who are also unequivocally and unjustly oppressed. When the nature and logic of these two parties in conflict are manifested in a definite way, there comes a moment when negotiations have to be interrupted, and the only possibility to keep alive is: flight. The only life possible is that which stands outside of the slave work camps.

One does not negotiate with such oppressive empires: if we want to save ourselves we should escape because those who try to negotiate and condescend to make compromises will one day find themselves in the role of the *slave masters*, forgetting about the poor, their cry and the first promise. We do not manage to free ourselves from too many emperors because we do not recognise what they really are and enter into negotiations governed by their logic, accepting their donations and sponsors to take care of their victims, so in the end we do not liberate anyone and end up aggravating our slavery and that of others, too.

The empires of the past were obvious and evident, they clearly extended above all the people on the horizon. Our empires are not visible anymore, and they manage to present themselves as good and generous kingdoms where the poor will get liberated. Much of the liberty and justice of our time derives from our spiritual and moral capacity to see and call our empires by name, to recognise the plagues and to flee from them. But as long as we resist, try not to perish and hope for liberation, we shall never forget that behind the many forms of spiritual deafness and missed liberation we see around ourselves there may be some great pain found, produced by our visible and invisible empires. Reducing the suffering of the peoples, loosening and breaking the chains that bind us to forced labour may allow many of the poor to finally listen to the prophets and set out on the road to the sea together.

Chapter 31
The Greatest Liberation

The plagues did not stay the cruelty of the Egyptian oppressors toward the Hebrews. It continued unabated until the very end of their sojourn in the land. On the day of the exodus, Rachel the daughter of Shuthelah gave birth to a child, while she and her husband together were treading the clay for bricks. The babe dropped from her womb into the clay and sank out of sight. Gabriel appeared, moulded a brick out of the clay containing the child, and carried it to the highest of the heavens...

(Louis Ginzberg, *The Legends of the Jews, Vol 2*)

Abstract In the unfolding of the ten plagues there is not only the role of YHWH; there is, essentially, also that of Moses and Aaron who, notwithstanding the hardened heart of the pharaoh, continue to ask him to convert. If we keep to the basic logic of the Bible, we should think that Moses and Aaron would have been probably struck after each plague. They knew that the pharaoh's heart was hard but they couldn't possibly know how far his obstinacy could take him. His stubborn inconvertibility is revealed again and again as they go to see him after each plague. And they had to assist to and resist through all this, up until the death of the children, a death they would not have wished to see. YHWH, their God of life, was the one who had blessed the midwives of Egypt years before, and in them, all the children of the Hebrews, the Egyptians...all the children in the world. The death cry of the firstborn that seems to annul the cry of life of the newborn saved by God and by the women from the hands of another homicidal pharaoh makes us dig deeper into this until we find a more profound trace.

The plagues of Egypt are the normal state of idolatrous empires – and so for ours, too. In such regimes, the water does not quench the thirst of the living beings and the soil is not fertile. It is in a state of decay and it generates frogs, gnats and flies... and the animals die. The sun does not manage to penetrate through the dust clouds over the lands, everything is covered by darkness. The empires of the idols have no

L. Bruni, *The Economy of Salvation*, Virtues and Economics 4,
https://doi.org/10.1007/978-3-030-04082-6_31

descendants; their firstborn die because the idol is seductive but it is also sterile. When the empires show off their invincible idolatrous nature, when no plague is able to convert the pharaoh, when the only condition possible in the land of the empire is slavery, Exodus tells us that this is not the end for the poor yet, there remains still a possibility.

Even in this terrible state – what can be more terrible than the death of children? – there exists a way of salvation if we are ready to believe the prophets and persist until the very end: '*Yet one plague more I will bring upon Pharaoh and upon Egypt. Afterward he will let you go from here.*' (11:1).

In the unfolding of the ten plagues there is not only the role of YHWH; there is, essentially, also that of Moses and Aaron who, notwithstanding the hardened heart of the pharaoh, continue to ask him to convert. If we keep to the basic logic of the Bible, we should think that Moses and Aaron would have been probably struck after each plague. They knew that the pharaoh's heart was hard but they couldn't possibly know how far his obstinacy could take him. His stubborn inconvertibility is revealed again and again as they go to see him after each plague: '*Thus says the Lord, the God of the Hebrews, »How long will you refuse to humble yourself before me?«*' (10:3) And they had to assist to and resist through all this, up until the death of the children, a death they would not have wished to see. YHWH, their God of life, was the one who had blessed the midwives of Egypt years before, and in them, all the children of the Hebrews, the Egyptians...all the children in the world. The death cry of the firstborn that seems to annul the cry of life of the newborn saved by God and by the women from the hands of another homicidal pharaoh makes us dig deeper into this until we find a more profound trace. In the meantime, however, we should not get out of touch with the terrain of history, with the collective memory of climactic, extraordinary events of the last years of the Hebrews in Egypt, or perhaps of a pest that hit the country and the children (our reading always transforms facts into signs). The historical memory of the pain felt over the ten plagues remained alive in Biblical tradition (in the evening of the *Pèsach*, or Passover, in the Hebrew houses they spill ten sips of wine from the cup: that non-fullness of the cup is the living place of memory that brings sadness into the holiday).

These difficult, terrible and wonderful chapters of Exodus should be read like a great lesson on idolatry – this is the most profound trace that we are in search of. The Bible has no mercy for this pharaoh because in order to save itself and ourselves, it has to be ruthless to idols. The first truth about YHWH is not being one of the many idols of man. Israel has always fought against idols around and inside itself, including those that they had seen in Egypt and were fascinated by. By placing a creator God and man created to his likeness to the beginning of Genesis, the Bible wanted to make a radical and fundamental choice. It unearthed a most profound cut between itself and the idolatrous culture where god is created to the likeness of man who is short of transcendence. The idol is the anti-YHWH, but also the anti-Adam because an idolatrous culture first of all denies man, and makes him end up being a slave and life-long brick maker in service of the idol he himself created. To believe in the idol no faith is needed, because it is just too obvious in the streets and markets everywhere. Biblical faith, however, is trust placed in a voice that one cannot see, only "hear". And so it is that the idol-emperor is struck by the plagues, and the great liberation is first of all the escape from idolatry. The children who have to die are the children of the idols and their empire who have been with us throughout our history and the history of salvation, too.

Today we live in a great era of idolatry, probably the greatest of all, because is interpreted as a higher humanism. We have reduced the transcendent into manufactured, we filled the "heavens" with things that will never satiate us because they are produced not to take away but to increase our hunger for hungry idols – the idols always have to eat, they end up eating up their adorers and are never satiated. The closest historical system to the culture of idolatry is financial-consumer capitalism, a creation of ours. It is enough to go to its places, talk to its important agents, assist in its liturgies to get some absolutely clear verification about it. It is a system that knows and feeds only the culture of itself, one that recognises only one goal: the maximization of the production of bricks to erect its own towers of Babel or pyramids, growing higher and higher. The purely idolatrous empires don't last long: the time of this consuming type of capitalism will soon be over, too. But our plagues are not over yet, and with them the loud cry of the oppressed peoples continues.

Therefore, it should not surprise us that the first two words of the Law that will be given to Moses on Mount Sinai are faith in a *God who grants his people liberation* from Egypt and the *radical rejection of the idols*. A god who does not liberate us is an idol (even inside our religions), but the biblical God is not an idol *because* he is a liberator, he delivers his oppressed people crying out from the work camps. And it is not the biblical God, only a stupid idol we are experiencing (one of the clear marks of every idol is their radical stupidity) if we are not saved from slavery by the encounter with him, be it our own slavery or that of others. Religious experiences without slavery and without liberation may be easily reproduced be the magicians of Egypt and by the legions of our new magicians in an attempt to make profit.

After the tenth plague, which is the most terrible one, the people may finally depart: '*Then he [the pharaoh] summoned Moses and Aaron by night and said, »Up, go out from among my people, both you and the people of Israel; and go, serve the Lord, as you have said. Take your flocks and your herds, as you have said, and be gone, and bless me also!«*' (12:31–32) And as soon as they leave Egypt we realise that the holiday the people want to celebrate in the desert is exactly *Pèsach*. For the people of Israel, the tradition of *Pèsach* was there before Egypt, the Passover holiday was part of the culture of the ancient nomadic tribes that used to offer a lamb to God, who, in turn, would bless them and their flocks. The pharaoh did not allow the people to celebrate that ancient nomadic three-day holiday, but YHWH transformed the feast day of shepherds into the great holiday of liberation of the people and all the oppressed who suffer from idolatrous pharaohs. This is how the holiday that was a great one even before Egypt became the most important one after Israel's liberation from slavery. The new Passover becomes "*the beginning of months*" because it is the beginning of the new Israel. It is the origin of a new history. But it is also the recapitulation of the first alliances and the promise of YHWH. In that great night there is, in fact, Noah and in him the entire humanity; but there is also Jacob, the patriarchs, his sons and the 12 tribes symbolised by

Joseph's "bones": '*Moses took the bones of Joseph with him, for Joseph had made the sons of Israel solemnly swear, saying, »God will surely visit you, and you shall carry up my bones with you from here.«*' (13:19).

The plagues and the sea that swallows the chariots and horse riders of the Egyptians are also the image of a new flood where the waters of the Nile and the Red Sea become the places of death again. But also this time there is a man (Moses) who is saved from the flood and, together with his family, animals are saved, too (Moses did not want to leave without taking their livestock, too: 10:26). Once again, a rainbow shines above the earth.

But in that new Passover we can glimpse Jacob, too. Among the many possible meanings of the ancient word Pèsach there is also the verb limp (*psh*). And for the Bible to say limp is to say Jacob, who became Israel during a night struggle at a river (Jabbok) when he was wounded in the fight with YHWH at the sciatic nerve, and was made lame and given a new name. The first Israel was born from a night struggle with Elohim amidst waters, the new Israel is reborn from a great night struggle while the people of the first Israel crosses the waters of slavery. From a first, personal wound there came a first blessing, from a great wound (the plagues), there flourished a great blessing (liberation) – and one day the greatest of wounds will generate an endless blessing. Jacob walked with a limp all his life, slavery and the plagues are still present in the lives of the children of Israel, the Risen One carries the marks and stigmas of the cross. Every wound transformed into a blessing is a fertile one.

There is no greater feast than that of Pèsach, Passover, Easter. No liberation is greater than the liberation from the idols.

Chapter 32
Gratuitousness Speaks

> *Keeping away from idolatry means not evading the question of our sons and daughters, asking: »what is this ritual for, what is this moral commandment for, why love the one God?« And it also means not to back out of answering.*
>
> (Jean-Pierre Sonnet, *To Generate is to Narrate*)

Abstract The first, fundamental characteristic of all idolatrous regimes is precisely the lack of gratuitousness, which is instead the first dimension of biblical faith. Creation is a gift, the alliance is a gift, the promise is a gift, the fight of the prophets against idolatry is a gift. Gratuitousness is the other name of God. The culture of the idol hates gifts. In fact, it is his number one enemy on earth, because the idol knows that the contact with the spirit of gratuitousness would kill it, it would take away its power of enchantment. Therefore, when idolatrous kingdoms are created, the first operation of the pharaohs is to try to remove all traces of true gifts from their sacred space, and fill it all and only with objects and merchandise. In our time this cancellation is attempted by oversimplifying and mocking gratuitousness, considering it a childhood nostalgia of wrongly educated adults. It is then transformed into the gadgets of the pharaoh, in his discounts, fidelity cards and harmless little gifts permitted only during his holidays. But the most insidious attempt to wipe out gratuity is to confine it in the realm of the non-profit, to entrust it as a monopoly to philanthropic institutions or sponsors who, like a scapegoat, should bear all the gift-giving/gratuitousness of the village, take it outside and let it die in the desert.

One night was enough time for the pharaoh to forget the great pain of the plagues, and the bricks and the "service" of the Israelites were right back as the only concern of the empire: '*When the king of Egypt was told that the people had fled, the mind of Pharaoh and his servants was changed toward the people, and they said, »What is this we have done, that we have let Israel go from serving us?« So he made ready his chariot and took his army with him...*' (14:5–6). The dawn of a new day reveals to us that there was no gratuitousness in the liberation we just saw.

L. Bruni, *The Economy of Salvation*, Virtues and Economics 4,
https://doi.org/10.1007/978-3-030-04082-6_32

The first, fundamental characteristic of all idolatrous regimes is precisely the lack of gratuitousness, which is instead the first dimension of biblical faith. Creation is a gift, the alliance is a gift, the promise is a gift, the fight of the prophets against idolatry is a gift. Gratuitousness (giving for free) is the other name of YHWH. The culture of the idol hates gifts. In fact, it is his number one enemy on earth, because the idol "knows" that the contact with the spirit of gratuitousness would kill it, it would take away its power of enchantment. Therefore, when idolatrous kingdoms are created, the first operation of the pharaohs is to try to remove all traces of true gifts from their "sacred" space, and fill it all and only with objects and merchandise. In our time this cancellation is attempted by oversimplifying and mocking gratuitousness, considering it a childhood nostalgia of wrongly educated adults. It is then transformed into the gadgets of the pharaoh, in his discounts, fidelity cards and harmless little gifts permitted only during his "*holidays*". But the most insidious attempt to wipe out gratuity is to confine it in the realm of the "*non-profit*", to entrust it as a monopoly to philanthropic institutions or sponsors who, like a scapegoat, should bear all the gift-giving/gratuitousness of the village, take it outside and let it die in the desert.

And so, the village remains silent. The idol cannot speak. And so his worshipers also end up losing the gift of speech – it is always heartbreaking to see the deafening silence that reigns in the slot halls that are occupying our cities, or on tobacconists' stands, in roadside restaurants, bars, and (alas!) at the post offices, where men, many women and just too many elderly people are busy "*scratching*" in religious silence and desperate solitude, kept there mercilessly by new pharaohs to do forced labour: '*...and they themselves* [the idols] *are gilded and laid over with silver; yet are they but false, and cannot speak.*' (Baruch, 6:7). For this is the infinite value of the word of YHWH, who is not an idol because he speaks, he is not an image but a voice that can also hear our voice and our cry.

The day that we manage to outsource all giving-for-free to its professionals, separating it from the ordinary life of the city and the businesses, the idolatrous/separating empire will be at its complete. When each bank will have formed its foundation, when the multinationals of gambling and weapons have funded all treatments of their victims, the poison (gift) injected into the capitalist body as a vaccine will have achieved its goal, and we will be finally saved from gratuitousness. The new cult will be all-out, in every hour of every day. But they will not succeed, because gratuitousness has a great resilience, as it is nestled in the deepest and truest part of the human heart. It is the invincibility of our vocation for gratuitousness that, sooner or later, makes the empires collapse. And our hope is in giving freely so that we can do so today, too.

The vision of the horses and chariots of the Egyptians was the first test of the Jews outside of Egypt: '*...the people of Israel...feared greatly ... [they] cried out to the Lord. They said to Moses, »Is it because there are no graves in Egypt that you have taken us away to die in the wilderness? What have you done to us in bringing us out of Egypt? Is not this what we said to you in Egypt: "Leave us alone that we may serve the Egyptians"? For it would have been better for us to serve the Egyptians than to die in the wilderness.«*' (14:10–12).

This is the point where the "*complaints*" and "*murmuring*" of the people freed from slavery in Egypt begin, but it will take a long time before they can break free from the memory of Egypt and from the benefits of slavery. They immediately understand that once they are free, the risk of dying increases ('*are there no graves in Egypt?*'). With freedom, the possibility of death is closer. Outside of the work camps, paradoxically, an increased vulnerability is experienced, since in all cases of slavery a form of alliance is created between oppressor and oppressed: the slave is kept alive because he has to produce bricks. No rational master (and empires are such) kills his profit tool: it is good to keep them alive to exploit them to the end. For this reason, if we are afraid to risk our lives, we will not liberate anyone – as the martyrs of yesterday and today know it very well.

Freedom is a delicate and complex "*good*". We seek it, desire it, crave for it in times of slavery, but as soon as we are liberated we realize that the new condition, too, has some costs, its typical sufferings and hardships. And so, almost always, we end up sighing for slavery and its "*goods*" (which during the trials of freedom get amplified and idealized).

The main effort of those who live or accompany processes of liberation is to remain free after being liberated, because the time spent in slavery does not prepare us for the laborious management of real freedom. It is difficult to get rid of a dead relationship with a violent man; but it is even harder to resist and not to return to him during the nights spent alone in tears ('*it would have been better for us to serve the Egyptians than to die in the wilderness*'). It was very difficult to break free from the masters that guaranteed contracts and jobs to the company that I had inherited from my family; it is even harder not to return today to knock on those old and secure doors, when the economic crisis is deep, there is no more work, and the Egyptians are catching up with us ('*Is not this what we said to you in Egypt: »Leave us alone that we may serve the Egyptians«*'). The processes of true liberation are very long, and once out of the land of slavery we are just beginning the journey. And without a "*Moses*" (a friend, an association, a public institution, a mother, a son...) who continues to believe in the promise and value of liberation, without someone to believe for us we often end up returning to being slaves.

The book of Exodus, therefore, is a great spiritual and ethical exercise not only for those who launch processes of liberation, but also for those who must persist, resilient, in their freedom, in the long journey after leaving Egypt. It is also for this reason that the God of the Bible is not the god of space (space is occupied by idols); instead, he is the God of time who calls us to go out, to walk through the deserts towards a promise that is always beyond the confines of our beliefs and fears.

This first test of the people and Moses near the sea also contains a teaching addressed in a special way to those who create (but also to those who must continue to run) communities, works, movements and organizations based on ideals. They answer a call, start a major process of liberation for themselves and for many, they set out on a journey towards the sea. But at the end of the night of liberation there is not a way of salvation but a wall that seems impossible to climb. The pharaoh is behind us, the sea is in the way, and even the people that we have saved are protesting, and they seem to want to go back nullifying the meaning and the pain of the history of salvation. These faithful solitudes are the typical tests of the founders, which you can only pass if you are able to imitate Moses: '*And Moses said to the people, »Fear not...«*' (14:13). Moses, too, was probably afraid, maybe more than all the others, but he managed to encourage and hearten them: '*Fear not...*' These tests involve the entire community (all are afraid), but the founder/leader goes through a double test: fearing for everyone's possible impending death and also for their own abandonment by the community. It is only possible not to die and cross the sea if at least "*Moses*" continues to believe, to hope, to resist, feeling and acting in the opposite direction to that which the community in fear would take.

There are decisive moments in the life of communities and institutions when salvation arrives if there is a virtue/capacity in the leaders not to give up and not to indulge in the collective fears, to keep rowing against the current, to resist the discouragement of the people, to continue to believe in the promise that is being dimmed by an imminent and very realistic fear. Those who govern always looking for the consent of all or the majority of the people may be good leaders in the ordinary life of the "labour camps", but they do not save anyone in times of great collective trials where you need wisdom to persist in moving on amidst difficulties and in solitude, in directions different from those that the community taken by fear and murmuring would like to follow. This wisdom/capacity of continuing to move in the obstinate and contrary direction is particularly valuable for the art of politics in times of great crises – an art that is entirely gratuitous, and therefore very rare in the times of idolatry.

And those who are crushed between the Egyptians and the people and are able to resist may witness the miracle of the sea that from impenetrable wall turns into the open gate to the land of promise: 'And the people of Israel went into the midst of the sea on dry ground, the waters being a wall to them on their right hand and on their left.' (14:22).

Chapter 33
Salvation Is Dance and Eyes

The Book of Exodus is full of kolòt, voices. ... Kalòt is the word that indicates the sounds produced by a ram's horn, the rattle of a priestly dress, or the sounds of thunder. ... But in the poverty of a single word there is something to cherish: the sacred language recognizes that the creation speaks incessantly, from the crash of a thunderbolt to the tinkling of a bell. For reasons of humility and a nostalgia the same word is used, admitting to being unable to hear those voices and remembering the time when the word Adam meant created to the letter.

(Erri de Luca, *Exodus/Names*)

Abstract After the miracle of the waters comes the great Song of the Sea. This grand hymn celebrating liberation ends with the song of Miriam, the prophetess and sister of Aaron. Once again, we see women return in the adventures of Moses. They were the protagonists in his first salvation from the waters of the Nile – the midwives, the mother and the sister of Moses and the pharaoh's daughter –, and now we find them again, at the end of the liberation from slavery, beyond the sea, as he sees and experiences another salvation from other waters. This image of women celebrating is beautiful. How many times have we seen them dance, cry and sing at the end of wars and famines. After the great suffering of all, they were able to use their special friendship with life to start over again, to get us back, again, to hope. We carry the rhythm and singing in our souls because we danced in the amniotic fluid first, and then also in their arms and inside the crib. We have learned to walk and for many years we fell asleep dancing and listening to the songs of women – and perhaps we will also depart from this earth with a final dance of the soul. Miriam is the first dancer and singer of the Bible, and she is an elderly woman.

The liberation of the oppressed people in Egypt began with the whip of the superintendents on the workers, and now it ends beyond the sea with the tambourine and the dancing Miriam. Where there is no space for the rhythm of the dance, sooner or

L. Bruni, *The Economy of Salvation*, Virtues and Economics 4,
https://doi.org/10.1007/978-3-030-04082-6_33

later the rhythm of the whip appears. It is the humble and meek beauty of the tambourine that celebrates freedom and saves us.

After the miracle of the waters comes the great Song of the Sea: '*Then Moses and the people of Israel sang this song to the Lord, saying, »I will sing to the Lord, for he has triumphed gloriously«*' (15:1). This grand hymn celebrating liberation ends with the song of Miriam, the prophetess and sister of Aaron. Once again, we see women return in the adventures of Moses. They were the protagonists in his first salvation from the waters of the Nile – the midwives, the mother and the sister of Moses and the pharaoh's daughter –, and now we find them again, at the end of the liberation from slavery, beyond the sea, as he sees and experiences another salvation from other waters: '*Then Miriam the prophetess, the sister of Aaron, took a tambourine in her hand, and all the women went out after her with tambourines and dancing. And Miriam sang to them: »Sing to the Lord, for he has triumphed gloriously; the horse and his rider he has thrown into the sea.«*' (15:20–21).

This image of women celebrating is beautiful. How many times have we seen them dance, cry and sing at the end of wars and famines. After the great suffering of all, they were able to use their special friendship with life to start over again, to get us back, again, to hope. We carry the rhythm and singing in our souls because we danced in the amniotic fluid first, and then also in their arms and inside the crib. We have learned to walk and for many years we fell asleep dancing and listening to the songs of women – and perhaps we will also depart from this earth with a final dance of the soul.

Miriam is the first dancer and singer of the Bible, and she is an elderly woman. The Jewish people would celebrate, dance and sing for years in Egypt, during slavery and forced labour (you do not survive in any job if you do not party every now and then, if you do not dance and sing). The daughters of Noah would dance and sing on the earth after having been saved from the flood. Of course, there would be dancing during the wedding of Jacob and Rachel, and a great party with dancing and singing in Egypt after the brotherhood was re-established between Joseph and his brothers. But the Bible wanted to preserve and cherish the word 'dance' up until the desert of Shur, and we were taken over the sea till we could see it used for the first time for Miriam to describe the feelings of women lauding in celebration.

There is a natural affinity between dance, song, music and women. There are many women in the Bible who sing hymns (Deborah, Anna, and finally another Miriam: Mary), and many dance (among them also the daughter of Herodias [Mt 14:6], a 'different' kind of dance that reminds us of the ambivalence of many, perhaps all really great things of the human realm). This is also the talent of women.

Miriam is not young. She was the sister of Aaron, whom the Exodus presents to us as a man of 83 years (7:7). Not only young men and women dance. There were many girls in that camp, but Miriam was the one to grab the tambourine, to sing the song and start the dance. It is always nice to see someone who dances and sings in praise. It is nicer if it is a woman who dances and praises. One of my most intense and vivid memories in life is an offertory during a mass in Kenya, where the bread and wine of the poor were accompanied to the altar by the chorus and dances of dozens of African girls. But it is even more beautiful to see an elderly woman dance and sing to life. There is no song that could be more beautiful and full of hope than the one that rises from the sunset of life, because it says that life is a gift in all its seasons, and the last song is the most beautiful of all. That of Miriam is the dance of gratuitousness, that of a body which in its essential nature is able to speak words of beauty, the ones that her years of youth and her different and more powerful dances did not know and could not say. Today Miriam does not dance and does not sing the refrain, because our culture does not make her dance, does not like her body that is not appealing any more to our senses that have stopped seeing different and greater beauty. So, we lose the purest of dances, the one that only a fragile and worn body can give us, making space by retreating.

After Miriam's 'Song of the See', '*Moses made Israel set out from the Red Sea, and they went into the wilderness of Shur.*' (15:22) This is where the story of the desert starts, in a place that immediately evokes another woman in the attentive reader's mind: Hagar. It was in this same Desert of Shur that the servant-mother wandered as she was fleeing with her son (Ishmael). There she was consoled by the first angel sent from YWHW on earth (Gen 16:6–7), and there she quenched her thirst from a spring. But that water and that consolation that Hagar, the Egyptian servant (16:3) in the house of Abraham found in the desert is not found by the descendants of Abraham who are now freed from the Egyptians: '*When they came to Marah, they could not drink the water of Marah because it was bitter ... And the people grumbled against Moses, saying, »What shall we drink?«*' (15:23–24).

There are protests before and after the miracles. The natural and very real experience of thirst pushes the extraordinary experience of the miracle of the sea into crisis. Even if we can see the waters of the sea divide in front of our eyes, if the trust and faith in salvation is not born anew each morning inside our daily hungers and thirsts, those miracles may be a true memory but they are incapable of changing our lives here and now. Miracles can make us leave, they may be the dawn of our liberation, but even the greatest miracles are insufficient for us to reach the promised land. To cross the desert, we have to become capable of transforming the bitter waters of everyday life into waters that quench our thirst on the tables of our kitchens and on those of work. In our actual human progress, miracles of the simple, humble water at home are no less important than the parting of the Red Sea.

The sign of Marah is a humble piece of wood: '*And he (Moses) cried to the Lord, and the Lord showed him a log, and he threw it into the water, and the water became sweet.*' (15:24–25). In the episode of the bitter water made sweet, YWHW, the God who has a voice, does not speak. The people murmur against Moses, the prophet cries out (how many cries are there in the book of Exodus, and the exoduses of today), but YWHW simply shows him a log. That piece of wood was perhaps already visible to all the people, but only the eyes of the prophet could now "*see*" it. Every prophet has a great relationship with the word, himself almost exclusively consisting of words. He speaks, he says different and big words because those words are not his private property or manufactured article, but a gift received and passed on as a gift to the people. It is the generosity of the word that makes the difference between Moses and the many false prophets of all times who are using the techniques of the word to their own advantage.

This first test at Marah reveals to us something about the importance of the eyes of the prophet. The prophet sees differently and he sees more. He also talks while looking at things in a different way. Many people, more than we can imagine, continue to save the world just by looking at it differently, to transform the discarded logs into instruments of salvation by the way they look at it. They save them because they are able to "*see them*", to recognize them in their vocation and beauty, so they may become assets for all – we would see so much beauty in the people around us if only we were able to look at them, and really see them. There are many logs of salvation abandoned along the banks of our cities and in our schools, because no one has ever seen them, looked at them, transformed them or loved them through their eyes. Not being watched by anyone, not having someone, at least one person that sees us, knows and recognizes us is the greatest poverty.

We will save our businesses if we learn to look at them differently, and if we start to see and look at workers differently. But we would need more prophets, more artists, poets and writers (and less human resources experts) in our places of work. That way we would be more able to turn the bitter waters of our crisis into fresh waters that save and create jobs again. We could glimpse an oasis in the middle of the desert and believe that no desert is endless: '*Then they came to Elim, where there were twelve springs of water and seventy palm trees, and they encamped there by the water.*' (15:27).

Chapter 34
The Law of Daily Bread

> *... (Moses) taught them the prayer in which they were to offer thanks after eating manna, which read: "Blessed be Thou, O God our Lord, King of the world, who in Thy bounty, dost provide for all the world; who, in Thy grace, goodwill, and mercy, dost grant food to every creature, for Thy grace is everlasting. Thanks to Thy bounty we have never lacked food, nor ever shall lack it...*
>
> (Louis Ginzberg, *The Legends of the Jews*, Vol. III)

Abstract We have reached the great episode of the manna. The phenomenon of the "manna" is a sweet and aromatic resin produced by two parasites of a plant (tamarix mammifera) in the central area of the Sinai. Coming from Egypt, the people could not know the manna, and so they ask, 'What is it?'. And Moses answers and explains. Without the eyes and words of the prophets our 'What is it?'-s remain unanswered, or, more simply, we seek and we find other cheap answers that leave us hungry. The greatest form of free gift is the one that comes down from heaven every morning together with the dew. The world is surrounded by gratuitousness. In fact, it is more real and present than evil that is also present. It dwells in our midst, we can find it in the trees, in our families, in the bushes, under our warehouses and offices, in the markets, in the streets, in hospitals, in schools and deep in the hearts of our people. It is here, in the amazement of ordinariness, that we may find the type of gratuitousness that saves us. Crossing our deserts would be much more bearable if only we knew how to recognize, with the help of the eyes of the prophets, the providence that surrounds us, that we can feed and that feeds us.

The greatest form of free gift is the one that comes down from heaven every morning together with the dew. The world is sourranded by gratuitousness. In fact, it is more real and present than evil that is also present. It dwells in our midst, we can find it in the trees, in our families, in the bushes, under our warehouses and offices, in the markets, in the streets, in hospitals, in schools and deep in the hearts of our

L. Bruni, *The Economy of Salvation*, Virtues and Economics 4,
https://doi.org/10.1007/978-3-030-04082-6_34

people. It is here, in the amazement of ordinariness, that we may find the type of gratuitousness that saves us. Crossing our deserts would be much more bearable if only we knew how to recognize, with the help of the eyes of the prophets, the providence that surrounds us, that we can feed and that feeds us.

Once they left the desert of Shur, the quenched people resumed the journey to Sinai, through the desert. And the tests are continued: '*And the whole congregation of the people of Israel grumbled against Moses and Aaron in the wilderness, and the people of Israel said to them, »Would that we had died by the hand of the Lord in the land of Egypt, when we sat by the meat pots and ate bread to the full, for you have brought us out into this wilderness to kill this whole assembly with hunger.«*' (16:2–3). People have always cried during the famines of bread and water, and they still do so. These are the first cries of life; we learn that again and again from our children. But it is even more true that the Psalms and all the prayers in the world resort to the vocabulary of hunger and thirst to express the feelings and the deepest passions of the human soul.

Those who have known true hunger and thirst could reach the true dimensions of the human condition that have been donated to them in the tragedy, some greater words that have enriched their anthropological and spiritual repertoire. They can speak better than satiated people, they know better how to pray and sing. This is also one of the paradoxes of the earth: suffering opens new horizons for humanity, but we must not rest until all the eliminable sufferings are erased from our society. There will always be those that cannot be done away with, the ones for which we still lack a culture to turn them into songs and psalms, to transform at least some of them.

Suffering, hunger and thirst naturally produce complaints, and they are one of the last resources of the poor (the biblical murmurings are not the chatter and gossip that, however, are always wrong). People who are ill complain, and they tend to feel nostalgic even about the worst past. Pain, especially pain that lasts long, makes us forget the gifts received, the sea that parted for us, the greatest miracles – and it transforms even the memory of slavery. Each murmuring hides a message, even when it is generated by much pain. It is even worse when there is a manager who does not want or cannot hear the murmurings of the people who hunger and thirst for water, bread, work, because they neglect a major source of truth about life and people: they cannot make the right choices in favour of life, and so the manna does not fall from the skies during our famines.

In the wilderness Moses and Aaron are learning to listen to the language of their people who can speak with the tambourine and the dancing of women, but also with that of the murmurings of all. And YHWH is there in the midst of them, hearing their complaints and their nostalgia: '*And the Lord said to Moses, »I have heard the grumbling of the people of Israel. Say to them, "At twilight you shall eat meat, and in the morning you shall be filled with bread."«*' (16:12) And so, '*In the evening quails came up and covered the camp, and in the morning dew lay around the camp. And when the dew had gone up, there was on the face of the wilderness a fine, flake-like thing, fine as frost on the ground. When the people of Israel saw it, they said to one another, »What is it?« For they did not know what it was. And Moses said to them, »It is the bread that the Lord has given you to eat.«*' (16:13–15).

It is normal that there should be and there were quails resting in the desert during their seasonal migrations, and the phenomenon of the "*manna*" is a sweet and aromatic resin produced by two parasites of a plant (*tamarix mammifera*) in the central area of the Sinai. Coming from Egypt, the people could not know the manna, and so they ask, '*What is it?*'. And Moses answers, '*It is the bread that the Lord has given you to eat.*' (16:13-15). Without the eyes and words of the prophets our '*What is it?*'-s remain unanswered, or, more simply, we seek and we find other cheap answers that leave us hungry. The truest and best answers to our deepest 'what is it?'-s are given to us by prophets. They make us feel and understand that everything that happens around me happens for me; that the manna is not only the resin secreted by parasites. The wonder of existence is to be able to see the manna in the resin, the infinite in the dew.

It is to discover that reality is greater than what our or even the prophets' eyes can encompass.

In Exodus, together with the manna, there comes a command, too: '*This is what the Lord has commanded: »Gather of it, each one of you, as much as he can eat. You shall each take an omer, according to the number of the persons that each of you has in his tent.« (...) And Moses said to them, »Let no one leave any of it over till the morning.«*' (16:16–19) Perhaps in the symbolic code of western culture there is nothing that says gratuitousness as eloquently as the word "manna". It comes from the sky, it is not linked to any merit on our part, and we meet it again in the gospels when Gratuitousness made flesh turns into bread, too. Still, manna comes together with rules, free gift (*donum*) comes together with obligations (*munus*). Gratuitousness without rules of communion and without obligations degenerates into the gadgets of the supermarket, into an individual and therefore small, useless experience. The most important type of free gift is the gratuitousness of duty, because that is the basis of our institutions, politics, family, business, social and fiscal pacts as well as our labour contracts. The Bible knows that a free gift that is not accompanied by community and social rules does not contribute to the common good. On the contrary: it has a destructive effect on it.

The management of the gift of manna in fact follows a definite law. All are entitled to the same amount of manna, which is distributed according to the number of family members, that is, on the basis of needs: '*whoever gathered much had nothing left over, and whoever gathered little had no lack. Each of them gathered as much as he could eat.*' (16:18) As for bread, as for the primary goods of existence, we are and we must all be equal. And it is the communion that does not let the manna and the daily bread rot. There have been some able ones in that camp and also those who were less adept at gathering the manna before the arrival of the sun that would melt it; but at the moment of its consumption the merits, strength, age or social status do not count any longer. Moses, Aaron, Miriam, the boy Levi, the pastor Joseph and his wife, Leah – they all have the same portion of manna, because they are all human beings.

There must be something that makes us equals prior to the many differences. There must be goods that we can enjoy even if we cannot buy them – yesterday in the desert towards the Sinai, now in the deserts of financial capitalism. The manna is a symbol of this kind of primary good, which feeds each only if it feeds all. Every time someone dies because they do not have the purchasing power to buy themselves bread and other basic necessities of life, we are denying the fundamental law of the manna. Many have dreamed of a society where every human being could enjoy goods not as a consumer and customer but as a human being: when will we realize this? We have no shortage of bread, what we are missing, more and more, is respect for the law of the manna. Furthermore, the manna cannot be accumulated, and therefore it cannot become the subject of trade: '*But they did not listen to Moses. Some left part of it till the morning, and it bred worms and stank.*' (16:20) Fresh bread can only be the daily bread. The gratuitousness/manna lives and it does not die and does not fade in the sun only if it remains a free gift. The manna can only feed us if it is received as a gift and not transformed into a commodity. The law of the manna reminds us that not all goods are economic goods, and that the only way for economic goods not to become "evil" is if other goods are kept non-economic.

Many goods are also merchandise, and it is good that they are. However, there are goods that cease to be goods (good things) if they become merchandise. Friendship is no business, prayer is no magic, a person is no human resource, if and until they remain things that are gratuitous. And the manna/gratuitousness has its own very firm law: it does not let you use it for profit, and it rots in the hands of those who would want to abuse it. That's how it has been saved even under the worst empires, and it is still there, surviving in all places of the human, continuing to feed the poor of the earth: '*The people of Israel ate the manna forty years, till they came to a habitable land. They ate the manna till they came to the border of the land of Canaan.*' (16:35).

Chapter 35
The Different Words of Equals

The Lord said to Moses in Midian, 'Go, return to Egypt'. (...) So Moses took his wife and his sons (...) (Aaron) went and met him on the mount of God, and (...) he asked him, 'Who are they?' Moses said: 'They are the wife I married in Midian and my children.' 'And where are you taking them?,' added Aaron. 'To Egypt,' he said. 'We are saddened by the Jews who are in Egypt, and you will bring them too?' So it was that Moses said to his wife, 'Go home to your father', and she took with her his two sons and left.

(Rashi, *Commentary to the Book of Exodus*)

Abstract On the earth, mixed in a sea of providence and goodness, there are also the enemies of the weak and the poor crossing the desert to the promised land. These enemies attack suddenly, sometimes for no reason. Many poor, yesterday and today, can be saved because someone is holding their hands up, praying, calling, crying with them, for them or in their place. And because there are those that stand beside the prophets and support them when they are exhausted by the length and hardness of the battle and their arms start to give in. However powerful and cunning evil is not as deep and true as the good is: this is a great message of biblical humanism. Life is greater and stronger than death. This is the word that anyone who fights for life and for good can still place their hope in, and their hope cannot be in vain. After hunger, thirst makes a return to Massah and Meribah and with it return the protests as well.

On the earth, mixed in a sea of providence and goodness, there are also the enemies of the weak and the poor crossing the desert to the promised land. These enemies attack suddenly, sometimes for no reason. Many poor, yesterday and today, can be saved because someone *is holding their hands up*, praying, calling, crying with them, for them or in their place. And because there are those that stand beside the

L. Bruni, *The Economy of Salvation*, Virtues and Economics 4,
https://doi.org/10.1007/978-3-030-04082-6_35

prophets and support them when they are exhausted by the length and hardness of the battle and their arms start to give in.

However powerful and cunning evil is – this is a great message of biblical humanism – it is not as deep and true as the good is; life is greater and stronger than death. This is the word that anyone who fights for life and for good can still place their hope in, and their hope cannot be in vain.

After hunger, thirst makes a return to Massah and Meribah and with it return the protests as well (17:1–7). In that desert of Rephidim there happens the attack of Amalek, too, and the people liberated from Egypt experience the first war. It was won by Israel because Moses was able to keep his arms up for the duration of the battle. He managed to do so with the help of Aaron and Hur who '*held up his hands, one on one side, and the other on the other side.*' (17:12). When certain enemies show up, Moses' strength is not enough to stay alive. We also need the arms of Aaron and Hur, other, equally essential '*charismas*' so that the people do not perish. The prophets can and should pray and sometimes scream, but without the people and the institutions who believe in that prayer and act, you cannot win the battle because the arms of the prophet alone cannot make it. Today, too many poor people continue to die not only because there are no 'Moseses' among them; they die due to the missing Aarons and Hurs, or because even if they are there, they are not strong and resilient enough to get through the day and to sunset. And so, despite the cries of the prophets, we continue to die at the thousands of Lampedusas of the world.

Jethro, the priest of Midian, Moses' father-in-law, heard of all that God had done for Moses and for Israel his people... (18:1) With his father in law, his wife Zipporah joins the camp (Moses had taken her for his wife during his exile in Midian), and their two children, too. And now in that scenario of the desert, hunger, thirst and war, there opens a glimpse of heaven, one of those pieces of paradise we may see and experience only through being in family: *Moses went out to meet his father-in-law and bowed down and kissed him. And they asked each other of their welfare and went into the tent.* (18:7) They kiss each other and inside the tent the story of liberation, the miracle of the sea, the holiday celebrated in the desert and Miriam's tambourine is told. And *Jethro rejoiced* (18:9).

Although he is also the heir of Abraham (because of Keturah, his second wife: Genesis 25:1–4), Jethro belonged to another people and worshipped other gods. But he had accepted the fugitive Moses in exile, had given him his daughter in marriage, and they worked together (Moses was pasturing his flock): he certainly loved him. Above all he knew and saw the call of Moses in Horeb, and told him, '*Go in peace*' (3:18). He could not hear the voice that had called his son-in-law, but he felt it was a real voice.

The family of the prophets are often, almost always in possession of the gift of understanding that the voice calling their son, brother or mother is a voice that is good and true. Maybe they do not know it, belong to another culture and other religions, but the natural flow of love and grace in the family allows them, often through pain, to sense that that voice came into their family for salvation. The meeting of Moses with his family also reveals the absence of Zipporah and her children during the liberation of the people from the pharaoh. We had left them on the way between

Horeb and Egypt, when Moses was saved by the mysterious action of Zipporah from the attack by God who he wanted to kill him (3:24–26). But during his mission to Egypt Moses had no wife and no children with him.

There is a mystery of loneliness at the heart of biblical prophecy. The prophetic vocation is not – lest we forget – a call to a happy personal life, but a consignment to perform a task of liberation and happiness for others. There is certain happiness in following the voice, but it is a different and mysterious type of happiness that we should call *truth*. When a person receives this type of call, they know that if they respond by saying '*here I am*', from that point on the presence of their affections and their typical and sublime happiness will not be ensured. In the call of the prophet there are no promises of company during the plagues and the journey of exodus; there is only the certainty that you are following a voice that is true and good for yourself and for all, and you are surprised to see an open sea and a pillar of fire pointing the way, and to hear the clouds talk. This form of loneliness, filled and accompanied only by a voice that cannot be seen but only heard, is an essential part of the prophetic vocation, even when you stay in the house surrounded by your family.

Jethro stays at the tent of Moses for the following day and sees him in the everyday of his ministry (and mystery). And he asks him, '*What is this that you are doing for the people? Why do you sit alone, and all the people stand around you from morning till evening?*' (18:14) Moses answers, '*Because the people come to me to inquire of God; when they have a dispute, they come to me and I decide between one person and another...*' (18:15–16). Jethro replies, '*What you are doing is not good. You and the people with you will certainly wear yourselves out, for the thing is too heavy for you. You are not able to do it alone.*' (18:17–18).

The typical look of family members and friends on the prophets is important, and so is their mysterious but real authority ('*What you are doing is not good.*') The people and the elders had another way of looking at Moses, as he was their liberator and their guide, the interpreter of God's will for them, the wise one who administered justice for them. Jethro comes from outside, he loves Moses, and he got to know him as a young man, he saw his blossoming affections and his vocation. So, he can see that the way Moses lives now is not sustainable. Without a wife, children or parents who would look at us differently and tell us, '*If you go on like this, you will certainly wear yourself out*' we do not understand that our work and our job is making our lives worse. It is not our colleagues or clients who can say these different words to us, let alone the people who see us as their guide. But without these 'different' words we do not reach the promised land, we get lost in the wilderness, we lose the way. These looks are essential not only for the prophets. They are also important for the leaders of religious and civil communities, for the founders of movements and associations, for all those who have moral and spiritual responsibility for others. One gets lost and does not manage to accomplish their task without the different looks on them by their family and friends, at least one of them.

Family members, true friends, even those from cultures different from our own, even those who do not believe in our God but wish us well have a kind of prophetic blessing. They can speak to us, they speak in the name of God; and if we listen to them, they help us a lot in carrying out our mission. For this reason, communities that do not have other onlookers outside of the *internal* ones, are rarely the places of salvation.

The presence of external looks of natural love allows the *prophet* to experience the reciprocity between equals, which can and is often missing, among members of the community that he is the guide of. A parent, a wife, a father can give him the experience of '*eyes on par*', that Genesis has set as the fundamental law of humanity (2:18). The prophet is Adam first and only then is he Moses. Even the greatest prophets need to experience "son-hood" thanks to someone who can give them another authority with effective advice. Even the prophets should obey some people.

'*Now obey my voice,*' Jethro continued, '(...) *look for able men from all the people, men who fear God, who are trustworthy and hate a bribe, and place such men over the people as chiefs of thousands, of hundreds, of fifties, and of tens.*' (18:19–21) Moses '*did all that he had said*' (18:24).

Later Jethro *went away to his own country* (18:27) and Zipporah returned to the background of the Bible story. It is part of the blessing of the family members and friends of the prophets to know when the time for leaving has come. But first, using their own experience and special savoir faire, they can look at them in another way and help them bring their task to completion.

Chapter 36
Words of Heaven and Earth

The mountains among themselves were fighting for the honor of being chosen as the spot for the revelation. One said: "Upon me shall the Shekinah of God rest, and mine shall be this glory," whereupon the other mountain replied: "Upon me shall the Shekinah rest, and mine shall be this glory." The mountain of Tabor said to the mountain of Hermon: "Upon me shall the Shekinah rest, mine shall be this glory..." (...) Mount Sinai was given the preference not for its humility alone, but also because upon it there had been no worshipping of idols; whereas the other mountains, owing to their height, had been employed as sanctuaries by the idolaters.

(Louis Ginzberg, *The Legends of the Jews, Vol. III*).

Abstract The first reform and social organization of the people of Israel originates from the advice of Jethro, Moses' father in law, a foreigner of a different faith. Between the escape from the idols of Egypt and the receiving of the gift of the Torah at Sinai, the Book of Exodus wished to include a picture of a good believer who is not idolatrous, and placed it at the heart of an event of crucial importance for the life of the people. It is a message of great openness and hope that reaches us today when believers in the God of life should unite and have a greater self-esteem, to free and protect ourselves from the thousands of idolatrous cults of our time. The elderly, Aaron, the wise men of Israel, had definitely seen the strain in Moses and his difficulties in dealing with a numerous and complex people all alone. But to put into force the new organizational structure that would prepare the people for the great theophany of Sinai it took a different view of an outsider, someone of another people and another faith who still respected YHWH despite not being his God.

The first reform and social organization of the people of Israel originates from the advice of Jethro, Moses' father in law, a foreigner of a different faith. Between the escape from the idols of Egypt and the receiving of the gift of the Torah at Sinai, the Book of Exodus wished to include a picture of a good believer who is not idolatrous,

L. Bruni, *The Economy of Salvation*, Virtues and Economics 4,
https://doi.org/10.1007/978-3-030-04082-6_36

and placed it at the heart of an event of crucial importance for the life of the people. It is a message of great openness and hope that reaches us today when believers in the God of life should unite and have a greater self-esteem, to free and protect ourselves from the thousands of idolatrous cults of our time.

The elderly, Aaron, the wise men of Israel, had definitely seen the strain in Moses and his difficulties in dealing with a numerous and complex people all alone. But to put into force the new organizational structure that would prepare the people for the great theophany of Sinai it took a different view of an outsider, someone of another people and another faith who still respected YHWH despite not being his God.

Moses does not consider his father-in-law an idolater. He knows he does not believe in YHWH, but despite this he listens to and obeys him, because he recognizes that he is right. Moses would never have listened to and loved an idolater, nor would he have obeyed them. Having a different faith from my own is not what makes the other person idolatrous. Jethro is not idolatrous because he respects the God of Moses. The first sign that tells us that we are dealing with idolatry and not a faith is the contempt for the beliefs of others. Even today we can only talk, meet and even pray together with representatives of the different religions and faiths if none of us thinks that the You the person next to me is praying to is an idol, and if everyone believes or hopes that the faith of the other person is an authentic reflection of the one God of all, who is too "*other*" to be expressed or possessed only by "*my*" faith. The spiritual poverty of our time does not depend on the proliferation of faiths in our cities, but on the impressive growth of the idols in the space left empty by religions and ideologies. We wanted to fight the piety and simple faith of our grandparents, but when we woke up from the "*slumber of reason*" we found ourselves in a world populated by new totems and not in the land of the free. The many faiths make the world more beautiful and colourful, and protect it from idolatry.

The reform of governance in the desert of Rephidim was a crucial event for Israel. In it, there hide many messages and many truths. Its importance is also evidenced by the number of versions that we find in the books of the Pentateuch. In the story of the reform that we find in the Book of Numbers, there is an element that reveals much of the deeper meaning of this organizational decentralization: '*So Moses went out and told the people the words of the Lord. And he gathered seventy men of the elders of the people and placed them around the tent. Then the Lord came down in the cloud and spoke to him, and took some of the Spirit that was on him and put it on the seventy elders. And as soon as the Spirit rested on them, they prophesied.*' (Numbers 11:24–25)

Here we find something very important to every process of decentralization and delegation. It is the same Spirit that is given to those who will perform the functions of governing the people. The principle of power and wisdom is not the talent of the prophet, but it is the spirit that had been given to him before and that is now being shared with others. This decentralization and delegation require that the *prophet* (founder, manager) does not feel the holder or the source of the spirit, but the beneficiary of a gift that he does not consider a possession to be jealous of. The prophet acknowledges that others called to govern with him/her have the same light and wisdom, because they all have received it from the same source (the spirit).

Delegation and shared responsibility then, before being pragmatic or technical, are very serious things, spiritual events; and it is always true for them, but especially when they have to do with ideal-motivated organizations and charismatic initiatives. Without interpreting delegation as participation and sharing of the same gift-charisma, whoever decentralizes does nothing but reinforce the hierarchy of the community, because delegation increases the asymmetry between those who delegate and the people. In these delegations without the gift and without spirit, the creation of hierarchical intermediate steps only increases the distance between the head and the base– the number of castes and ranks in a company or an organization is always proportional to the degree of hierarchy. The creation of intermediate levels of power in human communities is no guarantee of greater democracy and participation in government. If the person who delegates is convinced (or was convinced) that his "*spirit*" is different and purer than what those who were selected to work with him will receive, the decentralization process only creates new castes and new shamans, who in turn become simple stools to increase the height of the throne of the supreme ruler. The increase in staff next to the heads often ends up making leaders more powerful and more distant from the people, by multiplying the veils between them and their subjects. There are many community leaders who create intermediate orders of government for the sole purpose of increasing the height of their own pyramid, at the top of which there is always the only, true pharaoh.

After the intervention of Jethro, the spirit of shared reform, the people finally arrive at the foot of Sinai: *They set out from Rephidim and came into the wilderness of Sinai, and they encamped in the wilderness. There Israel encamped before the mountain, while Moses went up to God. The Lord called to him out of the mountain...*" (Exodus 19:2–3) YHWH spoke again to Moses, on the same mountain where he had called him for the first time, where he revealed his vocation as a liberator of the oppressed people in Egypt – the Bible knows that places are not all alike when it comes to listening to and understanding voices. Now, after the plagues, the liberation, the open sea, hymns, hunger, thirst, war, Moses returns to that same mountain, and, once again, the Voice speaks to him: '*And the Lord said to Moses, »Behold, I am coming to you in a thick cloud, that the people may hear when I speak with you, and may also believe you forever.«*' (19:9) And again, God speaks to Moses involving nature in his speech. YWHW had always talks resorting to the language of nature: the bush, frogs, hail; and then the open sea and the wood in Mara. Now, before the big event of the Alliance, with the voice of YWHW there arrive also the clouds, thunder, lightning, smoke, fire, the loud sound of the horn. Natural sounds that become words, shades of the same voice that had called him by name, kept speaking to him during the liberation and the Exodus; the one that continues to answer to him: '*On the morning of the third day there were thunders and lightnings and a thick cloud on the mountain and a very loud trumpet blast, so that all the people in the camp trembled. (…) Now Mount Sinai was wrapped in smoke because the Lord had descended on it in fire. The smoke of it went up like the smoke of a kiln, and the whole mountain trembled greatly. And as the sound of the trumpet grew louder and louder, Moses spoke, and God answered him in thunder.*' (19:16–19)

For the biblical man, that Adam, the son of heaven (Elohim) and earth (Adamah), human voices are not enough to be able to speak and live. He wants to involve the whole universe and its many voices in his dialogue. In the great theophanies – and the one of Sinai is certainly one of the greatest theophanies of humanity – only a symphony of voices may be adequate to communicate with the God of the voice. Human words were not enough to tell what was happening on the mountain. Not even those of YHWH were enough: other words of the earth were needed.

Nature takes part in the events of people. We have no other place where to give life to our stories. But it is particularly felt during the celebration of alliances (Moses and the people here are going to renew the alliance with YWHW), that these are events that are too great to be expressed only with our words. The discourse of life is an encounter between the words of the sky, men and all things on earth.

A wedding or a pact reconstructed after years of pain involve nature, the earth, the sky. And everything talks and talks to us, and everything goes into the photos and the memories: and we remember everything, human and natural details. The rainbow after the rain that soaked the bride was a powerful language, just like the words and tears that we had exchanged that day. Fraternity in the world is the greatest fraternity among humans: Brother Sun, Sister Moon.

If nature is created, then it is alive, living as we are; and if it is alive it can communicate, speak, participate in and accompany all human affairs. But you need eyes able to see the signs and ears able to recognize these other sounds that are too simple to be true and understood by our culture of the virtual and of consumption. Let us learn again to look at nature through the eyes of children, poets, prophets, mystics, who can see and hear differently and perceive more. Because the earth and the sky did not stop to talk to us, they are just waiting to meet our words again.

Chapter 37
The Only True Image

Then the Lord spoke to you out of the midst of the fire. You heard the sound of words, but saw no form; there was only a voice.

(Deuteronomy, 4:12).

Abstract At the foot of Mount Sinai, maybe the most important event in the history of Israel, all the earth and all the skies talk, interact with each other. The Adam, the tree of life, Abel, Cain and Lamech, Noah, Abraham, Hagar, Jacob, the Yabbok, Joseph's coat, the midwives, the women, the plagues, the open sea, Miriam, the manna and Jethro. Now they are all there, with the people, in front of Mount Sinai. The words of Sinai are not the laws of just a people. They are the ethical law of all, the first words for anyone who wants to be and remain human and free, on their way to a promise. He had done this when he spoke from the burning bush, but this time it was with a new solemnity and finality. Elohim, the deity reveals his name to the people: the name of the voice is YHWH. There have always been, and still are, religious experiences that stop at Elohim, faith in the existence of a God who is somewhere. But if the day when that generic deity reveals his name does not come, faith does not change our life, let alone that of others. Biblical faith is faith-trust-loyalty to a voice with a name that called his prophets by the name and that man was able to call them by the name.

Human history is not a uniform and monotonic straight line. Some events have the power to bend time, to fold it or sometimes break some paths from it, opening up new dimensions for humanity. As the old Greek remind us, *Kronos* and *Kairos* are the two axes of the time, *chronology* crosses *chairology*. The voice of Sinai is one of those instants. The words spoken there and given to a nation of former slaves freed and pilgrims in a desert allow humanity to enter into a new moral and religious era. An era that is entirely to be created still, one that will always remain unfinished. So, it is still ahead of us, waiting for us, calling us.

L. Bruni, *The Economy of Salvation*, Virtues and Economics 4,
https://doi.org/10.1007/978-3-030-04082-6_37

At the foot of Mount Sinai, all the earth and all the skies talk, interact with each other. The Adam, the tree of life, Abel, Cain and Lamech, Noah, Abraham, Hagar, Jacob, the Yabbok, Joseph's coat, the midwives, the women, the plagues, the open sea, Miriam, the manna and Jethro. Now they are all there, with the people, in front of Mount Sinai. The words of Sinai are not the laws of just a people (Israel). They are the ethical law of all, the first words for anyone who wants to be and remain human and free, on their way to a promise: *And God spoke all these words, saying, 'I am the Lord your God, who brought you out of the land of Egypt, out of the house of slavery.'* (20:1–2). He had done this when he spoke from the burning bush, but this time it was with a new solemnity and finality. Elohim, the deity reveals his name to the people: the name of the voice is YHWH. There have always been, and still are, religious experiences that stop at Elohim, "*faith*" in the existence of a God who is somewhere. But if the day when that generic deity reveals his name does not come, faith does not change our life, let alone that of others. Biblical faith is faith-trust-loyalty to a voice with a name that called his prophets by the name and that man was able to call them by the name. Outside of this "*encounter of calling by the name*" there are only the intellectual faiths of philosophy, or the non-faiths of believing in idols.

YHWH is presented as the liberator from slavery. He could have said many other things (*'I am the God of Abraham, the creator of the world, the giver of the manna in the wilderness...'*); instead he just said, *'I'm the one who brought you out of the land of Egypt.'* These few introductory words are enough to give content to the name of Elohim. You do not understand the words of Sinai, the Torah (the Law), perhaps the entire Bible, if you do not read them from the perspective of the labour camps in Egypt and liberation: *'You shall not make for yourself a carved image... You shall not bow down to them or serve them'* (20:4–5). You shall not *serve* idols because you have been liberated from the state of "*servant*". Liberation, if it is the true type, is a single one.

This anti-idolatrous command is a great religious and anthropological revolution, and it is a great gift for the defence of freedom. With the first commandment, the Bible not only wanted to separate YHWH from the other gods worshiped by the Canaanite peoples ('You shall have no other gods before me' (20:3)); it wanted and had to do everything possible to prevent his God from being transformed into an idol by the people – and it won't ever happen, after all. The prohibition of portraying God is a novel one that bursts into the history of mankind straight from Sinai and one that we do not find in any of the surrounding cults. And it's wonderful, because it says that the only eye that can give visible form to the speaking voice is that of faith. A god who can be seen has no need for faith in him, and therefore is but an idol. The biblical God disappears if looked at, or the man who catches sight of him dies, because the moment he is seen he becomes an object, an obsession or both. The anti-idolatry commandment is the most transcendent one, but it is also at the core of the human experience. The human being is a spiritual and religious animal because the earth with its visible things is not enough in his life. He also wants the invisible. Therefore, by his nature he is exposed to idolatry, in and outside of religions, because the idol is both an illness and a replacement of the religious experience.

The biblical God is a voice that speaks and reveals his name. He could not have done anything more to help us not to become slaves of idols. But he could not do even less, because YHWH is a God who is close to us and speaks and communicates to us because of his nature. By speaking and revealing his name, however, he becomes vulnerable and prone to abuse. Hence the third command- word: '*You shall not take the name of the Lord your God in vain*' (20:7). The Bible is not one of the many texts of the mystery religions, the purpose of which is to confine the divine in a sacred space that's inaccessible or accessible only for the professionals of the cult. The Bible is a re-velation, a lifting of the veil from Elohim, a formerly silent and distant deity who draws near, speaks, and even tells us his name, his intimate reality. Knowing the name may also produce idolatry: YWHW can also be reduced to an idol through the manipulative use of his name. All forms of magic use names to try to manipulate the deities. Even the name has a face, and so using it can build an image for the deity by invoking him '*in vain*'. The violation of the third commandment – the one regarding the name – is a form of idolatry that is typical of the religious man who knows the name of Elohim. The authentic religious experience is always sober about the use of God's name. A sign of authenticity in the Bible is the sobriety of the religious lexicon. When God and his name are "*used*" too much and in vain, they end up being "*abused*", and religious experience is gradually transformed into idolatry. Behind the prohibition of the abuse of God's name, there is, once again, the great theme of gratuitousness hiding (which is anti-magic). The biblical God is not an idol because he is the giver of free gifts. If we really want to meet him and don't want to end up meeting a dumb idol then we have to be moving within the coordinates of non-idolatry and gratuitousness.

Within these coordinates the Sabbath can be understood, too: '*Remember the Sabbath day, to keep it holy. Six days you shall labor, and do all your work, but the seventh day is a Sabbath to the Lord your God. On it you shall not do any work, you, or your son, or your daughter, your male servant, or your female servant, or your livestock, or the sojourner who is within your gates.*' (20:8–10)

If the prohibition of reproducing images is new, then equally new and amazing is the commandment about the Sabbath. Perhaps only a people that had conserved very vivid memories of the slavery in Egypt and then the Babylonian Exile could understand the value of the Sabbath, and place it at the heart of the Decalogue, converting it into a main wall of their own civilization. Slavery, servitude and forced labour are the denial of man also because they deny rest, feasting and the value of non- work. It is the denial of the value of the Sabbath that is the most telling about the idolatrous nature of the type of capitalism that we are experiencing. The logic of the profit does not know rest, and therefore it does not recognize the real human being, and so it ends up asking women to freeze their ovum in exchange for money. The experience of work without rest in Egypt was so strong and fundamental that it made a commandment on "*non-working*" and rest be entered into the core of the theophany of Sinai and the new law of the world. It was so strong and fundamental to be extended to all human beings, animals, to the whole of creation; beyond status, beyond the asymmetries of the other 6 days. The fraternity among the inhabitants of the earth is only possible in a world freed from idols.

It is then Adam being freed here, and in him the liberation of the earth taking place in the first part of the Decalogue. It is the '*jealousy*' (20:5) for this masterpiece and culmination of creation that inspired the first words: you've been lead out of Egypt, never to return to the slavery of the idols. The idols do not know and do not recognize the Sabbath, let alone Sunday. Their cult is perennial, and with it our slavery, too.

Finally, there is a strong and explicit link between Mount Sinai and the first chapters of Genesis. Not only because *in six days the Lord made heaven and earth, the sea, and all that is in them, and rested on the seventh day* (20:11) But because the deepest root of the prohibition to create images of God is the nature of Adam: the human being is the image of God, it is only there that a true reflection of YHWH can be seen. If you want to find an actual image of the God of the Bible you have to look for it in Andrea as he is working in his workshop; in Fatima who has lost her job; in the labour room of the hospital in your town; in Giovanna who is terminally ill with Alzheimer's and is resting in another department of the same hospital. And in all the crosses. You will not find any better image in the universe.

And you have to have that Adam in mind, an image and likeness of that same Elohim revealed as YHWH, freed from idols and from forced labour, loved jealously, as you read the second part of the Decalogue: '*Honour your father and your mother, that your days may be long in the land that the Lord your God is giving you. You shall not kill. You shall not commit adultery.*

You shall not steal.

You shall not bear false witness against your neighbour.

You shall not covet your neighbour's house; you shall not covet your neighbour's wife, or...anything that is your neighbour's.' (20:12–17). If man is the only possible image of God, because of being the only true one, then you have to honour him, you should not kill him, you should respect him and you must not betray him in his fundamental relationships.

The "*Ten Words*" of Mount Sinai are still in front of us. Every day we tread on them, the idols are multiplying, and thus our freedom decreases. But that image has not vanished; the covenant of Sinai has not been changed. The hope in the era of fraternity cannot be in vain.

Chapter 38
The Dowry of the Earth Is Pure Gift

If a man contracted a debt and gave his wife, sons, daughters in exchange or handed them over to be slaves, for three years they will work in the house of their purchaser or to the person who keeps them in slavery; but in the fourth year they will recover their freedom.

(Code of Hammurabi).

Abstract To understand and live again, here and now the great message of the Ten Words donated by YHWH-Elohim, we would need a culture of the covenant, a civilization of faithful promises, capable of pacts that recognize the value of the word 'forever'. Instead, a big sign of our time is the transformation of all the pacts into contracts, a sign that resonates louder and louder until it covers all the other sounds of the concert of community life. We see this extremely vividly in the context of family relationships, but also in the labour market where work relations in the twentieth century were designed and described using the relational register of pacts but today they are increasingly being flattened to the shape of contracts only. As if money could compensate for dreams, plans, expectations, human flourishing, especially in young people. We are losing the basic principle of any civilization capable of a future: that young people should be given credit, confidence must be given to them when they do not deserve it yet because they cannot possibly earn it yet. If they receive this confidence-credit, they can and should, give it on to the new young generation in turn.

To understand and live again, here and now the great message of the "Ten Words" donated by YHWH-Elohim, we would need a *culture of the covenant*, a civilization of faithful promises, capable of pacts that recognize the value of "forever". Instead, a big sign of our time is the transformation of all the *pacts* into *contracts*, a sign that resonates louder and louder until it covers all the other sounds of the concert of community life. We see this extremely vividly in the context of family relationships, but also in the labour market where work relations in the twentieth

L. Bruni, *The Economy of Salvation*, Virtues and Economics 4,
https://doi.org/10.1007/978-3-030-04082-6_38

century were designed and described using the relational register of pacts but today they are increasingly being flattened to the shape of contracts only.

As if money could compensate for dreams, plans, expectations, human flourishing, especially in young people. We are losing the basic principle of any civilization capable of a future: that young people should be given credit, confidence must be given to them when they do not deserve it yet because they cannot possibly earn it yet. If they receive this confidence-credit, they can and should, give it on to the new young generation in turn. Work grows and lives in this friendship and solidarity across time, it feeds off of this inter-temporal reciprocity. Without this generous relay between generations, work is not born or it is born in the wrong way, because it lacks the bedrock of gratuitousness and pacts. But we do not understand this anymore, and so we're missing out on it. Maybe we need to see the cloud and fire again and hear the thunder of Horeb; we need prophets, their eyes and their voice.

While Moses is listening to the Ten Words inside the cloud of Sinai, the people "see" the signs of God's presence, and fear: *and (they) said to Moses, 'You speak to us, and we will listen; but do not let God speak to us, lest we die.*' (Ex 20:19). Moses said to the people, '*Do not fear…*' (20:20) The same words come back here, at the foot of the mountain – '*do not fear*' – that he had spoken near the Sea, when the people felt entrapped between the Egyptians and the wall of the water (14:13). Prophets are always needed, but they are essential in times of collective fear.

Out of Egypt, the people are slowly getting used to the idea of a different Elohim, the one that freed them from slavery, the one that loves them and is merciful. But the process is long and difficult because the ancient man's religious experience, including that of the peoples around Israel, is primarily one of fear, anxiety and guilt. The best of the animals should be sacrificed to the gods and the first fruits gathered should be offered to them so that they suppress their wrath and become benign to the people. YHWH is offering his people another type of religious experience, another type of 'fear of God' (20:20) that from fear of the deity is more and more becoming '*fear of exiting from the covenant with YHWH*'. This revelation of another face of God has been a slow and bumpy process that took place in real time and space.

This historical and geographical dimension of the Torah emerges with great force and clarity in the so-called "*Code of the Covenant*", the long and admirable collection of standards, recommendations and laws – a sort of commentary on the application and realization of the Decalogue. In these chapters of Exodus an echo (sometimes a really sharp one) of the laws of the Semitic peoples of the Code of Hammurabi may be heard, and the great popular wisdom matured in the pain and love of the people through the centuries and millennia. That people of a different God, Elohim who speaks and cannot be seen, wanted to put those words of wisdom-pain-love next to the Ten Words of YWHW, giving them the highest possible dignity. They wanted those terrestrial words to respond to the gift of the heavenly words. It is the dowry of the earth, the wedding gift for the Covenant, the response to the gift of the Law. The Covenant is reciprocity because it is a dialogue between heaven and earth, where new and unusual words that pierce the clouds come together with the earthly words, created in the image of the voice that uttered the Ten Words.

The Book of Exodus tells us that the donkey exhausted by the weight put on it, the ox that gores and kills people, the foetus of the slave woman and the harvest feast can all be very close to the 'You shall not kill' and 'You shall not make idols'. All these words are those of salvation and freedom. Here, in this mixture of words from heaven and words from earth is the heart of biblical humanism.

Imbedded in this great '*Code of the Covenant*', there are some real eternal pearls of civilisation that must reach and penetrate our days, too, to change them or at least shake them to send a challenge to our certainties. *When you buy a Hebrew slave, he shall serve six years, and in the seventh he shall go out free, for nothing* (21:2). Even in Israel there were slaves (although, significantly, only after the monarchy). Even among the people of the God who presents himself at Mount Sinai as a liberator from slavery, who is the anti-idol since he is the enemy of slavery, there were slaves. It is one of the paradoxes of the Incarnation of the Word in history, but it tells us a lot. These slaves were people "bought" (*qnh* is a word used for purchases for currency), they were insolvent debtors who lost their freedom because they could not repay their loans. And along with them, their wives, sons, and especially daughters often ended up in slavery, too (21:3–5).

This form of debt slavery is still alive and growing in our capitalism, where entrepreneurs, citizens, almost always those who are poor, plummet into the conditions of slavery just because they cannot pay their debts. So today, too, they lose their freedom, home, properties, dignity, and often even their lives. Among the debt slaves, there always have been, of course, naive people, clumsy speculators, credulous persons; but there are also entrepreneurs, workers and citizens who have simply fallen victim of hard times – the Bible reminds us, and it's enough just to think of Job, that even the righteous may fall in hard times, through no fault: not all debtors are guilty. People who are reduced to slavery not only by the mafia and the usurers, but also by financial companies and banks protected by our "laws" that are written all too often by the powerful and against the weak. But we, unlike the people of Sinai, dare not call these unfortunates by the name ("slave"), and no law frees them at the end of the seventh year. Yet the ancient Law continues to repeat to us for thousands of years that no slavery should last forever, because before being debtors, we are first and foremost inhabitants of the same earth, we are children of the same sky, and so, in fact, we are brothers and sisters. Because the wealth we have and lend to another person, before it is our private property it is a gift received, it is providence, because '*all the earth is mine*' (19:5). The recognition that the wealth and the land that we have are not in our absolute possession since they are gifts is the inspiration for all the biblical laws on money and goods. If, however, we now believe that our wealth is only individual achievement and merit, then debts will never be repaid, slaves will never be freed and justice becomes philanthropy. The absolute possession of the individual over things about is an invention that is typical of our civilization, but it is not the logic of Sinai, it is not the true law of life.

It is within this larger frame that the words of the Code of the Covenant on the duties towards the enemy, the prohibition of claiming an interest on money lent to the needy and the law of the cloak should be read: *If you see the donkey of one who hates you lying down under its burden, you shall refrain from leaving him with it;*

you shall rescue it with him (23:5). It is not enough to lift the collapsed donkey out of pity for the poor beast: that incident should become an occasion for reconciliation with the enemy-brother who hates you. No enemy ceases to be a brother, and the pain of the humble donkey should become a way of re-composition of the broken fraternity.

If you lend money to any of my people with you who is poor, you shall not be like a moneylender to him, and you shall not exact interest from him (22:25). To the poor one is not supposed to lend money for profit, you should not speculate on poverty. But in the economic system that we have built outside the Covenant, it is mainly the poor, not the rich or the powerful to be enslaved by wrong and indefensible interests. And the poor continue to cry out. *If ever you take your neighbour's cloak in pledge, you shall return it to him before the sun goes down, for that is his only covering, and it is his cloak for his body; in what else shall he sleep? And if he cries to me, I will hear, for I am compassionate* (22:26–28).

We should try to write up a new economy based on the '*law of the cloak of the poor man*'; or at least imagine, dream or desire it, if we want to be worthy of the voice of Sinai. We should print and post these words of Exodus on the doorposts of our banks, on the doors of the revenue authorities, in the courtrooms, in front of our churches. Too many poor people are left "*naked and without a cloak*" in the night, and they die in the cold of our opulent cities. But their cry is not unheard: there are many people, even today, who are animated by charismas and provide blankets to cover many poor of the thousands of the world's Termini Stations (i.e. Rome's biggest, central railway station, a well-known gathering place of beggars and homeless people) every night. They are not enough to cover the multitude of those who are still left bare skinned day and night. But their presence brings those ancient words of life back into life, so they can talk louder to us, shake us, let us sleep less comfortably in the warmth of our many cloaks.

Chapter 39
The Treasure of the Seventh Day

In Montgomery, Alabama, in a small Baptist church, I heard the most extraordinary sermon ever: the topic was the book of Exodus and the political struggle of the black in the South. From his pulpit the preacher mimed the exodus from Egypt, and he expounded the similarities with the present; he bent his back under the whip, he defied Pharaoh, he fearfully hesitated in front of the sea, he accepted the covenant and the law at the foot of the mountain.

(M. Walzer, *Exodus and Revolution*).

Abstract The types of humanism that have shown themselves capable of a future have flourished thanks to non-predatory relationships with time and with the earth. Time and the earth are not our creation; they can only be received, kept, cared for and managed by us, as a gift and a promise. And when we don't act like this and use time and land for profit, the future horizon of all gets cloudy and smaller. We are not the masters of the world. We live on it, it loves us, nourishes us and gives us life, but we are guests and pilgrims here, residents and owners of a land that is entirely ours, and entirely foreign to us, where we feel at home and as travelers at the same time. The earth has always been a promised land, a goal that is in front of us and is never reached. And it is also the land on which we built our house, where our neighbourhood is, where the crops grow in our field.

The types of humanism that have shown themselves capable of a future have flourished thanks to non-predatory relationships with time and with the earth. Time and the earth are not our creation; they can only be received, kept, cared for and managed by us, as a gift and a promise. And when we don't act like this and use time and land for profit, the future horizon of all gets cloudy and smaller.

Biblical humanism had translated this dimension of the radical gift nature of time and land with the great law of the Sabbath and the Jubilee, with the culture of the fallow land: *For six years you shall sow your land and gather in its yield,*

L. Bruni, *The Economy of Salvation*, Virtues and Economics 4,
https://doi.org/10.1007/978-3-030-04082-6_39

but the seventh year you shall let it rest and lie fallow, that the poor of your people may eat; and what they leave the beasts of the field may eat Six days you shall do your work, but on the seventh day you shall rest; that your ox and your donkey may have rest, and the son of your servant woman, and the alien, may be refreshed. (Ex 23:10–12)

We are not the masters of the world. We live on it, it loves us, nourishes us and gives us life, but we are guests and pilgrims here, residents and owners of a land that is entirely ours, and entirely foreign to us, where we feel at home and as travelers at the same time. The earth has always been a promised land, a goal that is in front of us and is never reached. And it is also the land on which we built our house, where our neighbourhood is, where the crops grow in our field.

At the roots of the biblical culture of the fallow there is only a wise and sustainable technique of the cultivation of the land. In the Book of Exodus we find the fallow along with the Sabbath and the jubilee year, and it is an expression of a deeper and more general law concerning nature, time, animals, social relations; it is a radical prophecy of human and cosmic brotherhood. You can use the land for 6 days, not seven; you can get help from the work of other men for 6 days, not seven. You can and you have to work, but not always, because we only worked always when we were slaves in Egypt. The domestic animals work 6 days for you, but the seventh is not for you. The stranger is not a stranger every day, on the seventh day he is a person of your houselike all the others. There's a part of your land and your "*stuff*' that is not yours, and you have to leave it to the wild animals, to the stranger, to the poor. What you have is not altogether and only for you. It also belongs to another one who is never too "other" to be left out from the horizon of "*us all*". All true goods are common goods.

But if there is a stigma of gratuitousness imprinted on things and on human relationships, then every property is imperfect, every dominion is secondary, no foreigner is really and only a foreigner, no poor is poor forever. Prophetically, Christianity has sent the '*letter*' of the law of the Sabbath into crisis, but not to reduce the seventh day to the level of the other six. In the '*Kingdom of Heaven*' where the poor are called happy and the servants friends, the first 6 days are called to convert into the prophecy of gratuitousness and universal brotherhood enclosed in the last day.

Therefore, the law of the seventh day tells us that the animals, the earth, nature are not only valuable in relation to us humans, they are also valuable in themselves. Land and lakes must be respected, and so left to rest free from our dominion and our acquisitive instinct, not only because their fruits shall be more healthy and good for us this way; they should be respected for their intrinsic value and dignity that we should recognize and never offend even when a land is not cultivated, or when there is no fish to catch in a lake. Because fields, lakes and forests are created and given as gifts, just as we humans, animals and the world is. It's the fraternity of the earth that inspired the law of the fallow, the Sabbath, the Jubilee. The radical diversity of the seventh day reminds us that the laws of the 6 days, the asymmetries and inequalities are neither the only nor the most true ones, because the seventh day is the judgment over the justice and humanity of the other six. The degree of humanity and civilization of any concrete society is measured using the difference between the sixth and seventh day. The last day then becomes the perspective from which the other 6 days, as well as their ethical, spiritual and human quality can be viewed and judged. When there is no seventh day, work becomes slavery to those who work; it becomes servitude and lack of breath for the land and the animals; the stranger never becomes a brother and the poor remain short of redemption of themselves and the city. Empires have always tried to eliminate the very idea of the seventh day and the concrete utopia contained in it, thinking of eliminating the judgment on the injustices perpetrated by them throughout the 6 days – it's nice to think that while the Jewish priests wrote the Book of Exodus, or at least some pieces of it, they were slaves in Babylon, with no Shabbats. For this reason, they loved it and longed for it as a great hope and promise of freedom from all idols and empires, and as a judgment on their time: the prophecy of a different '*day*' has always reappeared in the midst of suffering and slavery, and it can be born yet again in our time.

As long as we save the prophecy of the seventh day, there might be hope for the poor and the oppressed and all those who are not happy with the slavery and humiliation of the 6 days of history. And let's say that we do not want those injustices to last forever.

The law of the seventh day challenges every aspect of life. As individuals, it invites us not to consume and possess ourselves fully, to make room in our soul that is not occupied by our projects so that some seeds that we don't even know how to receive can shoot up and flourish in there. Without this dimension of gratuitousness and respect for the mystery that we are, life is missing that space of freedom and generosity which is the dwelling place of the spiritual humus that matures the "*already*" from the "*not-yet*". It's the intimate and precious space for the most fruitful kind of generativity. It is there, in the land of the free that is not only a "*source of income*" for us, where the big surprises of life reach us that will change it forever, it is there that true creativity is born. It is from that piece of uncultivated and untapped land of the garden that we can see the top line of the horizon between heaven and earth, where our eyes so sickly fixed on the infinite may finally relax and find rest.

But the logic of the fallow (?the Italian word for fallow is "maggese", originating from the word "maggio" or *May*, the month in which fields were left to rest in the Roman world?) has important messages also for communities and institutions. A community without fallow land has no time for feasts, is not a welcoming community, takes possession of people and goods, does not know fraternity, so the breath of the '*breathing*' of the spirit cannot be felt in it. However, wherever its indicators are clear and strong: the hierarchies and power only last 6 days there the gratuitousness of the feast and the efficiency of work have the same dignity. The children and the poor always feel at home, because there are areas of unoccupied houses that are left free for them.

The culture of the fallow is not the culture of capitalism that we live in, which by its idolatrous nature builds on a permanent and totalitarian cult that needs consumer-workers 7 days a week: *Pay attention to all that I have said to you, and make no mention of the names of other gods…* (23,13). And so, a great need of our generation, perhaps the greatest, derives from the death of the seventh day, that was made to disappear from our collective symbolic code. Because the value of the seventh day is not only one seventh of the total: it is the yeast and salt in all the others, without it they remain unleavened and saltless. It is only the non-yoke of the seventh day that makes the yokes of all others sustainable, even easy and light.

We have let the seventh day be stolen from us, we bartered it with the culture of the weekend (where the poor are even poorer, the animals even more subdued, foreigners even more foreigners). And the night of the seventh day is inexorably darkening the other six. The earth has stopped breathing, and we miss its air. We have a duty to restore its breath to it and to ourselves, giving it back to our children who are entitled to live in a world with one day more that is different, to repeat the experience of the gift of time and earth.

But we can still hope. The prophecy of the seventh day is not dead – the Bible has preserved it for us. It also kept the judgment on our 6 days that have become seven identical days and has preserved its promise for us, too. The word is alive, it generates and regenerates us forever. It gives back time and land to us, it widens our horizons, it makes us feel and see the clearest skies: *Then Moses and Aaron, Nadab, and Abihu, and seventy of the elders of Israel went up, and they saw the God of Israel. There was under his feet as it were a pavement of sapphire stone, like the very heaven for clearness.* (24:9–10)

Chapter 40
The Desire to Entrap God

So the king [Rehoboam] took counsel and made two calves of gold. And he said to the people, "You have gone up to Jerusalem long enough. Behold your gods, O Israel, who brought you up out of the land of Egypt."
And he set one in Bethel, and the other he put in Dan. Then this thing became a sin, for the people went as far as Dan to be before one.

(Book 1 of Kings, 12:28–30).

Abstract On Sinai an anthropological, cultural, social and epochal revolution took place. There, humanity has reached a new stage in its process of humanization, thanks to a religious experience that was radically different from that of the other peoples, with their simple gods or dumb idols of wood. But at the foot of that mountain there also took place what was the biggest crisis of the people that had come out on a journey to the promised land, and it contains an extraordinary teaching on the most serious disease of every religious experience or ideal: its reduction to idolatry. The transformation of YHWH in a golden bull is a strong message addressed to all those people, communities, institutions that are given a "charisma", all those that were once reached and inhabited by a voice that called them to a task and announced them a different and larger promise. In these experiences and in these people there is always a powerful appeal to resize and normalize the call and the promise, to reduce the mystery to trivial evidence. It is a charm-temptation that acts and operates throughout life, and becomes particularly tenacious in the last phase of it.

Biblical faith is not only necessary for people: it also serves YWHW not to be turned into an idol, not to return to the state of an ordinary, nameless Elohim.

Indeed, on Sinai an anthropological, cultural, social and epochal revolution took place. There, humanity has reached a new stage in its process of humanization, thanks to a religious experience that was radically different from that of the other peoples, with their simple gods or dumb idols of wood. But at the foot of that

L. Bruni, *The Economy of Salvation*, Virtues and Economics 4,
https://doi.org/10.1007/978-3-030-04082-6_40

mountain there also took place what was the biggest crisis of the people that had come out on a journey to the promised land, and it contains an extraordinary teaching on the most serious disease of every religious experience or ideal: *its reduction to idolatry*. The transformation of YHWH in a golden bull is a strong message addressed to all those people, communities, institutions that are given a "charisma", all those that were once reached and inhabited by a voice that called them to a task and announced them a different and larger promise. In these experiences and in these people there is always a powerful appeal to resize and normalize the call and the promise, to reduce the mystery to trivial evidence – it is a charm-temptation that acts and operates throughout life, and becomes particularly tenacious in the last phase of it.

The God who had revealed himself to Moses, was not to be seen or touched, he was not there to satisfy the senses. Not even Moses saw him (and he will only see him for a second and even then only from behind), he only listened to his words. YHWH was, and continues to be, a voice. All other peoples had gods with clear, natural and immediate figures. All but the people of Israel, who had received the gift of the Covenant by a God who was completely different and completely new. To "see" and "feel" him, they needed double faith: partly in Moses and partly in the voice speaking to him. The more difficult religious struggle for Israel was not the one fought not to abandon YWHW and surrender to the gods (Baal or Astarte). YHWH was in the roots of the people, with the same identity kept up, and even after the betrayals the people could return to their one and only God. The great temptation was different: losing the novelty of their faith, reducing that different and new God to a simpler god who is more understandable, more manageable with just common sense and easier to tell about to others and to themselves.

This is the great and perhaps the main message of the episode of the 'golden calf', one of the most extraordinary stories of the entire Bible. That calf built by Aaron and the people at the foot of Sinai is not another god, nor is it an idol: the name of the handmade calf is YHWH: *And they said, "These are your gods, O Israel, who brought you up out of the land of Egypt!" When Aaron saw this, he built an altar before it. And Aaron made a proclamation and said, "Tomorrow shall be a feast to the Lord.*" (32:4–5)

After the gift of the Decalogue, the Code of the Covenant and the seventh day, Moses comes down from the Mount to receive the solemn "yes" to the covenant from the people: "*All the words that the Lord has spoken we will do.*" (24:3) And so, *early in the morning* (24:4), he climbs the mountain again, called by the same voice, as Abraham did when he went up on Mount Moriah with Isaac, or when he got up *early in the morning* to prepare Ishmael before abandoning him with his mother Hagar in the Wilderness of Sur: *Moses entered the cloud and went up on the mountain. And Moses was on the mountain forty days and forty nights.* (24:18) Moses stays on the Sinai for long; he receives very detailed instructions from YHWH on the building of the ark, the temple, the altar, the lampstand, then on the clothes of the priests (chaps. 25–31), and he is given indications that end with the gift of the tablets of stone (31:18). The calf is erected during the absence of Moses, who *delayed to come down from the mountain*.

We, the readers of the Bible know that Moses stays on the mountain for 40 days and then goes down. But the people did not know either if or when he would return. And if we really want to relive the experience of the people, if we want to feel the wrong but strong charm of the god who is simple and visible, and then take it again, after being wounded, the road home, we also have to read these pages this time as if for the first time. We should do this not knowing whether the God of Israel will always remain trapped in the golden calf, nor if and when Moses is returning from the mountain.

So while on the Mount the dialogue on building the ark and the sanctuary is on course, the people at the foot of it do exactly the opposite of what they had solemnly promised to Moses-YHWH just a few days before. ("*All the words that the Lord has spoken we will do.*") In the absence of their prophet, uncertain of his return, the people who had seen the signs and the cloud on the mountain, Aaron, the 70 elders who had even "seen" God, give an image to their God: *When the people saw that Moses delayed to come down from the mountain, the people gathered themselves together to Aaron and said to him, "Up, make us gods who shall go before us. As for this Moses, the man who brought us up out of the land of Egypt, we do not know what has become of him." ... all the people took off the rings of gold that were in their ears and brought them to Aaron. And he received the gold from their hand and fashioned it with a graving tool and made a golden calf.* (32:1–4)

The liberator, the God of the voice, the different God is transformed into a stupid calf built with their gold that was supposed to serve for the building of his Ark (25:3). The worship of the calf-idol is a very grave sin; even graver is the worship of the calf-YHWH.

The people of Israel have always made a great effort to save their different type of faith-religion. Theirs is the God of life but he cannot be represented by the symbols of life and fertility (bulls, women); he is the God of the voice that, however, only Moses can hear; he is the God who has revealed his name, but that name is unpronounceable. He is too different, too new.

The main effort and the greatest labour of those who – whether as individuals or communities – have received a vocation – whether it is artistic, civil, scientific or religious ... – is not resisting the temptation to imitate the vocations of others (there is also this, but it is not the most dangerous one if their vocation is true), but rather reducing or eliminating the creation of a specific result of the charisma-call received. Because during the crisis – and during the absence of the prophets – the temptation to simplify and normalize one's own task and vocation is always strong. So is the possibility of losing faith in the gift that one has received and the trust in that gift with a name and a voice. Faith, this faith, is also a fully anthropological experience: it means to continue to believe in the best part of oneself, of ourselves, not to reduce it to the tastes of "consumers" and "customers", to contain it all within the horizon of our limitations – it is for this reason that a culture without faith cannot flourish.

Those who received a true vocation know and feel that that vocation-charisma is inscribed in their being. This type of "identity-forging" vocation is not one that you can simply leave. Here the real, meaner type of temptation is to reduce it to something else, leaving the "name" and changing the contents. One can leave an alliance, a call or a charisma but not by simply walking away: the exit with no return is that of those who remain in something different that, however, is still calling them by their old name from youth. Through these exits-with-no-exit you will never return "home." Until YHWH remains YHWH and the calf remains an idol, it is possible to convert and return even after long time periods of keeping distance. It is when YWHW is reduced to a calf that the possibility of conversion is lost forever, that no conversion or re-conversion is possible any longer. We can hope to return home until we don't lose the ability to distinguish the acorns for the pigs from the food of the father's table. From the road that we have taken to follow the seductions of our idols one can always return home, because the way back is alive in the flesh of our longing for truth. It is the vocation-charisma reduced to our image and likeness from where there is no way back, because there is no place to return to. We can get back to love the truth again until we distinguish it from lies, those of others and our own. The fatigue of those who keep a vocation is in not calling our comfortable and innocuous artifacts by the name of the first voice that we have manufactured in the meantime, even when, over time, those artifacts had become the only companions for us not to die of loneliness.

The golden calves almost always arrive during the absence of the prophets. This is also a strong message of this great chapter of the Book of Exodus. The right and true idea of God and ourselves is very much tied to the radiant face of the prophets that illuminate our days and our souls. As long as they are among us, we can glimpse without seeing the true face of Elohim and our own, we can perceive some sounds of his good and real voice inside and outside of ourselves and we can recognize signs of life and fecundity everywhere. But when they are not there, the golden calves pull in to fill a void that becomes too large. Perhaps we would have less idols and less servitude today if the "prophets" had been more present in politics, economics, in the ordinary places of living.

The Bible has saved us from inevitable idolatry by cherishing an idea of God for us that is not reduced to the measures of our artifacts. But without the presence and without the faces of prophets we end up transforming faiths into idolatry, vocations into simple crafts, losing our way home.

Prophets, please return to us, come down from the mountain. Do not stay in the temples and shrines: get out to our streets, schools and businesses, reach to our wounded enterprises. Come back and tell us about your different Elohim, to deliver us from our cults that are too trivial to be good, real or liberating.

Chapter 41
The Weight of Common Words

With Judaism I share the journey, not the arrival. I am not in the promised land, my residence is on the edge of the camp … If I could choose where and how to be born, and I would opt for the same again and again: at the Sinai, as a stranger.

(Erri de Luca, *And He said*).

Abstract The prophet is not saved without his people. The charismatic is lost without his community and without the poor and so is the artist without his art and his works. Gratuitousness could not become a social, political and economic experience if there were no prophets, charismas and artists to reveal its nature to us. The crucial moment in their lives, however, is the test of the 'golden calf', when the ultimate and sole sense of one's vocation is perverted. That the world keeps moving forward and does not die is because prophets, charismas and artists are able to care for even the people that failed and for the communities that have lost their way, using their weakened and silent talent. The Exodus tells us that the presence and action of the prophets may even make God relent, and they can soften and soothe the effects of our words and our grievous gestures. But it also tells us something else: the prophets can also prevent that our words and our actions be actually realised and then produce consequences. The day when the people under the Sinai decided to deny and break the alliance, reducing YHWH to an artefact of molten metal, to that calf, those dances and mistaken feasts have appeared on the world's grand stage. No one can deny their existence, no one can erase the consequences of those acts and those words spoken in the days of the golden bull.

Without prophets, charismas and artists we are doomed to perpetual adoration of the golden calves. We would reduce religion to idolatry, the religious communities to spiritual consumerism and works of art to mere merchandise. These testimonies of "gratuitousness by vocation" recall by their mere existence the nature of the gift of life, because they force us to look up above them if we want to find the source of the gifts that inhabit them.

L. Bruni, *The Economy of Salvation*, Virtues and Economics 4,
https://doi.org/10.1007/978-3-030-04082-6_41

The prophet knows how to speak in the name of an Other and tells us that it is not him/her to liberate us from the Pharaoh of Egypt. The true prophets know that they are not the owner of the Voices. They are inhabited by a voice that they do not control and obey to.

The artist knows he is not the owner of the best part of himself, and that the gift that he has is not his property (and when he appropriates it, both the gift and the artist perish). When there are no prophets, charismas and artists, the world gets necessarily filled with idols. Leaders, entrepreneurs, politicians and priests become "gods" for their followers, their employees, voters and their faithful. In the absence of a higher sky, the ceiling of their homes becomes the ultimate horizon of all existence. To avoid reducing YHWH to a calf, priests (Aaron) are not enough, and neither is the wisdom of the fathers (the elderly). Without the prophets they, too end up building the gods of gold with the people to worship them, to dance and have feasts in their honour.

While the people were immersed in the festivities to their new YWHW, who was finally reduced to a simple and trivial god, Moses was on the mountain, dialoguing with his different God: '*Go down, for your people, whom you brought up out of the land of Egypt, have corrupted themselves.*' (Exodus 32:7) YHWH discloses to him his decision to punish the people: '*Now therefore let me alone, that my wrath may burn hot against them and I may consume them…*' And he renews the promise to Moses: '*…I may make a great nation of you*' (32:10). It is during this great crisis in Israel's history that one of the most beautiful passages of the Bible begins, the one that makes us understand even more what a true prophetic vocation is and opens another slit through which we may glimpse the "*face*" of the biblical God.

Moses, however, does not '*let YHWH alone*', he does not accept his decision. He is not satisfied by just saving himself, he wants to be in solidarity with his disloyal people: *But Moses implored the Lord his God and said, 'O Lord, why does your wrath burn hot against your people, whom you have brought out of the land of Egypt…? (…) Turn from your burning anger and relent from this disaster against your people. Remember Abraham, Isaac, and Israel…*' (32:11–13) During the greatest betrayal it is the words of a man, those of Moses that make him relent and remember his earlier deeds and promise. And the unthinkable happens, something impossible for the god of philosophy – but not for the God of the Bible: '*And the Lord relented from the disaster that he had spoken of bringing on his people.*' (32:14)

The prophet, however, is not interested in his individual salvation, because the very sense of his existence is the salvation of a people. Moses did not depart from the burning bush of Horeb to Egypt to seek his personal happiness. The prophets are like that: they get saved only through saving others, they do not care about their own fulfilment. And his interest is not born out of vocation and nature, neither out of altruism or philanthropy. The meaning of their life is something different. The pursuit of individual happiness, which is at the centre of modern humanism, is not the drive that moves the prophets. They are there because they have to and want to perform a task.

This note of the prophetic vocation is also found in the charismas and, in a true sense, in the artists. Those who received the gift of a charisma – be it civil, spiritual or political – feel that they have a talent to be implemented while waiting for the "*return*" of the giver of gifts, whose only question will be if the talents have been multiplied. They will not be asked if they were more or less happy during their lifetime only if those talents have borne fruit. They did not receive a gift for their own "*consumption*" but to multiply it and "*produce*" more of it for others. Artists, too, go through something very similar. They received a vocation that is a free gift entirely, one that they house in themselves, must care for and serve.

The prophet is not saved without his people. The charismatic is lost without his community and without the poor and so is the artist without his art and his works. Gratuitousness could not become a social, political and economic experience if there were no prophets, charismas and artists to reveal its nature to us. The crucial moment in their lives, however, is the test of the '*golden calf*', when the ultimate and sole sense of one's vocation is perverted. That the world keeps moving forward and does not die is because prophets, charismas and artists are able to care for even the people that failed and for the communities that have lost their way, using their weakened and silent talent.

The Exodus tells us that the presence and action of the prophets may even make God relent, and they can soften and soothe the effects of our words and our grievous gestures. But it also tells us something else: the prophets can also prevent that our words and our actions be actually realised and then produce consequences. The day when the people under the Sinai decided to deny and break the alliance, reducing YHWH to an artefact of molten metal, to that calf, those dances and mistaken feasts have appeared on the world's grand stage. No one can deny their existence, no one can erase the consequences of those acts and those words spoken in the days of the golden bull. Not even YHWH. Because if we were to deny it, we would make our dignity and our freedom shrink away, and we would be denying our vocation. The self-image imprinted by Elohim onto Adam is also expressed in his ability to betray – to betray himself and then suffer the consequences, in his ethical duty of having to answer for the actions he does and for the words that he says. Of being *responsible*.

The word is efficacious – this is a great principle of the Bible – even when that word is wrong, idolatrous or unfair. Of all words, those that are spoken have a special, strong status. Alliances and pacts are, by their nature, effective social acts; they are events that forever change our lives. Marriage, the foundation of a community – they all leave traces in our flesh as individuals and on a collective level, they affect and transform us. Agreements may get loose and alliances can be broken, but the signs that we have been abandoned remain with us forever. And if the words and actions of the pacts change us regardless of our loyalty, betrayals and broken pacts also have their effect on us and around us, living their own life.

Great instances of forgiveness can heal even the deepest relational wounds, but the effects operated by the betrayal remain alive because history is true and never misleading. The price to pay for a meeting of two 'yes'-es pronounced to create a new reality is the reality of the effects of our 'no'-s, because the words spoken above the bread and wine will also turn them into the food and drink of eternal life. This price is fair and good, because the only possible alternative to the world of efficacious words and our responsibility is the kingdom of the golden calf and all the idols, a world where all the 'yes'-es and all the 'no'-s are just like an empty sigh, because all the words are false. A great temptation of our idolatrous times is emptying the words of their truth. We no longer have the virtues that make us able to assume all the consequences of the words we say, but instead of converting and trying to take up responsibility again, we prefer to reduce the words to mere chatter, to puffs of wind that we can deny, withdraw and cancel because they have lost all contact with reality, and so did we with them.

It is only within this culture of the word and the efficacious words that we may understand the scene that takes place under the mountain, when Moses comes down from the Sinai and sees what is taking place around the calf: '*And as soon as he came near the camp and saw the calf and the dancing, Moses' anger burned hot, and he threw the tablets out of his hands and broke them at the foot of the mountain. He took the calf that they had made and burned it with fire and ground it to powder and scattered it on the water and made the people of Israel drink it.*' (32:19–20) And so '*...the sons of Levi did according to the word of Moses. And that day about three thousand men of the people fell.*' (32,28)

Moses attained the repentance of YHWH, but to place hope into a '*new covenant*', he had to correct and eliminate the effects produced by the people's betrayal. The forgiveness and repentance of YHWH was not enough to start over. Moses had to perform other gestures and say other words, because if he had not done so he would have denied the difference between the metallic calf and his God that is not an idol because he takes our words and actions seriously, and so he fills them with reality and truth.

Idols do not punish us, they do not relent or make alliances with us, because they are only puppets.

The inevitable effectiveness of the consequences of our actions tells us that our history and that of others is not a deception, and that the world is real. The prophets who know how to appease God cherish the alliances that we have broken and give us a chance to start over even after the construction of golden calves. This is also where the beauty and love of life and the world lie.

Chapter 42
The Back and the Face of God

Glory is a too violent presence for the human senses. Iod (YWHW) lets the perhaps more tolerable breeze of another emanation, goodness pass by the face of Moses. Even though it is immense, it is not more than a caress to humans.

(Erri de Luca, *Exodus – Names*).

Abstract Moses has the extraordinary privilege to see God. But he saw just YHWH's back, not the face. The presence of God in the world is in his goodness, in the goods that he gives us, in the 'milk and honey' of his – our land, in all his gift-and-creation. So, the only true exercise of those in search of the "face" and presence of God in the world is to be able to recognize it in his goods, but without transforming them into a god. Idolatries are always in front of us because in the goods of the world (people, things) there really is something divine – the contemplation of the Bible is a great help for those who do not want to commit this fatal mistake. Idolatry is easy because we prefer the great pyramids to the small and fragile mobile tents, and we like the gods that we can use and possess. That different God instead shows himself to us while passing fast, putting a hand over our eyes, rushing across our tent. All 'tents of the meeting' scattered over this world tell us about a real presence of God and not of an idol if they manage to cherish an absence in the pain-and-desire of waiting without wanting to fill it with the easy presence of idols. The access to the good mystery of life is a void of faces in an abundance of words.

The real hope of being able to start over after the great crisis is drawing on those truer words that we said in the best moments of our lives, the greatest and most generous gestures that we have ever done, returning to the promises of our mothers and fathers who generated us.

But without the presence of the prophets this "*return*" is not achieved, or it is only completed at high costs. On Mount Sinai, Moses manages even to attain YHWH's "*conversion*" by reminding him of his greater words and his old but never betrayed promise to the fathers: '*Remember Abraham, Isaac, and Israel, your servants, to*

L. Bruni, *The Economy of Salvation*, Virtues and Economics 4,
https://doi.org/10.1007/978-3-030-04082-6_42

whom you swore by your own self, and said to them, "I will multiply your offspring as the stars of heaven..."' (Exodus 32:13) That we still can work and live in a certain well-being today, we owe it in large measure to the promises and the covenants that our fathers and mothers have made with one another. Promises and pacts that created the republic, the cooperatives, businesses, institutions and cathedrals. But even before, their wedding vows that have allowed us to grow, being cared for and loved in the first years of life, those really decisive first years, receiving nurturing and love that have made us good workers and citizens, too. Promises kept often at very high cost, because those faithful '*forever*'-s were pronounced in a culture where the most important happiness was that of the children, not one's own – a truth that founded and nurtured our civilization over the centuries. The one that was threatened of being wiped out by only three short decades of individualistic hedonism.

Now Moses used to take the tent and pitch it outside the camp, far off from the camp, and he called it the tent of meeting. (...) Whenever Moses went out to the tent, all the people would rise up, and each would stand at his tent door, and watch Moses until he had gone into the tent. When Moses entered the tent, the pillar of cloud would descend and stand at the entrance of the tent, and the Lord would speak with Moses. (33:7–9) The first temple of YHWH on earth was a mobile tent. Moses received very detailed instructions on how to build the ark and the great temple, but the first house of God was a humble and simple tent. And if the first house of YHWH was a tent, the last will not be a big and mighty golden temple either, but something small and humble just like the first tent. The great cathedrals and the great and golden temples are things that come second and penultimate, because the first and last word on the "meeting" between men and God are those delivered under a small tent moving out and away from the camp. The Book of Exodus, then, not only tells us that the human condition is nomadic and pilgrim like: it also tells us that even God's house is nomadic and pilgrim like on this earth.

Inside that small, mobile and humble tent, however, the most unthinkable conference takes place: *Thus the Lord used to speak to Moses face to face, as a man speaks to his friend.* (33:11) This idea of God-as-friend comes to us as an absolute first – Greek philosophy (Aristotle) did not admit the friendship (philia) between man and God, but rather emphasized and saves the asymmetry of this relationship. The biblical God may instead be called a "*friend*" by Moses, by a man, and this will always be exposed to the risk of the greatest type of abuse: idolatry. For this reason, while Exodus is announcing this 'face to face' dialogue to us, it must immediately negate that Moses could see the face of God, even in the privacy and secrecy of the tent of the meeting. The only "*face*" that Moses will see during his life will be a voice (never forget that even in Christianity, where the biblical God takes on a human face, to recognize it and not confuse it the gardener of the tomb will need to hear and recognize a voice: "*Maria*", Jn 20:16).

How and where do we place ourselves in front of the words we are reading? We can approach these texts with the disenchanted modern attitude, stripping them of the pillar of cloud, the dialogue between Moses and his God, and all the details that accompany it. But we can also read these verses today by finding a place for ourselves on the threshold of a tent of that camp, and next to the women and men of the people, following the steps of Moses to the meeting with our eyes. Seeing really the pillar of cloud that covered the tent, waiting standing or prostrate on the ground for Moses, shining, to exit from the meeting, believing with the people that under that tent a meeting of true reciprocity is being held between the infinite and the finite, and that it is a dialogue of love (*'for you have found favour in my sight, and I know you by name.'* 33:17). Then rushing to meet Moses to tell us the words of the Voice, and hearing the words of life addressed to us, to me, in our time. Without our eyes next to the eyes of those ancient men and women, we do not see either Moses or his God, and we do not understand the tragedy of the golden calf, and we continue to call it YHWH.

At the height of this wonderful dialogue, Moses ventures to ask the impossible: '*Show me your glory!*' Moses knew (and certainly, the writer of Exodus knew) that their different God could not be seen by the living. As long as we are inside the story, we are so much inside God that we cannot see his face: we are like a baby in their mother's womb that can "*hear*" some sounds of her voice, can feel her around, but to see her face it has to be born first.

Moses, however, pushes his "*friendship*" with God to the limits of possibilities, and even here he seems to get an answer of reciprocity: *And YHWH said, 'I will make all my goodness pass before you*' (33:19). Moses asks to see his '*glory*' and YHWH allows him only to see his '*goodness*' passing. Just for a moment, and from the back: '*…you shall stand on the rock, …I will cover you with my hand until I have passed by. Then I will take away my hand, and you shall see my back, but my face shall not be seen.*' (33:21–23)

It is a wonderful passage that says many things, all precious and of the kind that we do not say enough to one another. The presence of God in the world is in his goodness, in the goods that he gives us, in the '*milk and honey*' of his – our land, in all his gift-and-creation. So, the only true exercise of those in search of the "*face*" and presence of God in the world is to be able to recognize it in his goods, but without transforming them into a god. Idolatries are always in front of us because in the goods of the world (people, things) there really is something divine – the contemplation of the Bible is a great help for those who do not want to commit this fatal mistake. Idolatry is easy because we prefer the great pyramids to the small and fragile mobile tents, and we like the gods that we can use and possess. That different God instead shows himself to us while passing fast, putting a hand over our eyes, rushing across our tent. All '*tents of the meeting*' scattered over this world tell us about a real presence of God and not of an idol if they manage to cherish an absence in the pain-and-desire of waiting without wanting to fill it with the easy presence of idols. The access to the good mystery of life is a void of faces in an abundance of words.

But there is one last pearl hidden in the soil of this great chapter of Exodus. When Moses, the greatest prophet, God's friend, the one who can speak "*mouth to mouth*" with him (Numbers 18:2) receives the extraordinary gift of seeing him for a moment sees him only from behind, not face to face. It is then possible that God is walking among us and we do not realize it because we see him only from behind. And it is also possible that the night of our culture, and many nights of the soul, are only darkness created by a good hand. But when that hand is removed, if we do not believe the words of the prophets we will only see the back of something running away from us. The prophets and charismas are the gifts that tell us that the darkness in front of our eyes may be love, that behind those shoulders fleeing there may be the face of life.

On this earth there are, especially in our depleted times of deep eyes many people who honestly seek what is good, beautiful and true and do not believe in God because, seeing only his back, they fail to recognize his face. This is the basis for a real and authentic solidarity and friendship among those seeking what's good, beautiful and true; and thanks to their faith they believe-and-hope that those shoulders are the back of YHWH, and those who follow it are after that same reality without recognizing it. We all follow the same "person", we all only see the same back of someone, that sooner or later, if our following is genuine, becomes love for the shoulders of those who are humiliated, bent, wounded by life and by those who are not looking for what is good-beautiful-and- true. It is not impossible, it is very likely indeed.

However, the possibility of continuing to walk side by side is there in the encounter between two ethical and the spiritual attitudes. Those who see only a 'back' should not deny that on the other side there will be a face, and those who believe-and-hope that there is a face hiding behind, must admit the possibility that someone might be right and true even if they do not feel the need to go beyond that "back" because they are happy with just walking towards a lay promise. It is this common sequel, mutually respectful and open to the mystery, that unites all the righteous in the mobile camp of life.

Chapter 43
The Veil that Reveals the False Ones

Between the separate commandments were noted down all the precepts of the Torah in all their particulars, although the tables were not more than six hands in length and as much in width. It is another of the attributes of the tables, that although they are fashioned out of the hardest stone, they can still be rolled up like a scroll. When God handed the tables to Moses, He seized them by the top third, whereas Moses took hold of the bottom third, but one third remained open, and it was in this way that the Divine radiance was shed upon Moses' face.

(L. Ginzberg, *The Legends of the Jews*, Vol. 3).

Abstract Forgiveness does not turn back time, nor does it delete words and deeds. But it has the power to make us reborn, to raise us to new life, to collect and receive our hurt body and turn it into a new and different one, where the scars are replaced by a face shining with light. The earth is still alive because every morning there are people who, forgiving and accepting forgiveness, are capable of new alliances after great betrayals, of writing new promises on new tablets after the first had been broken by our wickedness. It is also the capacity to forgive and restart that really makes something immense out of the human being, who is 'little lower than the heavenly beings' (Psalm 8). If there is a time when women and men are truly worthy of their divine image it is when they forgive. Forgiveness is the spiritual act that is closest to the creative act of God, because it re-creates our relationships from the nothingness where we let it fall and it generates new alliances.

Forgiveness does not turn back time, nor does it delete words and deeds. But it has the power to make us reborn, to raise us to new life, to collect and receive our hurt body and turn it into a new and different one, where the scars are replaced by a face shining with light.

The earth is still alive because every morning there are people who, forgiving and accepting forgiveness, are capable of new alliances after great betrayals, of writing

L. Bruni, *The Economy of Salvation*, Virtues and Economics 4,
https://doi.org/10.1007/978-3-030-04082-6_43

new promises on new tablets after the first had been broken by our wickedness. It is also the capacity to forgive and restart that really makes something immense out of the human being, who is '*little lower than the heavenly beings*' (Psalm 8). If there is a time when women and men are truly worthy of their divine image it is when they forgive. Forgiveness is the spiritual act that is closest to the creative act of God, because it re-creates our relationships from the nothingness where we let it fall and it generates new alliances.

The Lord said to Moses, 'Cut for yourself two tablets of stone like the first, and I will write on the tablets the words that were on the first tablets, which you broke.' (Exodus 34:1). The first tablets, those prepared and sculpted directly by YHWH, are no more there, the collective crime of the golden calf has broken and destroyed them forever. These new boards will have to be 'cut' by Moses, with his hands and with his work.

The verb "cut" (*psl*) has the same root as "image" (*pesel*). Therefore, there is a strong bond between the cut-out tablets and the absolute and unique prohibition on making any image of YHWH. The word is the only possible image of their different God, a word that now becomes written, too: it is turned into scripture.

To understand what the Scripture is and what its place is in biblical humanism, we must be aware that when we read the Bible we are repeating the experience of the voice that becomes writing; we return to the camp, and, still shaken and wounded by the betrayal of the golden calf, we are truly amazed and excited to see Moses coming down surrounded by light, with the words he heard on the mountain and written on two stone tablets in his hands.

Faced with the good image of the written and cherished word, all the poets, writers, composers, journalists, should exult with joy and gratitude. The Book of Exodus, with the gift of the voice made visible, thus poses a clear opposition between the golden calf (the wrong image) and the written word, and it teaches us that the cure of the tendency to idolatry which is there in each one of us is listening to the spoken word, but it is also the reading of the written word. It tells us that every reading of the written word is listening, dialogue; it is the exercise of the ears first and then of the eyes. We can save ourselves from fetishes by listening, but maybe we can also save ourselves from the many totems that take up our time by returning to read and by re-learning to write the words.

This chapter of Exodus then gives us an insight into why men and women receive some real salvation also by "listening" to great novels and "meeting" poetry. When the word of the voice decided to become written word, it elevated the ethical and spiritual status of every written word – and, likewise, that of the word (verb) that by becoming man elevated the value of every man and of all mankind. It increased the responsibility of our spoken and written words, the responsibility of all words. At the same time, Exodus tells us that this and every written word is only second, because the first written word, carved by YHWH personally, was broken by the rebellion of the people. The first written word is no more, and our words written after the golden calf in the camp of history carry a deep yearning imprinted in them for a first word that has been lost forever. Perhaps the labour pain of childbirth that generates real scripture and enduring poetry is also to be found here. But Exodus reminds us that even the second words are true and dictated by YHWH, but we must make the effort to cut the tablets for the word that is first dictated then written.

Anyone who writes or composes poetry knows that every true word born to them is dictated first: the realisation of receiving words is the first experience of each writer and poet; a discovery that should leave you breathless every time. It is not uncommon that the effort of the 'cutting of the tablets' makes us feel even the smells and see the fire of the theophany at Sinai.

Moses made the new tablets (he *cut two tablets of stone like the first* – 34:4), climbed Mount Sinai again, and asked YHWH's pardon for the people: '*If now I have found favour in your sight, O Lord, please let the Lord go in the midst of us, for it is a stiff-necked people, and pardon our iniquity and our sin...*' (34:9) Moses uses the grace he has conquered with his loyalty to obtain forgiveness for the people. This is the first "job" of every true community leader. And forgiveness, the new alliance and the gift of the tables duly arrived, too: And the Lord said to Moses, '*Write these words, for in accordance with these words I have made a covenant with you and with Israel.*' (34:27)

Moses comes down from Mount Sinai, with the tablets 'in his hands', but he *did not know that the skin of his face shone because he had been talking with God.* (34:29) This splendour of the face of the prophet is mysterious and wonderful. Moses is not aware that his face is glowing with a new and different light. The splendour of your face – all splendour – is a relational experience, others watching us are the ones that reveal it to us: *Aaron and all the people of Israel saw Moses, and behold, the skin of his face shone, and they were afraid to come near him.* (34:30)

Moses did not see the face of YHWH, he only listened to a voice; yet his human face bore the traces of that meeting and dialogue. Spiritual and mystical experience is always embodied experience. The bright face and shining eyes are the first sign (sacrament) that what we met is not an idol. Apart from enslaving us, the idols make us ugly and others can see it. The dialogue with the voice makes us more beautiful, and others must see this different beauty. We do not see the face of God, but we can see his light in our faces.

The prophet needs the community to find out that his face is shining. The faith of all is always a relational experience. Moses did not see the face of the voice that changed his face, he sees it only with the eyes of the people. It is the intersection of eyes (and looks) that makes us see God. The prophet lives in a typical loneliness that runs through the entire Exodus, but he needs others to see the signs of his vocation which blooms in fullness only through the faithful eyes of his companions of the same journey. Not being able to see the splendour of one's own face is a typical suffering of every truly prophetic vocation that in turn makes him a humble and perennial beggar of reciprocity.

And when Moses had finished speaking with them, he put a veil over his face. Whenever Moses went in before the Lord to speak with him, he would remove the veil, until he came out (34:33–34). This mysterious veil that Moses wore when he finished to tell the people the words he had heard suggests an important dimension of the prophetic vocation. After the Sinai there are "two types of words" of Moses: those uttered without the veil, when having listened to the voice in the 'tent of the meeting' its words are transmitted to the people, and the words spoken by Moses with the veil, when having concluded his prophetic meeting he lives his ordinary life and speaks different words.

To be able to distinguish the different words of the prophets, to be able to see their veil is a fundamental functioning in all religious communities, especially in movements and charismatic communities born from a founder (every charisma is prophecy). A serious – perhaps the most serious – disease of communities born around a 'prophet' starts to develop when the prophet or his companions begin to think that the words in the 'tent of the meeting' are of the same identical nature of the words spoken under the 'tent of the house'. This way the prophets become false prophets (or reveal their true nature). The prophet speaks in a different way because he first listens to a voice that is not his own. He is the guard of goods that are not his, since the prophet is in the service of a word that is not his. A first sign that indicates the nature of the false prophet is the nonexistence of the 'veil', the failure to distinguish between his words and those of the voice, the belief that every word that comes out of his mouth is the word of the voice. And so, the prophet turns into, or is transformed into an idol: every true prophet knows that the more difficult but crucial salvation that he must bring to his people is them being saved from the prophet himself whose voice should not take the place of the voice of YHWH – this is the great temptation of every prophet, the fatal risk of every prophecy.

Not all the words of the prophets are the words of YHWH. The Bible is not a "transcript" of all the words spoken by the prophets, but only of those heard and uttered on the mountain or under the tent of the meeting: *...the people of Israel would see the face of Moses, that the skin of Moses' face was shining. And Moses would put the veil over his face again, until he went in to speak with him.* (34:35)

The earth is full of people who – albeit in good faith – construct "spiritual" DIY itineraries and practices for themselves that should be leading to a dialogue with a "you" that has nothing to do with either YHWH or Elohim. The prophets, with their radiant face and with their 'veil' ensure us that at the end of our search for life we do not find a fetish and that the voice we hear is not only the echo of our own. And so, they continue to save us.

Chapter 44
Work Is Already the Promised Land

It's nice to see a handful of bricklayers who, when arrested by a difficulty, each reflecting on their own, indicate different means of action, and apply unanimously the method conceived by one of them, who may or may not have an official authority over the others. In such moments the image of a collective appears to be pure.

(Simone Weil, in G. Borrello, *Work and Grace*).

Abstract The blessing of Moses is a blessing to the mind and hands of work, which are two instances of the same intelligence and the same soul, the one at the service of the other. The real work is only one: hands at the service of intelligence and intelligence at the service of the hands. The body that becomes our works; the mind, the soul and the hands that give, together with those of others, shape the world. The artists are the great masters and witnesses of this incessant and essential dialogue of the mind, the soul, the hands, the hands that become the soul, the soul that turns into hands, the hands that become works. By praising and blessing the work of the hands, too, the Bible represents innovation with respect to the whole ancient culture that considered the work of the hands as impure activities, and therefore worthy only of slaves and servants. The value of this chapter of Exodus is still great, as it places the work of the hands at the centre of the new covenant, the subject of a specific blessing of Moses. Just as the tabernacle, the ark and the sanctuary.

There is a deep relationship between community and forgiveness. Community is not given without forgiveness, and forgiveness is the great generator and regenerator of communities. *Cum-munus* (reciprocal gift) and *for-give-ness*. The only social relations that do not need forgiveness are the functional, bureaucratic, anonymous, impersonal, contractual ones, where, since there are no un-mediated meetings, there is no need for forgiveness, and in turn it becomes just an out-of-tune and foreign word.

L. Bruni, *The Economy of Salvation*, Virtues and Economics 4,
https://doi.org/10.1007/978-3-030-04082-6_44

Here, the mediation of the superior, monetary compensation, appeals and court cases are sufficient. In communities, however, it is mainly the members to speak and meet; and so one gets hurt quite often, more intentionally, or less. Only forgiveness can truly heal the wounds of community relations (in families, but also in many companies), where the compensation in money, injunctive relief and courts are not of any help to start over, and do nothing but decree the death of communities and often also of people's souls. In communities, we should simply – and painfully – just forgive. It is forgiveness that transforms a people into a community. We were able to become a community in the instances when, after the crazy fratricidal wars, we forgave each other collectively, when we reconciled with each other, crying together over the graves of our dead, or rejoicing, singing and dancing at our parties. That's how we made economic 'miracles', too. Only the community-peoples can create great economies; the no-more-than-peoples are alive (if they are alive) thanks to their income from capital generated yesterday by other community-peoples. We shall see new economic and civil miracles only if we can go back to being a community, certainly in a whole new and different way, but remain communities: *cum-munus* and *for-give-ness*.

Moses assembled all the community of the people of Israel and said to them, '*These are the things that the Lord has commanded you to do.*' (Exodus 35:1) It happens after the golden calf, after the forgiveness requested and obtained by Moses from YHWH and after the new covenant that the word *community* makes an appearance in the book of Exodus. What was called the people ('*am*) has now become 'the community' ('*eda*) of Israel.

Moses summons them and transmits instructions for the construction of the house of YHWH in the midst of his people, the instructions he received at Sinai. Among these, unexpectedly, we find some wonderful words embedded about craftsmen, artists and human work: Then Moses said to the people of Israel, '*See, the Lord has called by name Bezalel the son of Uri, son of Hur, of the tribe of Judah*'. (35:30)

Here we find the deeper basis for work to be understood and lived as *vocation*: we need to be 'called by name' also in order to work, just as Bezalel. The same is true for being able to construct shrines, cathedrals, the Baglioni Chapel and Mahler's symphonies; but also for making tables and electrical installations, or for cleaning a bathroom thoroughly. YHWH places another worker next to Bezalel: Oholiab, who also receives the blessing (35:34). Their work is an activity of 'two or more'. No work is exclusively individual act, because there is always someone else nearby, before and beyond our work. YHWH has called those two architects-artists-artisans by name and *He has filled them with skill to do every sort of work done by an engraver or by a designer or by an embroiderer in blue and purple and scarlet yarns and fine twined linen, or by a weaver—by any sort of workman or skilled designer*. (35:35)

The blessing of Moses is a blessing to the mind and hands of work, which are two instances of the same intelligence and the same soul, the one at the service of the other. The real work is only one: hands at the service of intelligence and intelligence at the service of the hands. The body that becomes our works; the mind, the soul and the hands that give, together with those of others, shape the world.

The artists are the great masters and witnesses of this incessant and essential dialogue of the mind, the soul, the hands, the hands that become the soul, the soul that turns into hands, the hands that become works.

By praising and blessing the work of the hands, too, the Bible represents innovation with respect to the whole ancient culture that considered the work of the hands as impure activities, and therefore worthy only of slaves and servants. The value of this chapter of Exodus is still great, as it places the work of the hands at the centre of the new covenant, the subject of a specific blessing of Moses. Just as the tabernacle, the ark and the sanctuary.

Moses gives his blessing to 'work in every skilled craft': 'to devise artistic designs' and 'in cutting stones for setting, and in carving wood'. He blesses the artists, architects and craftsmen. The blessing on the work is one. Dignity is the same. The work of those who devise projects and the work of the artist and the craftsman who give shape and 'flesh' to those ideas receive the same spirit within the one blessing of work. Only one is the spirit of life, of all life. In biblical humanism there is a spirit for intellectual work (design) and a different one for manual work (carving). We are given a fraternity between different trades that are all reached by the same breath. The trades of men and those of women: *And every skillful woman spun with her hands, and they all brought what they had spun in blue and purple and scarlet yarns and fine twined linen. All the women whose hearts stirred them to use their skill spun the goats' hair* (35,25–26).

In a culture that no longer understands the body and so does not understand the ethical and spiritual value of manual skill, we must remember that the first act of intelligence is that of the hands. We know the world by touching it, we inhabit it with our hands. They are the first language that gives name to things, shapes and transforms them, the first instrument with which we come into contact with existence, life and with others. As children, as adults, as old or infirm people, always. Even when our hands do not move any more – or when they never move – we continue to imagine reality as if we still had them and as if we were able to get to know it through 'touching' it. Even when we are motionless in a bed and we can write poems and prayers with the movement of just one pupil.

There is a whole art of hands at the base of our real economy. It is easier to discover it in daily and humble work that make up the grammar of our civilian cooperation. We talk, we respect and serve each other and we meet first of all while working, that is, while talking, respecting, serving, and especially by meeting with our hands. It is the hands of the nurses, doctors, housewives, bartenders and architects, electricians, plumbers and masons, those of the men and women who clean our offices and our factories, the hands of the teachers, of the master carpenters, writers and journalists (that remain 'hands' even when typing on a keyboard or touch screen) that make us live and our society revive. We can take degrees, diplomas, we can attend ten masters, but as long as those abstract types of knowledge do not become awareness of our hands, we have not learned a trade yet, we are still waiting in the anteroom of work.

The Book of Exodus, and the entire humanism of the Bible tells us that the craftsmen, artists and workers in the economy of the new covenant of Sinai have the task of being the builders of the house of YHWH among the people. The construction of the sanctuary is the great work that embodies the alliance and brings the promise close: A construction that is possible only because there are craftsmen, artists, because there is human labour. Without the work of building the temple during the 6 days, no celebration would be possible on the seventh. This passage of Exodus should then be read together with Genesis that shows us Adam who works and transforms the world through his work. The work we do makes us become co-creators of the earth and of the temple. This is where the true secularism of biblical humanism lies: the first prayer of the workers is the construction of the 'sanctuaries' and not the construction of idols. Our first prayer is the one of our hands. The spirit fills the world thanks to human labour. This truth should be enough to look at work and workers in a different way.

The great law of the seventh day also tells us that work has a legitimate presence until the sixth day, the penultimate day, just as the sanctuary is part of what is penultimate. But it also reminds us that during the 6 days of history the blessing of work is inside the covenant, it is already promised land.

Not all human work, however, is blessed and filled with the spirit of God. There is work needed to build the golden calves, too. Those workers, the same artisans who are now to build the sanctuary, had built the golden calf in the camp at the foot of Mount Sinai. With those same hands and with the same talents. But that job had obtained the greatest curse. Artists, artisans, workers can build cathedrals but they can also build golden calves and idols. The hands, the intelligence and the work of craftsmen can also be used – they have been and still are used – to build land mines, the non- places of gamble or inhuman bingo halls. Today there are hands and minds in the service of the golden calves and idols, and other hands and minds that continue to build "cathedrals". That's the difference in the dignity of work that the Bible presents us, and that our consumer society no longer sees. The quality and the moral dignity of society should be measured – if we were to return to Exodus – by the reduction of work in the service of idols and by the creation, in their place, of work possibilities that build the good – and they are still the majority.

The world of work has a great hunger and thirst for blessings. Blessing: the Latin word for it (*bene- dicere*) means to talk well of someone, to say 'good words'. To bless work is to tell each other good words on work and workers. Work is part of the human condition, and so it is always at the centre of our words, words of good-diction or bad-diction (the important words are never neutral). Work is suffering now because we have surrounded it by bad words, those of disesteem and contempt. Let's bless work again: this is the premise of every good labour reform and all true humanism.

Chapter 45
No Liberator Is Crowned King

No one knows his resting place. For the men of the mountain, their tomb is located in the valley; for the men of the valley, it is situated on the mountain. It is everywhere and elsewhere, always elsewhere. No one was present at the time of his death. In a sense, he still lives in us, in all of us. Because, as long as there is a son of Israel, somewhere, who proclaims his Law and his truth, Moses lives through him, in him, as the burning bush lives, which consumes the hearts of men without consuming their faith in man and in his agonizing cries.

(Elie Wiesel, *Biblical characters through the Midrash*).

Abstract Moses, the deliverer from slavery, the one who revealed to the people the name of Elohim and his Law, the only man who spoke with God 'mouth to mouth', dies outside of the promised land. YHWH shows it to him from a distance, but he cannot reach it. The Patriarchs of Genesis had died otherwise, surrounded by their wives, sons, daughters, grandchildren, by the many 'stars' promised on the day of the call. They die at home, many of them are buried in the same cave of Machpelah, which was the only piece of the promised land owned by Abraham. Moses dies alone with no one to accompany him on the last trip, without the consolation of affections. He dies as he lived, in that lonely and continuous dialogue with the voice that had called him from the bush as he was herding, alone, the flock of Jethro his father-in-law at Horeb; the same voice that spoke to him again on the mountain, in the tent of the meeting, in solitude. We do not know if on that last trip to Mount Nebo the voice continued to talk to him, if it accompanied him or retired as it happened to many prophets who have died in the silence of the voice. Because, the most important happiness is not ours, but that of our children, that of the children of all.

L. Bruni, *The Economy of Salvation*, Virtues and Economics 4,
https://doi.org/10.1007/978-3-030-04082-6_45

To learn how to be born again we must re-learn to die, something we have forgotten. Consumer society is first and foremost a gigantic effort to exorcise death, the limit, old age; it is a huge, sophisticated industry of perpetual entertainment that should not leave us time and space to think that one day the big game of consumption will end and the carousel will come to its final lap.

So, we delete the last day from the horizon of our capitalism, and celebrate the cults of its idols that feed on our merchandise. The idols promise wrong exorcisms that are ineffective for death and pain. The Books of Genesis and Exodus are great, sublime and eternal songs to life, to all life, and because of this, they are also great teachings about death. Abraham, Isaac, Jacob and Joseph taught us to live and also to die 'full of days', with 'beautiful gray hair'. The death of Moses, a mysterious and completely different death, is the culmination of his life, the ultimate meaning of the words he heard from the 'voice', the complete unveiling of his vocation, and that of those who try to respond to a vocation of liberation and moving towards a promised land.

The Book of Exodus ends with the construction of the house, made possible by the blessed hands and minds of workers, and not with Moses' life events that are continued in the other books of the Torah: *Then Moses went up from the plains of Moab to Mount Nebo, to the top of Pisgah, which is opposite Jericho. And the Lord showed him all the land, Gilead as far as Dan, all Naphtali, the land of Ephraim and Manasseh, all the land of Judah as far as the western sea, the Negeb, and the Plain, that is, the Valley of Jericho the city of palm trees, as far as Zoar. And the Lord said to him, "This is the land of which I swore to Abraham, to Isaac, and to Jacob, 'I will give it to your offspring.' I have let you see it with your eyes, but you shall not go over there."* (*Deuteronomy* 34:1–4) Moses, the deliverer from slavery, the one who revealed to the people the name of Elohim and his Law, the only man who spoke with God 'mouth to mouth' (Numbers 12:8), dies outside of the promised land. YHWH shows it to him from a distance, but he cannot reach it: '*you shall not go over this Jordan*'. (*Deut* 3, 27).

The Patriarchs of Genesis had died otherwise, surrounded by their wives, sons, daughters, grandchildren, by the many 'stars' promised on the day of the call. They die at home, many of them are buried in the same cave of Machpelah (Genesis 23), which was the only piece of the promised land owned by Abraham. Moses dies alone with no one to accompany him on the last trip, without the consolation of affections. He dies as he lived, in that lonely and continuous dialogue with the voice that had called him from the bush as he was herding, alone, the flock of Jethro his father-in-law at Horeb; the same voice that spoke to him again on the mountain, in the tent of the meeting, in solitude. We do not know if on that last trip to Mount Nebo the voice continued to talk to him, if it accompanied him or retired as it happened to many prophets who have died in the silence of the voice. We can imagine him in the company of his God if we go back to the expressions of the Book of Exodus that suggest a relationship of true intimacy between Moses and YHWH: 'God's friend' (*Exodus* 33:11), '*you have found favour in my sight*', '*I know you by name*' (33,17). According to the midrashic tradition while Moses breathes his last YHWH kisses him on the mouth, continuing the mysterious and unique 'mouth to mouth' dialogue until the very end.

In this mysterious and painful death, the nature of the vocation of Moses is revealed in all its strength and fullness but also that of every founder of a community or a charismatic movement, or of great spiritual works. All prophets die out of the promised land, because the promise was not for them but for the 'people' that they liberated. Moses is the liberator from slavery and the guide through the desert, not the ruler of the new kingdom of Canaan. The prophets are the companions in the instances of exodus, in crossing deserts; they are the inhabitants of the mobile tent of the wandering Aramean. Their task is to take us out of slavery, to protect us from idols, to make us reconcile and start over after the collective betrayals, to bring us to the threshold of the new land, to make us see it. Without passing it, though. Their land is the one that is between the labour camps and Canaan, between the Nile and the Jordan. They are the men and women of the night ford of the river of liberation, the passage and the threshold. So, after the books of the Pentateuch, Moses almost disappears from the Bible. We do not find him in the genealogies of Jesus or in the liturgy of the Hebrew Passover, he is almost absent from among the Prophets, from the historical books or the Psalms. Moses was too great, and Israel felt the need to protect themselves from his greatness. It is a type of need that the Bible did not feel about other leading figures of salvation (from Abraham to David). But Moses was too big, the biggest of them all; so, it was necessary to 'make him die' and almost delete him from collective memory after the liberation. Moses is the prophet who dies upon God's command, that is how he disappears from the scene, albeit *His eye was undimmed, and his vigour unabated* (*Deut* 34,7). He does not die because of old age – he dies because his task has been completed and finished; he dies in order to make space for Joshua for he 'had laid his hands on him' (34:9).

There is a precise moment in time when the prophet must "die". It is the time when he must step aside, delete himself and be deleted, unless he wants to become an idol and take the place of the voice (this is the great risk that every prophet runs). This is the last great decisive act that says definitively, that the words the prophet has heard and transmitted to the people were not the words of his own voice, but he spoke in place of another (*pro-phetés*), that his words were great because they weren't his own.

All founders die before the Jordan, and if they go beyond it they become the kings of the new promised land, or else the land is not the promised land and they are false prophets. The land reached is that of the promise if the prophet does not reach it. And it is not because of a strange punishment of God (Moses was always righteous), but for the intimate nature of the vocation. Here Moses goes beyond Noah who also got into the ark that he had built. Moses built an ark that is not for himself, and this is why he is the greatest prophet of all: *And there has not arisen a prophet since in Israel like Moses, whom the Lord knew face to face…* (*Deut* 34:10).

In the death of Moses there is also a paradigm of biblical faith. You cannot see God and you cannot represent him. He is a voice that comes to us through the voice of the prophets. But the border between the voice that speaks to the prophet and the prophet's voice becomes increasingly nuanced and subtle over time, it almost disappears, and for the people they end up becoming a single voice. The prophet is distinguished from the false prophet because he knows how to step aside, disappear and cancel himself one day, saying: 'I'm not Elohim for you'. If Moses was the greatest of all, then biblical faith is not a possession. Faith is knowing how to inhabit the 'gap' between the promise and the end in the desert, being able to stay at the ford without being overwhelmed by the river's current. It is this gap that allows faith not to become idolatry, worship of idols, of others, of oneself. In the death of Moses there is, finally, a wonderful teaching on the human condition. No promised land is reached, because life is a journey, a pilgrimage, an exodus. There comes a moment – almost always before the last round of the carousel – when we see that the promises of life have not been accomplished. Even when life was wonderful, even when we have seen God 'face to face', the burning bushes, the manna fall from the sky, the cloud rests on our tent, we feel that the promise was something else, something beyond the Jordan. The story and the death of Moses tell us, however, that the gap between the promised land and the land reached is not a failure: it is simply life, our good human condition. That river ford we haven't crossed tells everyone, including Israel, that the real promise is not firm land but a nomadic journey across a desert, following a voice; to find out, in the end, that the promised land was nothing but the desert we were going through, because that's where our story of love took place (Hosea). There we saw the pillar of fire descend from the sky, there we heard the voice and received his words, there we freed slaves and protected them from idols, there we glimpsed the promised land, there we talked with God 'mouth to mouth'.

Therefore, what the conclusion of the life of Moses tells us, once again and finally, is the word that has accompanied us throughout the contemplation of the Book of Exodus: gratuitousness. The greatest free gift that the prophet experiences is the detachment from the promised land, and being able to see it without reaching it. Because the price for the gift given free to the prophet is to keep up that space between every land and every promise. It is in that gap that life is lit, it is there where wishes and great dreams feed from (the great deception of our time is to switch off the wishes of children by merchandise). It is this gap that reminds us that each promised land is for 'our descendants', not for us. The world will only live as long as we can still release someone from slavery and as long as we keep walking towards a promised land to give to our children and grandchildren, to the youth of today and tomorrow.

Since the most important happiness is not ours, but that of our children, that of the children of all.

References

Costacurta, B. 2014. *Lascia andare il tuo popolo. Riflessioni bibliche sul cammino dell'Esodo*. Milan: San Paolo.

De Benedetti, P. 1971. *La morte di Mosè e altri esempi*. Brescia: Morcelliana.

De Luca, E. (a cura di). 1977. *Esodo*, traduzione e commento a cura di M. Noth. Brescia: Paideia.

———. 1994. *Esodo/Nomi*, Feltrinelli, Milan.

———. 2011. *E disse*. Milan: Feltrinelli.

Molari, L. 2014. *Sulla stupidità dell'idolatria*. Brescia: Morcelliana.

Moro, C. 2011. *I sandali di Mosè*. Brescia: Paideia.

Quinzio, S. 2008. *Un commento alla Bibbia*. Milan: Adelphi.

Sonnet, J.-P. 2015. *Generare è narrare*. Milan: Vita e Pensiero.

Walzer, M. 1986. *Exodus and Revolution*. Basic Books.

Weil, S., in G. Borrello. 2001. *Il lavoro e la grazia*. Naples: Liguori.

Wiesel, E. 2007. *Personaggi biblici attraverso il Midrash*. Florence: Giuntina.

MIX
Papier aus verantwortungsvollen Quellen
Paper from responsible sources
FSC® C105338

If you have any concerns about our products,
you can contact us on
ProductSafety@springernature.com

In case Publisher is established outside the EU,
the EU authorized representative is:
Springer Nature Customer Service Center GmbH
Europaplatz 3, 69115 Heidelberg, Germany

Printed by Libri Plureos GmbH
in Hamburg, Germany